1.

Fourth edition

New Headw

Pre-Intermediate Student's Book

John and Liz Soars

OXFORD
UNIVERSITY PRESS

CONTENTS

LANGUAGE INPUT

SKILLS DEVELOPMENT

READING	LISTENING	SPEAKING	WRITING
Blind date *Looking for love* A newspaper organizes a date between two of its readers. How will they get on? (jigsaw) p10	**My oldest friend** Three people talk about their oldest friend p9 **Blind date** Sally and Dominic talk about their date p10	**Discussion** Talking about your friends p9 **Exchanging information** Talking about the couple on a blind date p10 **Social expressions** Acting out conversations p13	**Describing friends** Symbols for correcting mistakes ~~enjoing~~ Sp Writing about your best friend p104
The happiness quiz *How happy are you?* Find out how happy you are, and what you can do to make yourself happier p18	**Song** *Money* – the best things in life are free p18 **Getting on with your neighbours** Two neighbours gossip about each other. Do they see things in the same way? p20	**Discussion** What's most important to you – money, job, health …? p14 **Exchanging information** Ask and answer questions about three people p16 **Describing** My perfect day p17	**Writing a postcard** Adjectives *great, wonderful, amazing …* Writing a postcard about a holiday p105
The flight attendant who lost his cool *Stephen Slater* Day-by-day newspaper articles as a story breaks, goes global, then dies p26	**The news** Radio news items p25 **Dictation** Transcribing a news story p25	**Narrating** Retelling a news story p24 **Project** Research a news story that interests you – tell the class p25 **Discussion** Famous for fifteen minutes p26	**Narrative writing** Expanding sentences in a story *… a burglar broke into a large, expensive house. …* Picture story *A fishy tale* Comparing stories p106
Unusual places to eat *No ordinary place to eat!* Three extraordinary restaurants (jigsaw) p34	**Our diet** A couple talk about their diet p31 **Unusual places to eat** People talk about their experiences of eating in extraordinary restaurants p34	**Discussion** A good diet p31 **Exchanging information** Talking about a restaurant p34 **Roleplay** Acting out a conversation p36	**Writing an email** Linking words *but, although, however* *so, because* Writing an email to a friend p108
Hope for the future *The girl with two families* A girl from Belarus whose life changed when she visited Ireland p42	**How does it feel to be 20-something?** Three people talk about what it's like to be in their twenties p41	**Describing** Talking about someone in their twenties p41 **Discussion** Living at home/leaving home p41 **Roleplay** An interview with Palina p42	**Writing for talking** My dreams for the future *In five years' time I would like to …* *One day I hope to …* Writing about future plans – tell the class p109
Multicultural London *The world in one street* Four people from different cultures talk about living in the most cosmopolitan city in the world (jigsaw) p50	**My family** People talk about who they are like in their family p49 ***What's on?*** Deciding what to do in London p53	**Talking about you** Who are you like in your family? p49 **Exchanging information** Talking about an immigrant p50 **Project** Research the life of someone from a different country – tell the class p50	**Describing my hometown** Relative pronouns *who/that/which/where* Pittsburgh – the town where I was born Writing a description of your hometown p110

CONTENTS

LANGUAGE INPUT

SKILLS DEVELOPMENT

1 Getting to know you

Questions • Tense revision • Right word, wrong word • Social expressions

STARTER

1 Match the questions and answers.

Where were you born?	Two years ago.
What do you do?	Twice a week.
Are you married?	In Scotland.
Why are you learning English?	I'm a teacher.
When did you start learning English?	No, I'm not.
How often do you have English classes?	Because I need it for my job.

2 **T 1.1** Listen and check. Ask and answer them with a partner.

WHERE DO YOU COME FROM?

Tenses and questions

1 **T 1.2** Listen to **Anton Kristoff**. Where does he come from? Say one thing you can remember about his present, past, and future.

2 Complete the text about Anton with verbs from the boxes.

present	past	future
~~come~~	was born	'm going back
earn	arrived	'm going to study
have	had	
like	moved	
'm living	didn't speak	
'm working		
'm saving		

T 1.2 Listen again and check.

3 Work with a partner. Make sentences about him. Begin like this:

Anton comes from Canada, but now he's working in ...

4 Write one sentence each about your present, past, and future. Read them aloud to the class.

Anton Kristoff
from Toronto, Canada

present 'Hi! I'm Anton. I [1] *come* from Canada, but at the moment I [2] ________ here in New York. I [3] ________ as a bike messenger. I really [4] ________ New York, it's the center of the universe and it's very cosmopolitan. I [5] ________ friends from all over the world. I [6] ________ about $100 a day in this job. That's good money. I [7] ________ money for my education.

5 Look at the photo of **Rowenna Lee**. Where does she come from? What do you think her job is?

6 **T 1.3** Listen to Rowenna. What can you remember about her present, past, and future?

present	past	future

7 Complete the questions about Rowenna. Ask and answer them with a partner.

1 Where _does she_ live? Who with?
2 What __________ do?
3 What __________ doing at the moment?
4 When and why __________ to England?
5 How long __________ study law?
6 How much money __________ borrow from the bank?
7 How many children __________ have?
8 Why __________ excited?

T 1.4 Listen and check. Practise again.

past 'I [8] __________ in Toronto, but my parents are from Bulgaria. They [9] __________ to Canada thirty years ago. When they first [10] __________, they [11] __________ any English. They worry about me. Last month, I [12] __________ a bad accident on my bike, but I'm fine now.

future 'Next September, I [13] __________ home to Toronto and I [14] __________ for a Master's degree, and then I hope to get a good job.'

Rowenna Lee
from Melbourne, Australia

GRAMMAR SPOT

1 Find examples of present, past, and future tenses in **T 1.3** on p118.

2 Name the two tenses in these sentences. What is the difference between them?

He **lives** in Toronto.
He's **living** in New York at the moment.

3 Match the question words and answers.

What ...?	Because I wanted to.
Who ...?	Last night.
Where ...?	$10.
When ...?	A sandwich.
Why ...?	For two weeks.
How many ...?	In a small village.
How much ...?	My brother.
How long ...?	The blue one.
Whose ...?	It's mine.
Which ...?	Four.

▶▶ **Grammar Reference 1.1 – 1.3 p136**

PRACTICE

Asking questions

1 Read the interview with Serkan, a Turkish student in England. Complete the questions with question words from the box.

what	where	who	why	which
how often	how much	how many		

I Hi, Serkan. Nice to meet you. Can I ask you one or two questions?

S Yes, of course.

I First of all, [1]______ do you come from?

S I'm from Istanbul in Turkey.

I And [2]______ are you here in England?

S Well, I'm here mainly because I want to improve my English.

I [3]______ English did you know before you came?

S Not a lot. I studied English at school, but I didn't learn much. Now I'm studying in a language school here.

I [4]______ school?

S The Shakespeare School of English.

I A good name! Your English is very good now. [5]______'s your teacher?

S Thank you very much. My teacher's called David. He's great.

I [6]______ did you do back in Turkey?

S Well, actually, I was a teacher, a history teacher. I taught children from 14 to 18.

I [7]______ children were in your classes?

S Sometimes as many as 40.

I Goodness! That's a lot. [8]______ do you go back home?

S Usually I go every two months, but this month my brother is coming here. I'm very excited. I'm going to show him round.

I Well, I hope your brother has a great visit.

2 **T 1.5** Listen and check. Find examples of present, past, and future tenses in the interview. Roleplay the interview with a partner.

Who's or Whose?

3 *Whose* and *Who's* sound the same.
T 1.6 Listen and repeat.

> *Whose* ... asks about possession.
> *Who's* = who is
> 1 *'Whose phone is ringing?' 'It's mine.'*
> 2 *'Who's calling?' 'It's my brother.'*

4 Work with a partner. Choose the correct word.

1 '*Who's / Whose* brother is coming to stay?'
'Serkan's brother.'
2 '*Who's / Whose* talking to Serkan?'
'I think it's a reporter.'
3 '*Who's / Whose* dictionary is this?'
'It's Serkan's.'
4 '*Who's / Whose* going to Ben's party?'
'I'm not.'
5 '*Who's / Whose* is that expensive car?'
'It's my neighbour's.'
6 'Do you know *who's / whose* bag this is?'
'It's mine.'

5 **T 1.7** Listen to the sentences.

If the word is ***Whose?*** shout **1!**

If the word is ***Who's?*** shout **2!**

Questions about you

6 Each of these questions has one word missing. Write it in.

1 What you like doing in your free time?
2 Do you like listening music?
3 What kind music do you like?
4 What did you last weekend?
5 What you doing tonight?
6 What are you going do after this lesson?
7 How many languages your teacher speak?
8 What your teacher wearing today?

T 1.8 Listen, check, and repeat.

7 Ask and answer the questions with a partner.

T 1.9 Listen and compare.

LISTENING AND SPEAKING

My oldest friend

1 Write down the names of some of your friends.

- Why do you like them?
- When did you first meet them?
- Who is your oldest friend?

Discuss your list with a partner.

2 Three people are talking about their oldest friend. Look at the pictures. Who are they talking to? Who are they talking about?

3 **T 1.10** Listen to their conversations. When and where did they meet their oldest friend? What did they like about them? Make notes after each conversation.

Kenny ______________________________

____

______________________________.

Damian ______________________________

____

______________________________.

Katie ______________________________

____

______________________________.

4 **T 1.10** Listen again. Answer the questions about the people.

1. Who has a lot of friends on Facebook? How many?
2. Whose mums met before they were born?
3. Who's going to travel the world with a friend?
4. Whose oldest friend lives in Canada?
5. Who's talking to their oldest friend?
6. Who doesn't have many friends?
7. Which friends don't see each other very often?
8. Who named his son after the friend?
9. Whose friend is like a sister?
10. Whose brother is boring?

Check your answers with a partner.

5 Put the words in the right order to make sentences about the people.

1 Pete | after | best | son | named | his | friend | his | Ken

2 Toby | world | wants | the | brother | to | his | with | travel

3 Katie | friends | from | has | times | different | life | her | in

▶▶ **WRITING Describing friends** *p104*

READING AND SPEAKING

A blind date

1 In a survey, 10,000 couples were asked how and where they first met. How do you think most couples meet? Look at the chart and match a line with a percentage.

How did they meet?	%
at school or university	12%
at work	
at a bar or club	15% 20%
online	5%
through friends	8%
through family	13%
a blind date	4%
while shopping	
none of these	22% 1%

T 1.11 Listen to the survey results. Did anything surprise you? Talk about couples you know. How did they meet?

2 Each week the *Guardian* newspaper organizes a blind date between two of its readers. Look at the pictures and read the introduction.

- Who are the people? How old are they?
- What are their jobs?
- Where did they meet?

3 Work in two groups.

Group A Read what **Sally** says about **Dominic**.
Group B Read what **Dominic** says about **Sally**.

Answer the questions in your group.

1 Were they both nervous when they met?
2 How does he/she describe her/him?
3 What did they talk about?
4 Why was she/he embarrassed?
5 What did they use to eat their food?
6 What were the best things about him/her?
7 What didn't he/she talk about?
8 How did the evening end?
9 How did she/he travel home?

4 Compare answers with someone from the other group. What do Sally and Dominic have in common? What don't they have in common?

What happened next?

5 Do you think Sally and Dominic will meet again? Take a class vote.

6 **T 1.12** Listen to Dominic and Sally. What did they do? What are they doing now? What are they going to do?

Blind date

This week

Sally Fox, 25, tennis coach meets Dominic Evo, 29, actor.

They met in a Chinese restaurant called *Ping Pong*. Will they ever meet again?

Sally talking about Dominic

First impressions? He was friendly, tall, and attractive. We laughed together from the start, I think because we were both a bit nervous.

What did you talk about? So many things – places we want to travel to, such as South America. Sport, of course. Unfortunately Dom doesn't play much sport, but he's going to run the marathon this year. His acting – I don't often go to the theatre so I didn't have a lot to say.

Any difficult moments? I couldn't decide how to greet him when we first met. I shook his hand and he tried to kiss my cheek. That was a bit embarrassing, but we laughed about it.

Good table manners? Yes, very. He couldn't use chopsticks, but he tried.

Best thing about him? He was chatty and funny. He didn't just talk about himself, he asked me questions. It was nice to meet a guy who wasn't crazy about football.

Did you go on somewhere? Just to the square next to the restaurant. There was a piano with a notice 'Please play me' – so Dom did. He can play the piano very well. It was a great way to end the evening. He lives out of town, so he went to get his train.

Marks out of 10? I liked him more and more as the evening progressed. 8.

Would you like to meet again? Maybe. We swapped numbers, so we'll see.

Dominic talking about Sally

First impressions? She smiled a lot. She has a lovely smile and amazing green eyes. I think she was a bit nervous. I loved her red dress – it was very red indeed.

What did you talk about? Everything – travel, we both want to visit Chile; cooking, I love it, Sally hates it; sport, I hate it, Sally loves it, but I am training to run the marathon for charity; the theatre, I have a small part in a small theatre at the moment.

Any difficult moments? Not really. Oh yes, I could see that the waiter knew it was a blind date. That was embarrassing.

Good table manners? Very good. I like a girl who enjoys her food and she could use chopsticks. I was impressed with that.

Best thing about her? The green eyes! And she was really easy to talk to. She was interested and interesting. She didn't just talk about sport.

Did you go on somewhere? Well, we didn't go far. We found a piano – they are all over the city at the moment with signs saying 'Please play me'. I played, but I'm not very good. Sally sang, she can't sing at all. We made a terrible noise! It was good fun. Then she caught the bus home.

Marks out of 10? She can't sing, but I like her. 9

Would you like to meet again? Definitely. She left very hurriedly, but she has my number.

Vocabulary

7 Match the lines about Sally.

Sally was interest**ed**	because she was funny and made him laugh.
Sally was interest**ing**	so she asked him a lot of questions.

8 Complete the adjectives with *-ed* or *-ing*.

1 Thank you. That lesson was really interest______.
2 It's my birthday tomorrow so I'm very excit______.
3 Look at the view! It's amaz______.
4 I didn't like her new boyfriend. He was very bor______.
5 Don't be embarrass______. Everybody cries sometimes.

VOCABULARY

Right word, wrong word

Work with a partner. These exercises will help you think about how you learn new vocabulary. Use a dictionary.

Verbs of similar meaning

1 Choose the correct verb for each line.

1 **play** **go**
Can you _____ the piano?
Do you _____ running every morning?

2 **do** **make**
I _____ too many mistakes in English.
I _____ my homework in the evening.

3 **speak** **talk**
She can _____ three languages.
He can _____ forever! He never shuts up!

4 **say** **tell**
Pardon! What did you _____?
Can you _____ me the time, please?

5 **pay for** **buy**
How much did you _____ that meal?
Where can I _____ some sun cream?

Adjectives and nouns that go together

2 Underline two nouns that go with the adjective.

1	**important**	person / meeting / price
2	**delicious**	holiday / cake / meal
3	**high**	price / mountain / man
4	**long**	tree / journey / time
5	**heavy**	bag / sunshine / rain
6	**busy**	street / day / traffic

Prepositions

3 Complete the sentences with the correct preposition.

to from at about of on in with for

1 He comes _from_ Istanbul _in_ Turkey.
2 He's crazy ___ football, but I'm not interested ___ it at all.
3 I am married ___ John. I met him ___ university ___ 2007.
4 I live ___ my parents ___ a flat ___ the first floor.
5 He's very good ___ playing the piano.
6 I like going ___ a walk ___ the park.
7 This is a photo ___ me ___ holiday ___ Spain.
8 I got this jumper ___ my sister ___ my birthday.

Words with two meanings

4 Look at these sentences. What are the two meanings of *date*?

I met my husband on a blind **date**.
Dates and raisins are good for you.

5 Write two sentences that show two possible meanings for these words.

left		
train		
run		
rest		
kind		
flat		
mean		

T 1.13 Listen to some sample answers.

EVERYDAY ENGLISH

Social expressions

1 In everyday situations we use a lot of social expressions. Read the expressions. Where are the people?

1

A 'Hi, Anna. How are you?'
B 'I'm fine, thanks. How are you?'

2

C 'Thank you so much.'
D 'My pleasure.'

3

E 'Can I help you?'
F 'No, thank you. I'm just looking.'

4

G 'Excuse me! Is that seat free?'
H 'No, sorry, I'm afraid it isn't.'

T 1.14 Listen and repeat. Pay attention to stress and intonation.

2 Match a line in **A** with a line in **B**.

A	B
1 Good morning!	___ Bye! See you later!
2 See you tomorrow!	___ Of course. What's the problem?
3 How do you do?	___ Never mind. Perhaps another time.
4 Thank you very much indeed.	___ Thanks! Same to you.
5 I'm sorry. I can't come tonight.	___ Good morning! Lovely day again.
6 Can you help me with this exercise?	___ Yeah! About 9.00, in the coffee bar.
7 Bye!	___ It doesn't matter. You're here now.
8 Bye! Have a good weekend.	___ Don't mention it. My pleasure.
9 Sorry I'm late.	___ How do you do? Pleased to meet you.
10 Cheers!	___ Cheers! Here's to your new job!

Bye! See you later!
Of course. What's the problem?
How do you do?
Good morning!
Thank you very much indeed.

T 1.15 Listen, check, and practise.

3 Choose a line to continue the conversations.

a I don't know what this word means.
b Yes, it's really warm for the time of year.
c Pleased to meet you, too.
d Thanks a lot. I'm excited, but a bit nervous.
e It was so kind of you!
f I'm free tomorrow night. What about that?
g Fine. 9.00 is good for me too.
h Yes. Let's meet after class.
i Thanks. Are you doing anything special?
j Yeah. I missed the bus.

T 1.16 Listen and check.

4 With a partner, choose two of the conversations. Continue them if you can and act them to the class.

Good morning!
Good morning! Lovely day again.
Yes, it's really warm for the time of year.
They say it's going to rain again tomorrow! Enjoy it while it lasts!

2 Whatever makes you happy

Present tenses • *have/have got* • Things I like doing • Making conversation

STARTER

What is most important to you?
1 = most important, 6 = least important.

- ☐ good friends
- ☐ money
- ☐ a good job
- ☐ having fun
- ☐ being healthy
- ☐ family

Compare your ideas as a class.

For me, the most important thing is having a good job.

I LOVE WHAT I DO

Present tenses and *have/have got*

1 Look at the pictures of Ruth Flowers and Fraser Doherty. What's remarkable about them? Who likes going to clubs? Who makes jam?

2 **T 2.1** Read and listen to the article about Ruth. How old is she? What does she look like? What does her family think of her?

MAMY ROCK
the granny DJ

RUTH FLOWERS is not an ordinary grandmother. She's in her 70s, and has silver hair and bright-red lipstick. She's a DJ and works in clubs in Europe and tours festivals.

She lives alone in Bristol. She says, 'I've got a son and a grandson. They think what I'm doing is very cool!'

She likes rock bands such as Queen and the Rolling Stones, but she also plays electro and dance music. 'I love being with young people,' she says. 'They've got so much energy and enthusiasm!'

She's planning another European tour, and is currently making a new single.

'I'm having a lot of fun,' she says. 'I don't want it to stop.'

3 **T 2.2** Read and listen to the article about Fraser. What is his company? How old was he when he started it? What does his charity do?

the SuperJam millionaire

FRASER DOHERTY is an extraordinary young man. He has his own company, SuperJam, which he started when he was just 16. 'I earn more money than my parents,' he says. His company makes jam – 500,000 jars every year – using a secret recipe from his grandmother.

All the major supermarkets sell his products. The business is growing fast – four flavours at the moment, but more on the way. And he has a charity that organizes huge tea parties for old people with live music and dancing.

'At the moment I'm very busy. I'm writing a cookbook. I've got an idea for a TV programme. And we're trying to get into the American market.'

GRAMMAR SPOT

1 Which two present tenses are used in the texts? Find examples of both.

2 Look at the sentences. Which refers to all time? Which refers to now?

He **makes** a lot of money. He **has** his own company
She's **making** another single. She's **having** a good time.

3 Find the examples of *have* and *have got* in the texts. Is *have got* more formal or informal? More spoken or written?

▶▶ **Grammar Reference 2.1 – 2.4 p136–137**

4 Work with a partner. Ask and answer questions about Ruth and Fraser.

RUTH	FRASER
1 What/do? *What does Ruth do? She's a DJ.*	1 What/do?
2 Where/work?	2 How much/earn?
3 How many children/have?	3 How many jars/ every year?
4 What sort of music/like?	4 Whose recipe/use?
5 Why/like young people?	5 What/writing?
6 What/doing at the moment?	6 What/trying to do?

T 2.3 Listen and check.

5 **T 2.4** Listen to an interview with Ruth. Does she like being famous? What do her friends think of her job? Complete the sentences.

1 I'm just an old lady ____________.
2 I ________ an old woman in an old people's home …
3 Because it ________ me happy!
4 It ____________ how old you are.

6 **T 2.5** Listen to Fraser. What does he like about his work? What does he say about friends and family? Complete the interviewer's lines.

1 It ________ to me you really love what ________!
2 ________ any free time?
3 ________ you ________ a girlfriend?
4 ________ you ________ much of your parents?

7 Ruth and Fraser both use the expression *'It's none of your/their business!'* What does this mean? What are they talking about?

PRACTICE

Talking about you

1 Look at the speech bubbles with *have* and *have got* in the question, negative, and short answer. How are the forms different?

Do you have a car?
Yes, I do.
No, I don't.
Have you got a bike?
Yes, I have.
No, I haven't.
I don't have a camera.
I haven't got an iPod.

T 2.6 Listen and practise.

2 Work with a partner. Ask and answer questions about these things.

- any pets
- a bike
- a laptop
- a camera
- an iPod
- a credit card
- any brothers and sisters
- the teacher/a big bag
- your parents/a holiday home

Speaking – exchanging information

3 Look at the photos of Ilona, and Bill and Christina. With a partner, take turns to ask and answer questions about the people.

Student A Look at p151.
Student B Look at p153.

State verbs

4 Some verbs don't usually take the Present Continuous. Complete the sentences with a verb in the Present Simple in the correct form.

think	~~not know~~	not believe	look	not agree	love
mean	not matter	need	own	not understand	

1 'What time is it?' 'I __*don't know*__. Sorry.'
2 I'm thirsty! I ________ a drink.
3 I ________ your bag! Where did you get it?
4 'I ________ Thomas is stupid.'
'I ________. I think he's very clever.'
5 Her English isn't very good. I ________ her.
6 He's very rich. He ________ a house in Mayfair.
7 You ________ sad! What's the matter?
8 'Sorry I forgot your birthday!' 'Don't worry. It ________.'
9 'I'm 74 years old.'
'I ________ you! You don't look a day over 60!'
10 I don't understand *learn by heart*. What ________ it ________?

Check it

5 Tick (✓) the correct sentence.

1 ☐ Angela live with her parents.
☐ Angela lives with her parents.
2 ☐ Where do you go on holiday?
☐ Where you go on holiday?
3 ☐ She doesn't work here anymore.
☐ She no works here anymore.
4 ☐ He's at the bus stop. He waits for a bus.
☐ He's at the bus stop. He's waiting for a bus.
5 ☐ I'm liking black coffee.
☐ I like black coffee.
6 ☐ I don't have got a phone.
☐ I haven't got a phone.

▶▶ **WRITING Writing a postcard** *p105*

VOCABULARY AND SPEAKING

Things I like doing

1 Work with a partner. Match a **Verb** and a **Phrase**.

Verb	Phrase
play	emails and texts
go out	games on my PlayStation
download	music and films
send	with my friends

Verb	Phrase
shop	in front of the TV
have	friends for a drink
relax	for clothes online
meet	a lie-in

Verb	Phrase
listen to	music
go out	nothing
get	for a meal
do	a takeaway pizza

Verb	Phrase
read	a football match live on TV
chat	to the gym
go	magazines
watch	to friends online

T 2.7 Listen, check, and practise.

2 When and where do you do some of these things?

I like playing games on my PlayStation at home after school.

I just love having a lie-in on Sunday mornings.

3 Complete the sentences with words from exercise 1.

1 I like shopping in the High Street, but mainly I *shop online*.
2 When I hear a band I like, I ______ their ______ from the Internet.
3 I ______ on my iPod when I go jogging.
4 I spend hours ______, even though I'm with them all day at school!
5 Sometimes I like to chill out at home and ______.
6 I'm always so tired after work I just want to ______.
7 On Saturdays, I ______, and don't get up till midday.
8 Do you want to cook tonight, or shall we ______?
9 It's Pete's birthday tonight, so we're ______. Indian, I think.
10 I like keeping fit. I ______ three times a week.

T 2.8 Listen, check, and practise.

My perfect day

4 What is your idea of a perfect day? Make notes.

have a lie-in, go to a café, meet my friends

5 Work in groups. Talk about your perfect day.

For me, a perfect day is when I have a lie-in, and go to a café for breakfast. Then, I meet my friends …

READING AND SPEAKING

The happiness quiz

1 Look at the pictures. What are the people doing? Why are they happy?

2 Read the introduction to the quiz and answer the questions.
1 What does happiness depend on?
2 What do you need to know about yourself?
3 How can you learn to be happier?

3 Do the quiz and add up your score to see how happy you are. Do you agree?

4 The quiz is in four sections. Write one of these headings above each section.

Your enjoyment of life
Your health
Your relationships
Happiness with yourself

5 In which sections of the quiz did you score a high number? What do you need to do if you want to be happier?

What do you think?

6 Here are the results of a recent survey into happiness. Work in groups. Do you agree?
- £25,000 per year is all we need to make us happy.
- Buying things doesn't make us happy.
- Experiences such as holidays and living abroad *do* make us happier.
- Be happy with what you have. Stop wanting what you haven't got.
- Enjoy what you're doing.

7 **T 2.9** Listen to the beginning of the song, *Money*.
1 According to the song, what is more important, love or money?
2 'The best things in life are free.' Does the singer agree? Do *you* agree?

Project

Research the life of someone rich and famous in the news at the moment. Has fame and fortune brought them happiness? Bring information and pictures to class. Tell the others about your person.

How happy are you?

Your happiness depends on how you see yourself, what you want from life, and how well you get on with other people.

But you need to know yourself. What sort of person are you? What makes you happy? Do you know how to make yourself happier? If you can answer these questions, you can learn to change the way you think and behave. And you *can* actually be happier. It just needs practice.

Do the quiz and find out how happy you are. Write 1–5 for each statement.

1 = very true
2 = mainly true
3 = about 50/50
4 = not very true
5 = not true at all

1 ☐ I take every opportunity to play, laugh, and have a good time.
2 ☐ I usually have a holiday at least once a year.
3 ☐ I get pleasure from lots of different things – art, nature, sport, friends …
4 ☐ Sometimes I get really enthusiastic about things.

5 ☐ I have the things in life that I think are important.
6 ☐ I have a positive image of myself.
7 ☐ I am grateful for what I have, and appreciate it.
8 ☐ I don't often feel jealous or envious of other people.

9 ☐ I sleep well and wake up feeling ready for a new day.
10 ☐ I keep fit and I take care of myself.
11 ☐ I never feel stressed when I have a lot of things to do.
12 ☐ I don't feel afraid or depressed.

13 ☐ I have close friends and people I share interests with.
14 ☐ I get a lot of satisfaction from my work/study.
15 ☐ My life makes a difference to other people.
16 ☐ I try to help other people.

☐ Add up your score

Your score – How happy are you?

16–28	Extremely happy
29–40	Happy enough
41–52	About average
53–64	Not very happy
65–80	Cheer up! Life can't be that bad!

LISTENING AND SPEAKING

Getting on with your neighbours

1 What do you know about your neighbours?

They're called ...   *He's a ...*   *They've got ...*   *She's a ...*

How well do you know them?

Really well/not at all/just to say hello to ...

2 What makes a good neighbour? Read the ideas. Do you agree or disagree?

A good neighbour is someone who . . .

- always says hello.
- doesn't make too much noise.
- I never see.
- minds his/her own business.
- invites me to parties.
- feels at home in my house.
- sometimes comes round for coffee.

Discuss your ideas in small groups.

Two neighbours

3 **T 2.10** You are going to listen to two neighbours, Mrs Crumble and Alfie, talking about each other. Read the questions.

First, listen to Mrs Crumble. Answer the questions.

1 Where is Alfie's flat?
2 Do Alfie and Mrs Crumble speak to each other?
3 What does he wear? What *doesn't* he wear?
4 Has he got a job?
5 What time does he go to bed? What time does he get up?
6 How many people are staying in Alfie's flat?
7 Has he got a girlfriend? Where does she live?
8 Why does he make such a noise? What's he doing now?
9 What does Alfie think of Mrs Crumble?

Check your answers in small groups.

4 **T 2.11** Now listen to Alfie. How does he answer questions 1–9. What differences are there?

5 In your groups, discuss who you think is telling the truth.

Roleplay

Work with a partner. Roleplay a conversation between Alfie and Mrs Crumble where they actually get to know each other.

A Hello. I'm Alfie, your neighbour. You're Mrs Crumble, aren't you?
C Oh, Alfie, hello. I don't usually see you in the mornings ...

EVERYDAY ENGLISH
Making conversation

1 John and Maria

2 Maggie and Jean-Jacques

1 **T 2.12** It is the first day of a new school term. Listen to the conversations between two students and two teachers. The teachers are trying to be friendly. Which conversation is more successful? Why?

2 When you are having a conversation, it helps if you …

- add a comment
- don't just answer *yes* or *no*
- ask questions
- express interest

Find examples of these in **T 2.12** conversation 2 on p120.

3 Match a line in **A** with a reply in **B**.

A	B
1 What a lovely day it is today!	☐ a No, I didn't. I missed it.
2 Are you having a good time in London?	1 b Yes, beautiful, isn't it?
3 Have a good weekend!	☐ c Nothing special.
4 Did you have a nice weekend?	☐ d Thank you! They're new.
5 What are you doing tonight?	☐ e She's OK, thanks.
6 How's your mother these days?	☐ f Yes, I am. It's a very interesting city.
7 Did you watch the football last night?	☐ g Yes, I did. It was really good.
8 I like your shoes.	☐ h Thanks. Same to you.
9 If you have a problem, just ask me.	☐ i Thank you very much.

T 2.13 Listen and check. How does **B** keep the conversation going?

4 Practise the conversations with a partner. Cover **B**, then **A**. Remember the extra lines.

Keeping a conversation going

5 Work with a partner. Begin a conversation with one of these lines. Keep the conversation going as long as possible.

3 What's in the news?

Past Simple and Continuous • Adverbs • Saying when

STARTER

1 What is the Past Simple of these verbs? Which are regular? Which are irregular?

leave	take	become	begin
go	do	think	meet
walk	arrive	explain	end
want	decide		

2 Practise saying them around the class.

leave, left *take, took*

HE WALKED 6,000 MILES!

Past Simple and Past Continuous

1 Look at Ed Stafford's web page. What was he the first to do?

2 Read and complete the text with verbs from the *Starter* in the Past Simple.

T 3.1 Listen and check.

3 Work with a partner. Write the questions.

1 How far/Ed walk?

How far did Ed walk?

2 When/journey begin?
3 Where/journey end?
4 Which countries/go through?
5 How long/journey take?
6 Why/do it?

Now look at the map and read the text again. Answer the questions.

4 **T 3.2** Listen and check. Practise the questions and answers with your partner.

Home | Map | Videos | Photos | Team | FAQs

Amazing journey ends after 6,000 miles

Ed Stafford [1] ___*became*___ the first man in history to walk the length of the Amazon River from the source to the sea. He [2] ________ for 860 days.

The journey [3] ________ in April 2008 when Ed [4] ________ the town of Camana on the Pacific coast of Peru. It [5] ________ in August, 2010 when he [6] ________ in Maruda, on the Atlantic coast of Brazil.

He [7] ________ through three countries, Peru, Colombia, and Brazil. The journey [8] ________ nearly two and a half years. 'I [9] ________ it for the adventure,' says Ed.

5 Read **Cho's story**. Who is Cho?

6 Which tense are the verbs in **bold** in Cho's story? Complete these sentences.

1. Cho was working in the forest when he …
2. They were walking in a dangerous part of the forest when they …
3. The tribe didn't understand what Ed …

7 Write the questions. Ask and answer them with your partner.

1. What/Cho doing/when/met Ed?
2. Where/walking when/saw/tribe?
3. Why/tribe think/Ed/crazy?

T 3.3 Listen and check.

Cho's story

Home | Map | Videos | Photos | Team | FAQs

Ed didn't do the trip alone. His companion was Gadiel 'Cho' Sanchez Rivera, a forestry worker from Peru.

Cho said, 'When I first met Ed, I **was working** in the forest. I thought he was crazy, but I wanted to help him and be his guide.'

'One day we **were walking** in a very dangerous part of the forest when we saw a hostile tribe. They didn't understand what Ed **was doing** there. I explained he was an adventurer and he **was walking** the Amazon. They decided he was crazy, too.'

GRAMMAR SPOT

1. The Past Simple expresses a completed action in the past.
   Ed **walked** the Amazon. He **began** his journey in 2008.
2. Complete the question and negative.
   When ______ the journey begin?
   They ______ finish the journey until 2010.
3. The Past Continuous expresses an activity in progress in the past.
   Cho **was working** in the forest when he met Ed.
   Compare these sentences.
   I **had** a shower last night. (= simple, completed action)
   I **was having** a shower when the phone rang. (= interrupted activity)

▶▶ **Grammar Reference 3.1–3.3 p138** ▶▶ **Irregular verbs p158**

8 Read **Ed's blog**. Put the verb in brackets in the Past Simple or the Past Continuous.

Popular | Latest | Comments | Tags

Ed's blog

12 July

The day I nearly died

Today I [1]______ (walk) next to the river when I nearly [2]______ (stand) on a snake. I [3]______ (stop) immediately. The snake's fangs [4]______ (go) in and out. I was terrified. I [5]______ (not move). One bite and you're dead in 3 hours.

10 September

Knives and guns!

Early this morning we [6]______ (cross) the river by boat when we [7]______ (see) five canoes. The tribesmen [8]______ (carry) knives and guns. They were angry because we [9]______ (not have) permission to be on their land. We [10]______ (leave) as fast as we could.

24 November

The jungle at night

I [11]______ (lie) in my hammock last night trying to sleep, but it was impossible because the noise of the jungle was so loud. Monkeys [12]______ (scream) in the trees, and millions of mosquitos [13]______ (buzz) round my head. I [14]______ (take) a sleeping pill and finally [15]______ (fall) asleep at 3.00 a.m.

T 3.4 Listen and check.

9 Think of more questions to ask about Ed and Cho.

- What did they eat?
- How did they navigate?

Go online and find out more about Ed. Were your questions answered? What else did you learn? Tell the class.

PRACTICE

Pronunciation

1 Write the past tense in the chart.

stop	decide
stay	work
study	play
laugh	phone
want	mend
look	answer

/d/	/t/	/ɪd/
stay**ed**	stopp**ed**	decid**ed**

T 3.5 Listen and check.

2 **T 3.6** Listen and repeat the sentences you hear.

We stayed‿in a hotel. They stopped‿at lunch time.

3 **T 3.7** Listen and practise the sentences. Notice the pronunciation of *was* and *were*.

/wəz/
I was having dinner.

/wəz/
What was she wearing?

/wə/
They were playing football.

/wə/
Where were you going?

/wɒznt/
He wasn't listening.

/wɜːnt/
They weren't enjoying the party.

Discussing grammar

4 What's the difference between these pairs of sentences?

When we arrived, she **was making** some coffee.
When we arrived, she **made** some coffee.

I **read** a good book in bed last night.
I **was reading** a good book in bed last night.

5 Choose the correct verb form.

1 I *saw / was seeing* a good film yesterday.
2 While I *shopped / was shopping* this morning, I *lost / was losing* my wallet.
3 The police *stopped / were stopping* me on the motorway because I *drove / was driving* at 90 miles an hour.
4 'What *did you do / were you doing* when you saw the accident?' 'I *walked / was walking* down the street.'
5 'What *did you do / were you doing* when you saw the accident?' 'I *called / was calling* the police.'
6 'How *did you break / were you breaking* your leg?' 'I *was skiing / skied* and I *hit / was hitting* a tree.'
7 I *was cutting / cut* my finger while I *was cooking / cooked.*
8 *Did you have / Were you having* a good holiday?

Game – Truth or Lies

6 Write one true and two false sentences about where you were, and what you were doing at these times. Tell a partner.

- at 7.15 this morning
- at 10.00 p.m. last night
- at 1.00 p.m. yesterday
- at 10.00 a.m. last Sunday

Can your partner guess which sentence is true?

Talking about the news

7 Look at these newspaper headings. What do you think the stories are about?

Texting woman falls into fountain

Chinese vase sells for £53 million

The app that saved an iPad

Granny stops robbery

Choose one of the stories. Read the article on page 155.

8 Work in small groups. Tell your story to the others. DON'T read it! The other students can ask questions.

LISTENING AND SPEAKING

The news

1 How do you keep up to date with what's happening in the world?

Which of these news topics interests you most?

politics ... celebrities ... sport ... fashion ... culture ... the arts ... crime ... international news ... national news ... local news ...

Do you listen to the radio? Which station?

2 **T 3.8** Listen to five radio news headlines. What is the first story about? The second? Write a number 1–5.

☐ a strike ☐ a crime ☐ a death
☐ an explosion ☐ a football match

3 Which words do you think are from each story?

terrorists	thieves	guard	ex-wife
Picasso	cancer	goals	theft
half-time	higher pay	beat	protesting
injured	closed		

4 Write the question words.

______ planted the bomb?
______ paintings did they steal?
______ are they on strike?
______ times was he married?
______ was the score?

Work in groups. Choose one of the news stories. What else do you want to know? Think of more questions. Write the questions on the board.

5 **T 3.9** Listen to the news stories. Which questions were answered?

Dictation

6 **T 3.10** You will hear the story about the art theft at dictation speed. One student should write the exact words on the board. The other students help.

That isn't how you spell thieves.

You missed out a word.

She didn't say that. She said ...

Project

7 Find a news story that interests you. Do some research. In the next lesson, bring in pictures and articles. Tell the class about the story. Be prepared to answer questions.

READING AND SPEAKING

The flight attendant who lost his cool

1 Talk as a class. What makes you lose your cool?

Bad drivers. **My little brother.**

2 Look at the picture story about the flight attendant, Steven Slater. What made him lose his cool? In groups, write some sentences about the story. Compare ideas.

3 Read each article. After each one, answer the questions and have a class discussion.

4 Look at the pictures in 2 again. Retell the story in more detail.

What do you think?

1 After August 16, this story 'died'. Why was it such big news for a week?

2 Steven Slater appeared in court two months later.
Do you think he paid a fine or went to prison?
Look at the article on p155 for the answer.
Do you think this was fair?

3 The artist Andy Warhol once said, 'In the future everyone will be famous for fifteen minutes'. How does the Steven Slater story illustrate this?

Steven Slater

1 10 August

Emergency exit for flight attendant who lost his cool

Flight attendant Steven Slater made an emergency exit from an Airbus after he had an argument with a passenger.

The incident happened at New York's JFK Airport soon after the JetBlue flight from Pittsburgh landed.

As the Airbus A320 was taxiing slowly on the runway, a passenger stood up to get her luggage. Mr Slater told her to sit down, but she refused. The businesswoman was taking her case out of the overhead locker when it hit Mr Slater on the head.

He started bleeding, and it was then that the flight attendant lost his temper. He marched to the front of the cabin and spoke furiously over the plane's PA system, saying, 'That's enough! After 28 years in this business, I quit!'

He then took two beers from a fridge, opened the door and activated the plane's emergency chute and jumped onto it. Mr Slater then ran to his car and drove home.

Police arrested Mr Slater at his home a short time later.

1 When and where did the incident happen?
2 What did the female passenger do?
3 What did the flight attendant say to her?
4 What did she do to him? How did he react?
5 How did Steven Slater leave the plane?

Discussion

- Was this a very important story?
- Why do you think it was in the newspapers?

flight attendant

2 **11 August**

Angry flight attendant becomes Facebook hero

The flight attendant Steven Slater, who left his plane via the emergency exit, is becoming a folk hero in the US.

Last night a 'Free Steven Slater' page on Facebook had 170,000 fans. People wrote how much they admired him. 'I would dearly love to quit my job like you did!' is the message from many.

Tens of thousands of people, including other cabin crew, left messages of support.

'You only did what everyone else feels like doing,' wrote one.

Slater appeared in court in New York yesterday and pleaded not guilty to charges of criminal damage and endangering life. He could face up to seven years in prison.

1 What did people think of Steven the next day?
2 How did they show their support?
3 Why did the public admire him?
4 What did other cabin crew say?

Discussion

- Why did people think he was a hero?

3 **12 August**

Steven Slater thanks public

Flight attendant Steven Slater, 39, who left his job after an attack by a passenger, said he was amazed by the public sympathy he received.

Slater has messages from millions of people all over the world.

He said, 'I really appreciate this enormous support.'

As he was leaving a Bronx police station, people were shouting 'You're a hero!' T-shirts that read FREE STEVEN SLATER are on sale.

JetBlue confirmed that Slater was still an employee, but suspended from duty.

1 How did Steven feel?
2 How did people show their support?
3 Where was he?

Discussion

- How is it possible that this story went round the world in two days?

4 **15 August**

Folk hero Slater relaxes on the beach

Ex-flight attendant Steven Slater spent the weekend relaxing on the beach. He was having a couple of beers and enjoying his new worldwide fame as the latest American folk hero.

The 39-year-old was wearing a grey T-shirt, white shorts, and a baseball cap as he talked to excited fans on the beach near his home in New York.

Yesterday supporters shouted, 'Good for you, Steve!' and 'We love you!' as he sat down on a chair, took off his shirt, and put on his sunglasses.

1 What is Steven called in the headline?
2 What actually happened on the beach?

Discussion

- Why was this day's story in the papers?
- What did Steven Slater do to deserve being called a folk hero?

5 **16 August**

Ex-flight attendant to get TV Show

Steven Slater is in talks to get his own reality show. TV production company Stone Entertainment wants to give the flight attendant the chance to star in a program that shows unhappy workers how to leave their job.

1 How is Steven going to become more famous?
2 What will the program be about?

Discussion

- Why did a TV production company want to give him a show?

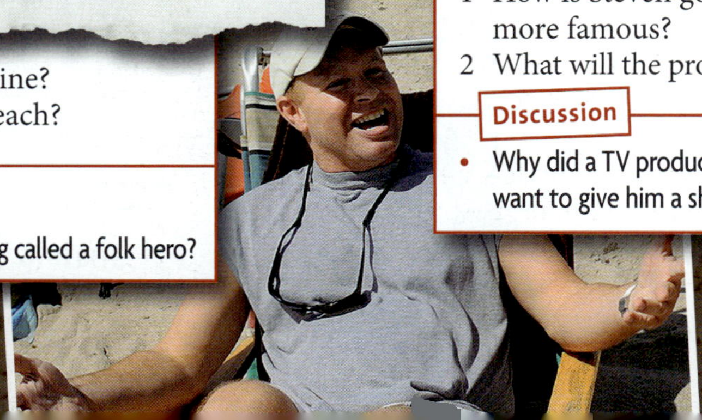

Folk hero

VOCABULARY
Adverbs

1 Look at these sentences from the articles on pages 26 and 27. Underline the adverbs.

… he spoke furiously …

… the Airbus A320 was taxiing slowly on the runway …

'I would dearly love to quit my job …'

2 Many regular adverbs end in *-ly*. Match a verb in **A** with an adverb in **B**.

A	B
1 drive	fluently
2 love	carefully
3 speak	patiently
4 rain	bravely
5 wait	heavily
6 fight	passionately

T 3.11 Listen and check. Try to remember the sentences.

3 What do you notice about the adjectives and adverbs in these sentences?

Is this a **fast** train to London?
Slow down! You drive too **fast**!

I work **hard** and play **hard**.
She's a very **hard** worker.

I got up **late** this morning.
We had a **late** breakfast.

4 What is the adverb from these adjectives? Complete the lines with the adverbs.

clear	quiet	slow	honest	perfect
complete	good	bad	easy	

1 play a game **well** and win
2 play a game … and lose
3 explain the rules …
4 shut the door …
5 forget something …
6 get out of bed …
7 play the piano …
8 pass an exam …
9 answer the questions …

Word order

5 Correct the word order in these sentences.

1 She speaks very well English.
She speaks English very well.
2 He started last week a new job.
3 Please read carefully the instructions.
4 Do you work still for the same company?
5 Never I can remember her name.
6 We had last year in Spain a holiday.

6 Put the adverbs in the correct place in the sentences.

1 My grandma is 75, and she goes swimming. (**nearly still regularly**)
2 'Do you love me?' 'I do. I will love you.' (**really of course always**)
3 I was relaxing with a good book when someone knocked on the door. (**just really loudly**)
4 My sister is three, but she can read, and she can write. (**only already too**)
5 Break the eggs into a bowl with some milk and butter. Heat it gently. When it is ready, serve the scrambled eggs with toast. (**first then immediately**)
6 All my friends have a mobile phone. They're on Facebook. My dad's on Facebook. (**almost as well even**)

T 3.12 Listen and check.

▶▶ **WRITING** **T 3.13** **Narrative writing** *p106*

EVERYDAY ENGLISH

Saying when

1 Answer the questions. Tell a partner.

- What's the date today/tomorrow/the day after tomorrow?
- When's your birthday?
- What's your date of birth?
- What year were you born?

T 3.14 Listen and compare.

2 Look at the two ways of saying the date.

A What's the date today? **B** It's the twenty-second of June.	**A** What's the date today? **B** It's June the twenty-second.

Practise saying these dates in two ways.

T 3.15 Listen and check.

3 **T 3.16** Listen to how Americans say the dates. What's the difference between British and American English?

4 Practise saying the years.

2012 2002 2015
2010 1980 1969
1994 1848

5 **T 3.17** Write the dates you hear.

1 ________ 3 ________ 5 ________
2 ________ 4 ________

6 What days are national holidays in your country?

7 Write down three dates that are important to you. Tell a partner.

July 25 – it's my wedding anniversary.

Time expressions

8 Complete the time expressions with *in/at/on*, or no preposition.

____ six o'clock	____ Saturday
____ 2004	____ Monday morning
____ last night	____ April
____ the weekend	____ yesterday evening
____ the evening	____ summer
____ January 18	____ two weeks ago
____ the 1960s	____ this morning
____ the other day	____ midnight

▶▶ Grammar Reference 3.4 p138

9 Work in small groups. When did you last ...?

- go to the cinema

I went to the cinema last Friday/on Monday evening/two weeks ago.

- play a sport
- go to a party
- do an exam
- have a holiday
- get a present
- buy some clothes
- go online
- cook a meal

4 Eat, drink, and be merry!

Expressing quantity • *something/no one ...* • Articles • *A piece of ...*
Can you come for dinner?

STARTER

1 What did you eat and drink yesterday? Make a list.

2 Compare your list with the class.
Who had the healthiest diet?

For breakfast I had a cup of coffee, some cereal, and ...

HOW TO LIVE TO BE 120!

Expressions of quantity

1 Read about Claus and Elvira Bonrich.

1. What is their extraordinary ambition?
2. What are their jobs?
3. What kind of food do they eat? Do they cook any of their food?

An extraordinary ambition!

Claus Bonrich (33) and his wife **Elvira** (28) are a successful young couple. Claus is a software programmer and Elvira works in a health food shop. In many ways their life is quite ordinary, but they have an extraordinary ambition. They want to live until they are 120. And they believe they can do this by following an American health plan called the 'Calorie Restriction Diet'. Claus and Elvira eat a lot of raw food. They steam some food but they don't fry, grill, or roast anything, and there are many things they don't eat at all.

'We want to live to be 120!'

2 Look at the nouns in the boxes. Which group can you count? Which can't you count? Label the nouns *Countable* and *Uncountable*.

________	
apples	grapes
carrots	prawns
vegetables	calories

________	
meat	fish
orange juice	coffee
tea	fruit
broccoli	alcohol

3 Work with a partner. Read and complete the questions and answers about the diet with the nouns from exercise 2.

"
1 **Q** Do you eat any ___*meat*___?
A No, we don't eat **any** ________ at all, but we eat **some** ________.

2 **Q** **How much** ________ do you eat?
A We eat **a little** white ________, but we love shellfish so we eat **a lot of** ________.

3 **Q** Do you eat **much** ________?
A Oh, yes, we eat **a lot of** fresh ________ – ________ and ________, everything.

4 **Q** And do you eat **many** ____________?
A Yes, of course, we eat **lots of** raw ____________.

5 **Q** Don't you cook **any** vegetables at all?
A We cook **some**. Sometimes we steam **a few** ________ and **a little** ________.

6 **Q** And what do you drink?
A Well, we don't drink **any** ________ or ________, and naturally there's **no** ________ in our diet, but we do drink **a lot of** ____________.

7 **Q** **How many** ________ do you have every day?
A About 1,500.
A That's about 1,000 fewer than most people. "

4 **T 4.1** Listen and check. Practise the questions and answers with your partner.

GRAMMAR SPOT

1 Look at the expressions of quantity in **A**, **B**, and **C**. Which group go with plural, countable nouns? Which go with uncountables? Which go with both?

A	B	C
How much ...? not much a little	How many ...? not many a few	some/any not any/no a lot of/lots of

Find examples in the interview in exercise 3.

2 *Much* and *many* are not usually used in positive statements. When do we use them? Correct the sentences.

There are ~~many~~ books in my bag. ✗
There's ~~much~~ homework tonight. ✗

3 Look at these sentences. Which is a request?

Is there *any* orange juice? Can I have *some* orange juice?

▶▶ **Grammar Reference 4.1 p139**

5 Work in small groups. Do you think the Bonrichs eat and drink the things in the box? Discuss with your partner and complete the lists.

~~cereal~~	~~bread~~	milk	cheese	butter
tomatoes	peppers	olive oil	nuts	rice
pasta	sugar	bananas	mangoes	biscuits
apple juice	potatoes	chips	crisps	wine
tap water	mineral water			

Do you think they eat any cereal?
Yes, I think so. Maybe just a little, not much.
What about ...?

✓ *cereal*

✗ *bread*

Compare your list with the class.

6 **T 4.2** Listen and find out if your ideas were correct.

7 What do you think of the diet? Will the Bonrichs live to be 120? Why/Why not?

PRACTICE

Discussing grammar

Work with a partner. Complete the sentences.

1 some / any

1 Have they got _____ children?
2 We don't need _____ olive oil.
3 Can you lend me _____ money.
4 Is there _____ petrol in the car?
5 Can I have _____ cake?

2 much / many

1 Have you got _____ homework?
2 We don't need _____ eggs. Just half a dozen.
3 Is there _____ traffic in your town?
4 I don't know _____ students in this class.
5 How _____ time have you got?

3 a little / a few / a lot of

1 I have _____ very close friends. Two or three.
2 He has _____ money. He's a millionaire.
3 'Do you take sugar in coffee?' 'Just _____. Half a spoonful.'
4 I'll be ready in _____ minutes.
5 She speaks good Spanish, but only _____ Russian.

something/someone/somewhere ...

4 Complete the lines with the correct word.

some any every no	+	thing one/body where

1 'Did you meet _______ nice at the party?'
'Yes. I met _______ who knows you!'
2 'Ouch! There's _______ in my eye!'
'Let me look. No, I can't see _______.'
3 'Let's go _______ hot for our holidays.'
'But we can't go _______ that's too expensive.'
4 'Where are my glasses. I can't find them _______.'
'What are they on the top of your head?'
5 'It was a great party. _______ loved it.'
'They did. _______ wanted to go home.'
6 'Did you get _______ nice in the sales?'
'No, _______. I couldn't find _______ I liked.'

T 4.3 Listen and check. Practise them with a partner.

5 **T 4.4** Listen. There is a word missing in each sentence. Call out what it is. Say the complete sentence.

THE SECRET TO A LONG LIFE

Articles – *a/an, the*

1 Do you know anybody who lived to be a great age? How old were they? Why do you think they lived so long?

2 **T 4.5** Read and listen to the text. Answer the questions.

1 How long did the grandfather live?
2 Where did he live?
3 What kind of shop did he have?
4 How many children did he have?
5 Why did everybody love him?
6 When did he stop work?
7 What was his secret to a long life?

My Grandfather's

My grandfather lived until he was **101** years old. He was a shopkeeper. He had a fish and chip shop in an old village near a big, industrial town in the north of England. He had a son and a daughter. The daughter is my mother. The family lived above the shop.

In those days, fish and chips was the most popular dish in the whole country. My grandfather made the best fish and chips in the area. People came to the village by bus especially to get them.

Everybody loved my grandfather because he was such a happy and contented man. He worked hard, but once a week he closed the shop and went to have lunch (not fish and chips!) with friends in the local pub. He didn't retire until he was 78 years old. He said that the secret to a long life was a glass of whisky before going to bed and lots of fish and chips.

GRAMMAR SPOT

Articles

1 Find examples of the definite article (*the*) and the indefinite article (*a/an*) in the text.

2 What do you notice about these phrases?

... came **by bus**.
... went to **have lunch**.
... before going **to bed**.

3 Read the rules in **Grammar Reference 4.2 p139**. Find some examples of these rules in the text.

PRACTICE

Reading aloud

1 Join the lines about the grandfather with *the*, *a*, *an*, or no article.

My grandfather was		shopkeeper.
He lived in		north of England.
He had a fish and chip shop in		old village.
His family lived above	**the**	shop.
He made	**a**	best fish and chips in the area.
Some people came by	**an** / **no article**	bus to the shop.
He closed the shop once		week.
He went to have		lunch with friends.
He liked to have		little whisky before bed.

T 4.6 Listen and check. Read the lines aloud to a partner.

Discussing grammar

Work with a partner.

2 Complete the sentences with *a/an*, *the* or no article.

1 He has ______ boy and ______ girl. ______ boy is 22 and ______ girl is 17.
2 His son is ______ engineer and his daughter is ______ student.
3 He always has ______ cheese sandwiches for ______ lunch.
4 All ______ family stayed at ______ Grand Hotel.
5 ______ few people came by ______ taxi to ______ party.
6 It was such ______ wonderful party. We had ______ best time ever.
7 I don't go out to ______ work. I work at ______ home on my computer.
8 I do all my shopping on ______ Internet. What ______ great way to shop!

Check it

3 Find *one* mistake in each sentence and correct it.

1 He's postman, so he has breakfast at 4.00 a.m.
2 The love is more important than money.
3 I come to school by the bike.
4 I'm reading one good book at the moment.
5 'Where are the children?' 'In a kitchen.'
6 I live in centre of town, near the hospital.
7 My parents bought the lovely house in the country.
8 I don't eat the bread because I don't like it.

READING AND LISTENING

Unusual places to eat

1 Are there lots of places to eat and drink in your town? What are they? Where did people in your country eat and drink hundreds of years ago?

2 Read the introduction. Look at the pictures and the Fact Files. What's unusual about the three restaurants?

3 Work in three groups.

Group A Read about *Dinner in the Sky.*

Group B Read about *Ithaa Undersea Restaurant.*

Group C Read about *'s Baggers Restaurant.*

Answer the questions about your restaurant.

1 Where is the restaurant?
2 In what ways is it unusual?
3 When did it open?
4 What's on the menu? Is it good?
5 How expensive is it?
6 Are there any problems?

4 Find a partner from the other two groups and compare the restaurants.

Listening

5 **T 4.7** Listen to people who visited the restaurants. Answer these questions after each person.

- Which restaurant did they visit? Who with?
- What was good about it?
- What wasn't so good?
- What do they say about the other guests?

Alexander **Hans** **Lucy**

What do you think?

- Which do you think is the *most* unusual restaurant?
- Which would you like to visit? Why?
- Do you eat out? How often? What's your favourite resturant?
- Do you know any unusual restaurants? Tell the class.

No ordinary place to eat!

Dinner in the Sky

FACT FILE
- 50m up in the air
- a table 9m x 5m
- diners hang from a crane
- there isn't a loo

Dinner in the Sky is for people who want more than a little excitement when they go out to eat. They sit at a huge table which hangs from a crane fifty metres in the air. It's not a good idea for people who are afraid of heights or for those who don't have much money. It costs £10,000. The twenty-two diners wear seat belts and relax and enjoy the views while the chefs prepare the finest food in front of them. The restaurant opened in Belgium in 2006, but now has branches in Paris, Dubai, Florida, and Las Vegas.

David Ghysels, the Belgian organizer says, 'We realized that people were bored with going to the same old restaurants. They wanted to try something different. The sky's the limit with us!'

The crane is checked carefully before every sitting. The table is 9m x 5m and weighs six tonnes. In the centre there is a sunken platform for the chef and two waiters. The food is delicious, but most guests don't feel like eating until after a few drinks! Then they also get the courage to look down at the ground where tiny people are looking up in amazement and waving.

Dinner in the Sky is very exciting and the food is good, but there are problems. For example, even in quiet weather conversation is difficult because of the wind. Guests shout to each other across the table. Also, the loo. You can't go to the loo until the table descends again. Difficult for some! But later, back on earth, after a visit to the loo, the guests have a great experience to talk about.

For hundreds of years when tired travellers stopped on their journeys, there were only a few places to eat and drink. Nowadays, streets are lined with restaurants, cafés, and snack bars, but some people want something more unusual.

Ithaa Undersea Restaurant

FACT FILE

- 5m under the sea
- a huge glass ceiling
- diners wear formal clothes
- they eat face-to-face with sharks

Welcome to the Maldives and the first underwater restaurant in the world. The ***Ithaa Undersea Restaurant*** on Rangali Island sits five metres below the Indian Ocean. Ithaa means 'pearl' in the Maldivian language and the guests are like pearls in a glass oyster.

It's not cheap – about £160 for dinner – and there aren't many seats, only a dozen, so it's not easy to get a reservation even if you've got enough money. However, it is easy to get to. You don't need to be a swimmer or a scuba diver, but you do have to wear formal clothes. You simply descend to the restaurant down some spiral stairs.

The manager, Carlton Schieck says, 'We have used aquarium technology to put diners face-to-face with the fish. Our guests are speechless at the colour and beauty of the underwater world. They can enjoy the views and the fine food and not get their feet wet.'

The views are spectacular. In the crystal-blue sea, a few metres from your head, there are sharks, sting rays, turtles, and thousands of tropical fish looking at you as you eat. There is also a fabulous coral garden to add to the colour. The experience is both romantic and magical – and you can guess what's on the menu!

The restaurant opened in 2004 and cost over £3 million to build. In April 2010 it also became a hotel. If you want more excitement and would like to sleep underwater with the fish, you can do this for just £7,500 a night!

However, an underwater building can't last forever. It is thought that it will have a life of about twenty years.

's Baggers Restaurant

FACT FILE

- no waiters
- food lands from above
- email as you eat
- eat now, pay later
- no tips

Germany likes to call itself *The Land of Ideas* and ***'s Baggers Restaurant*** in Nuremberg is certainly an amazing idea. It's a restaurant with no waiters to serve you. You do everything for yourself with touch-screen TVs and computers. It opened in 2007 and is the first automated restaurant in the world.

When you arrive you pick up an ***'s Baggers*** credit card and go to sit at a big, round table with three or four computer screens. You put your card into the computer and order your meal by touching the pictures on the screen. You don't see the chefs. They are in the kitchen high above you. They're real men, not machines (at least not yet). The food is all freshly cooked and when it is ready it is put in a pot and sent down a spiral tube where it lands on the table in front of you. This gives a new meaning to fast food! The TVs are connected to the Internet, so if you get bored while waiting, you can send and receive emails and text messages.

A businessman called Michael Mack had the idea for ***'s Baggers***. He decided that waiters were unnecessary and too expensive. 'You don't need waiters to run to and from customers taking orders to the kitchen and back.' Mack is planning to open more restaurants and now has the patent for the idea.

The meals are not too expensive – about €8 (£6) a portion. And if you want you can pay by direct debit at the end of the month. And something else that saves money – there is, of course, no need to leave a tip!

VOCABULARY AND LISTENING

A piece of …

1 Work in small groups. Match amounts in **A** with nouns in **B**. How many can you make?

A

a piece
a loaf
a bottle
a can
a kilo
a litre
a packet
a pair
a slice
a bunch

of

B

apples
bananas
beer
bread
cake
chewing gum
Coke
flowers
ham
tissues
jeans
milk
paper
petrol
sunglasses
socks
wine

2 **T 4.8** Listen and repeat the expressions. How much are some of these things in your country?

I think a large loaf of white bread costs about £1.00.

3 **T 4.9** Listen to six conversations.

1 Where is the conversation taking place? Choose from these places.
- a newsagent's
- a clothes shop
- a chemist's
- an off-licence
- a café
- a supermarket

2 What does the customer want to buy?
3 What numbers and/or prices do you hear? Write them down.

4 Who says these lines? What is each line about?

1 'No problem. I've got change.'
2 'Have you got any in blue?'
3 'I'm afraid there are only two slices left.'
4 'Take these three times a day.'
5 'Have you got any ID?'
6 'They're on the first aisle, over there.'

5 **T 4.9** Listen again and check. Work with a partner. Turn to page 123 and choose one of the conversations. Learn it by heart and then act it to the class.

▶▶ **WRITING** **Writing an email** *p108*

EVERYDAY ENGLISH

Can you come for dinner?

1 What is happening in the picture? What are the people eating and drinking?

2 Match a question in **A** with a response in **B**.

A	B
1 Would you like some more rice?	___ a Black, no sugar. Have you got any decaf?
2 Could you pass the salt, please?	___ b No, not at all. I got it online. I'll give you the website.
3 Can I have some water, please?	___ c Do you want still or sparkling?
4 Please, just help yourselves to the dessert.	___ d No, thanks. But could I have another piece of bread?
5 Would anybody like some more ice cream?	___ e Yes, of course. Do you want the pepper, too?
6 How would you like your coffee?	___ f No, but I'd love some more fruit. Is there any left?
7 This is delicious! Would you mind giving me the recipe?	___ g No, of course not. You're our guests!
8 Do you want some help with the washing-up?	___ h We will. It looks fantastic. Did you make it yourself?

T 4.10 Listen and check. What is the next line? Practise the conversations with a partner.

3 Complete the requests with *Can/Could I ...?* or *Can/Could you ...?*

1 __________ have some apple juice, please?
2 __________ tell me where Market Street is, please?
3 __________ see the menu, please?
4 __________ use your iPad for a few minutes, please?
5 __________ lend me £20, please?
6 __________ take me to school, please?
7 __________ help me with my homework, please?
8 __________ give me a lift to the station, please?

Practise the requests with a partner. Give an answer for each request.

Can I have some apple juice, please?

Sorry, we ...

Yes, of course. Would you like ...?

T 4.11 Listen and compare.

4 Make 5–8 in exercise 3 more polite using *Would you mind + -ing*?

Would you mind lending me £20?

No, not at all. Is 20 enough?

T 4.12 Listen and check. Practise saying them.

5 Request things from your teacher and other members of the class.

Can I borrow your ...?

Could you lend me your ...?

Would you mind helping me with ...?

5 Looking forward

Verb patterns • Future forms • Phrasal verbs • Expressing doubt and certainty

STARTER

Complete these sentences with ideas about you. Tell the class.

- *One day I want to ...*
- *Tonight I'm ...*
- *Right now, I'd like to ...*
- *This weekend I'm going to ...*

I'D LIKE TO ...
Verb patterns

1 Read what the people say. What do they do? What are their problems? What do you think they want to do?

2 Work with a partner. Which sentences go with which person.

1 'I'm going to study hard for my exams because I hope to get a well-paid job.' *Abby*

2 'I'd like to leave now and get a job, any job. I want to earn some money.'

3 'I'm thinking of applying for another job with a company in New York.'

4 'Now I like sleeping late and planning holidays on the Internet for me and my wife.'

5 'I'm looking forward to having a good break. We're going to Spain this summer.'

6 'I enjoy looking after the kids, but I'd love to travel, too.'

T 5.1 Listen and check. What else does each person say?

3 **T 5.1** Listen again. Complete the lines. Who says them?

1 I'd love *to work* there for a couple of years.
2 I'm planning ______ nothing but read on the beach.
3 I ______ owing so much money.
4 I get fed up with ______ at home all day. I'm looking forward to ______ back to work.
5 I'm pretty good at ______ a computer.
6 My mum and dad say that I ______ leave school.

GRAMMAR SPOT

1 Find examples in exercises 2 and 3 of:

verb + infinitive verb + *-ing*
prepositions *at*, *of*, *with* and *to* + *-ing*

2 What's the difference between these sentences?

I **like working** in New York.
I'**d like to work** in New York.

3 Complete the sentences with the phrase *work in New York*. Put the verb *work* in the correct form.

I want ... *to work in New York.*
I'd love ...
I enjoy ...
I'm fed up with ...
I hope ...
I'm thinking of ...
I'm looking forward to ...

▶▶ **Grammar Reference 5.1 p140** ▶▶ **Verb patterns p158**

PRACTICE

Discussing grammar

1 In these sentences, one or two verbs are correct, but not all three. Work with a partner. Tick (✓) the correct verbs.

1 I ___ to work in Paris.
a [✓] want b [ ] enjoy c [✓] 'd like

2 We ___ going to Italy for our holidays.
a [ ] are hoping b [ ] like c [ ] 're thinking of

3 She ___ leave work early tonight.
a [ ] wants b [ ] 'd like c [ ] can't

4 I ___ to see you again soon.
a [ ] hope b [ ] 'd like c [ ] 'm looking forward

5 He ___ playing sports games on the Wii.
a [ ] wants b [ ] 's good at c [ ] enjoys

6 Are you ___ learning foreign languages?
a [ ] want b [ ] like c [ ] good at

7 We ___ having a few days off soon.
a [ ] 're going b [ ] 'd love c [ ] 're looking forward to

8 I ___ doing housework.
a [ ] 'm fed up with b [ ] hate c [ ] don't want

T 5.2 Listen and check.

2 Make sentences with the verbs which *weren't* correct in exercise 1. Read them aloud.

T 5.3 Listen and check.

I enjoy working in Paris.

Making questions

3 Write the questions.

1 I hope to go to university. (*What/want/study?*)
2 One of my favourite hobbies is cooking. (*What/like/make?*)
3 I'm bored. (*What would/like/do?*)
4 I'm looking forward to the party. (*Who/hoping/see/there?*)
5 We're planning our summer holidays. (*Where/think/go?*)

T 5.4 Listen and check. How do the conversations continue? Practise some of them with a partner.

Talking about you

4 Ask and answer the questions with a partner.

- Where would you like to be right now?
- Do you like learning English?
- Would you like to learn any other languages? Which?
- Would you like to have a break now?

▶▶ **WRITING** **T 5.5** **Writing for talking** *p109*

HAVE YOU GOT ANY PLANS?

will, *going to*, and Present Continuous for future

1 Match questions 1–4 with an answer from Pete and an answer from Debbie. Who has got definite future plans? Who hasn't?

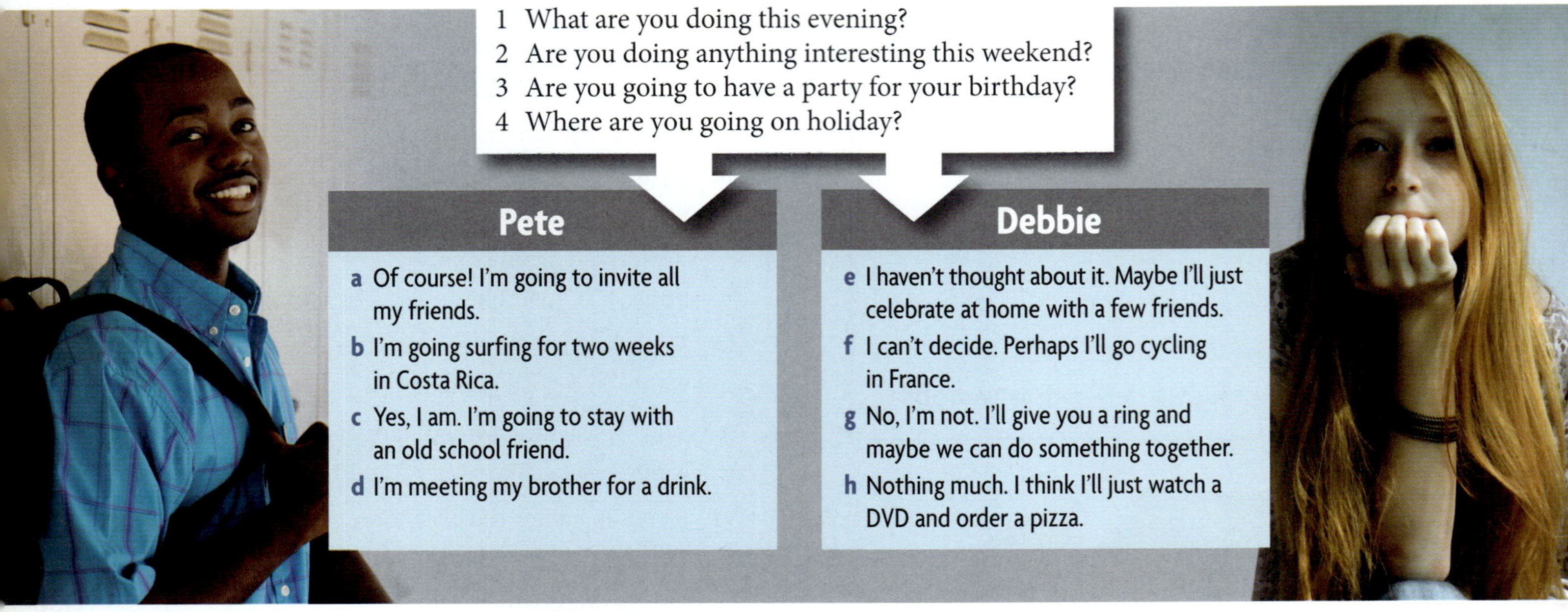

1 What are you doing this evening?
2 Are you doing anything interesting this weekend?
3 Are you going to have a party for your birthday?
4 Where are you going on holiday?

Pete

a Of course! I'm going to invite all my friends.
b I'm going surfing for two weeks in Costa Rica.
c Yes, I am. I'm going to stay with an old school friend.
d I'm meeting my brother for a drink.

Debbie

e I haven't thought about it. Maybe I'll just celebrate at home with a few friends.
f I can't decide. Perhaps I'll go cycling in France.
g No, I'm not. I'll give you a ring and maybe we can do something together.
h Nothing much. I think I'll just watch a DVD and order a pizza.

T 5.6 Listen and check.

2 Pete is talking to his friend, Ben. Debbie is talking to Ella. Answer the questions.

1 Why can't Ben go out with Pete and his brother?
2 Why is Pete going to visit his old school friend?
3 Where's Ben going on holiday?
4 Where's Ella going on holiday?
5 When's Debbie's birthday?
6 Why won't Ella stay late?

Talking about you

3 With your partner ask and answer the four questions in exercise 1 about you.

GRAMMAR SPOT

Will, *going to* and the Present Continuous can all refer to future time.

1 ***Will*** can express an intention decided *at* the time of speaking.
I'll give you a ring.
2 ***Going to*** can express a plan decided *before* the time of speaking.
I'm going to stay with a friend.
3 The **Present Continuous** can express an arrangement.
I'm working late this evening.

▶▶ **Grammar Reference 5.2 p140**

PRACTICE

Discussing grammar

1 Work with a partner. Choose the correct verb form.

1 A Have you decided which university to apply for?
B Oh yes, ***I'll*** / ***I'm going to*** apply for Oxford.

2 A I haven't got your mobile number.
B Really? ***I'll*** / ***I'm going to*** text it to you right now.

3 A We don't have any fruit in the house.
B ***I'll go*** / ***I'm going*** shopping this afternoon. ***I'll*** / ***I'm going to*** get some apples.

4 A My bag is really heavy.
B Give it to me. ***I'll*** / ***I'm going to*** carry it for you.

5 A Tony's back from holiday.
B Is he? ***I'll*** / ***I'm going to*** give him a ring.

6 A What ***will we have*** / ***are we having*** for supper?
B ***I'm going to*** / ***I'll*** make spaghetti bolognese.

T 5.7 Listen, check, and practise. What's the extra line?

What can you say?

2 **T 5.8** Close your books. Listen to the first line of six conversations. Respond to each one.

Why are you looking forward to the weekend?

Because I'm going to the theatre ...

3 **T 5.9** Listen and compare.

When can we meet?

4 Work with a partner. Arrange a time to meet in the next week.
Student A Look at your diary on p151.
Student B Look at your diary on p153.

What are you doing on Monday afternoon?

I'm ...

Will you, won't you?

5 Use the words in **A** and make sentences with *I think ... will ...* . Match them with a line in **B**.

A

1 you/pass your driving test
2 my team/win
3 it/warm today
4 I/join a gym
5 they/get divorced
6 I/go by train

B

__ I won't go on a diet.
__ You won't fail again.
__ You won't need your jumper.
__ I won't fly.
__ They won't stay together.
__ They won't lose this time.

6 **T 5.10** Listen and check. What is the extra line?

LISTENING AND SPEAKING

How does it feel to be 20-something?

1 Think of someone you know in their twenties. Tell a partner about them.
name • age • relationship to you • job • interests • ambitions

2 *The Times* newspaper ran an 'iGeneration' poll to find out how it feels to be a 20-something in the 21st century. What is a 20-something?

3 **T 5.11** Listen to three 20-somethings, Leo, Elsa, and Dan. Who is happy? Who feels grown-up? Who knows what they want to do in the future?

4 Complete the questions with the correct name.

1 How old is _Leo_'s nephew?
2 How much did ______ owe when he left university?
3 Why did ______ give up studying law?
4 How much does ______ earn as a junior reporter?
5 How long did ______ go travelling?
6 What question did ______'s nephew ask?

Ask and answer the questions with a partner.

5 **T 5.11** Listen again. After each 20-something, answer the questions.

Leo
1 Why was he shocked by his nephew's question?
2 Why is he happy?
3 What's he going to do next year?
4 When does he think he'll marry?

Elsa
5 Where did she go travelling?
6 What is she doing at the moment?
7 What question does her father ask?
8 How is her life different from her mother's at the same age?

Dan
9 Why is he a *boomerang kid*?
10 Does he think that his situation is unusual?
11 When does he think he'll marry his girlfriend?
12 Why is he fed up?

What do you think?

- When do you think is the best time for children to leave home?
- What are the pros and cons for parents if their children move back home?
- What are the pros and cons for the children?

READING AND SPEAKING
Hope for the future

1 Do you know the name Chernobyl? Do you know where it is? Find out about it on the Internet. Discuss with the class.

2 Read the introduction to **Palina – the girl with two families**.
- Where does Palina come from?
- When was she born?
- Why didn't her future look good?

3 Read **Life in the village of Polessye**. Are the sentences true (✓) or false (✗)? Correct the false ones.
1 Palina was born the same year as the disaster.
2 She grew up on a farm.
3 She was an only child.
4 Eight experts from Minsk came to her school.
5 There was a forest near the village.
6 The experts paid for the children to have holidays abroad.
7 Palina wanted to go to Ireland because she could speak English.

4 Read **Life in Ireland**. Answer the questions.
1 How did Palina communicate with the family?
2 Why was she so surprised in the shopping mall?
3 Was her English fluent at the end of the holiday?
4 How often did she visit the Irish family?

5 Read **Palina today**. Why is Palina lucky? What reasons can you find?

6 Read the sentences. Who do you think said each one?
1 'It's difficult to sell any of our produce these days.'
2 'We aren't going to pick any more mushrooms.'
3 'Would you like to have a holiday in Ireland?'
4 'I'm a bit worried about going.'
5 'Welcome to Ireland. We hope you'll be happy here.'
6 'Let's play in the garden!'
7 'We'll pay for your education.'
8 'One day I'm going to return as a doctor.'

What do you think?
- 'The disaster changed the lives of everybody in the village.' How do you think life changed?
- What do you learn about Palina and her family that suggests that they were poor?
- Do you think Palina was ever homesick?

Roleplay
Work in groups and think of questions to ask Palina about her life. In pairs take the roles of Palina and the interviewer. Ask and answer questions, begin like this.

Nice to meet you Palina. Can I ask you some questions?

Of course.

When and where were you born?

T 5.12 Listen and compare.

Palina

In the early hours of April 26 1986, the worst nuclear accident in history occurred in the Ukrainian city of Chernobyl.

Two years later and two hundred miles away, **Palina Yanachkina** was born in the village of Polessye, in northern Belarus. Like many others in her village she had a lot of health problems and her future didn't look good. Then a holiday in Ireland changed everything.

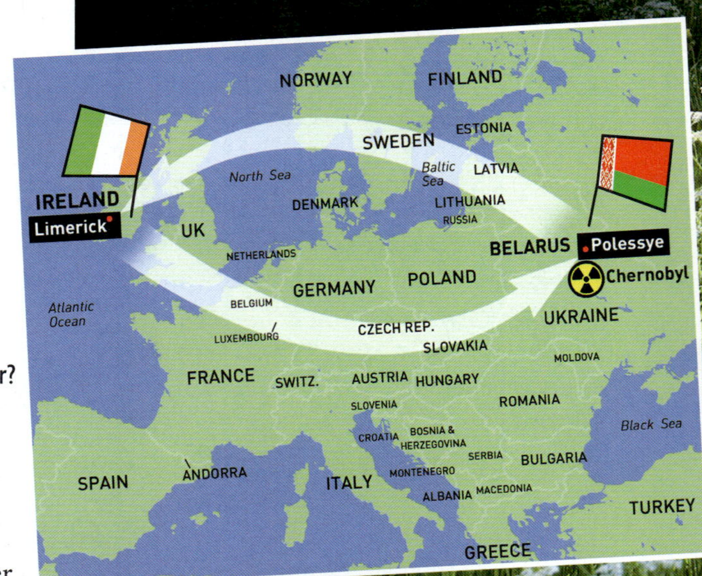

– the girl with two families

The Yanachkina family

The Quaid family

Life in the village of Polessye

The nuclear disaster changed the lives of everybody in the village. It took away all hope for the future. However, when Palina was born in 1988 her parents did their best to give her and her brother Micha a good life. They were farmers and before the accident, sold meat, fruit, and vegetables to the international market. After the disaster, no one wanted to buy anything.

The villagers were often ill and depressed. When Palina was eight, experts from the capital, Minsk, came to her school and did health tests on the children. The experts told them to stop picking the mushrooms in the forest because they were badly contaminated. When she was ten the experts returned with news of a charity that helped children like her have holidays abroad. They asked Palina if she would like to go to Ireland and stay with a family in Limerick. Palina felt a bit nervous about leaving home and she didn't speak a word of English, but she decided to go.

Life in Ireland

When Palina met her Irish family, she liked them immediately. John and Fiona Quaid and their two children, Chloe, three, and Evan, six, gave Palina a warm welcome. At first the only way to communicate was with a phrase book, but soon she became good friends with the children. They didn't need language to play.

So many things in Ireland surprised Palina. They visited a shopping mall and she couldn't believe her eyes, there was so much to choose from. She only knew her little village shop. She missed her family, but couldn't speak to them because they didn't have a phone.

By the time she went home, Palina could speak a few words of English and was delighted when the Quaids invited her back for Christmas. After that she started to visit the family twice a year and often spent three months with them in summer.

Palina today: 'I'm so lucky!'

When Palina was in her teens the experts returned to Polessye and checked her again. They couldn't believe how healthy she was. Her time in Ireland was improving her health and her English.

In her free time Palina helped run the farm. However, she didn't want to continue doing this for the rest of her life. She dreamed of becoming a doctor, but had no money to study. John and Fiona understood her problem. They offered to pay for her to study in Ireland and said she could stay with them full-time. Palina was amazed and delighted. It was hard for her parents, but they wanted the best for their daughter.

Palina is now studying biochemistry at the University of Limerick. She hopes to study medicine one day and return to Belarus to help those who are not as lucky as she is.

VOCABULARY AND SPEAKING

Phrasal verbs – literal

Phrasal verbs consist of a verb + adverb/preposition. Some phrasal verbs are literal. Look at these examples.

> *I wanted to* ***move back*** *home.* (move + back)
> *It* ***took away*** *all hope for the future.* (take + away)
> *She* ***grew up*** *in a small village.* (grow + up)

1 Complete the sentences with a word from the box.

out	at	down	on	back	off

1. Come in and **take** ______ your coat!
2. **Put** ______ something warm. It's cold today.
3. There's some ice-cream in the freezer. Can you **get it** ______?
4. If you don't feel well, go and **lie** ______.
5. **Look** ______ the countryside. Isn't it beautiful?
6. I'll lend you £20. **Pay** me ______ when you can.

2 Work with a partner. Take turns to mime one of these phrasal verbs. Can you guess what your partner is doing?

- throw something away
- try something on
- look for something
- turn something off
- turn round
- pick something up

3 Complete the sentences with a phrasal verb from exercise 2. Read them aloud.

1. I'm ______ my glasses. I can't find them anywhere.
2. I like these jeans. Can I ______ them ______?
3. Those jeans look great. ______ ______ so I can see the back!
4. Don't drop litter on the floor! ______ it ______!
5. Don't ______ ______ that newspaper. I want to read it.
6. Why are all these lights on? ______ them ______.

Phrasal verbs – idiomatic

Some phrasal verbs are idiomatic.

> *I* ***gave up*** *my job because I was bored.* (= stopped)
> *She* ***picked up*** *English from the children.* (= learnt bit by bit)
> *The plane* ***took off*** *late.* (= left the ground)

4 Match the phrases with the pictures.

look up a word	look after a baby	run out of milk
fall out with someone	get on well with somebody	

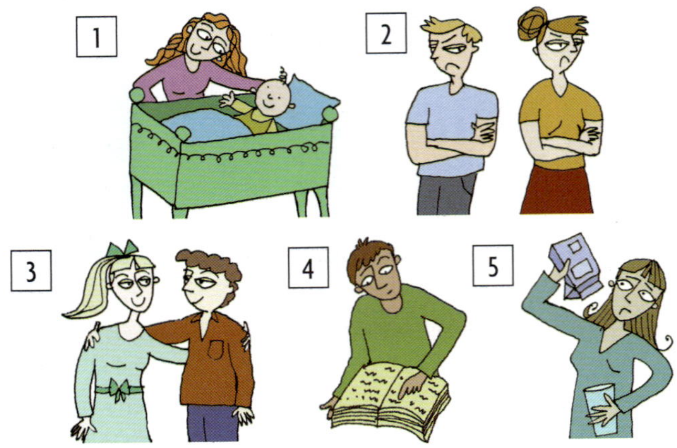

5 Complete the sentences with a phrasal verb from exercise 4. Read them aloud.

1. 'What does this word mean?' 'I don't know. I'll ______ it ______.'
2. My boss is a great guy. I ______ very well ______ him.
3. Leave little Emma with me. I'll ______ her while you're out.
4. It was a terrible journey – traffic jams all the way, and we nearly ______ petrol.
5. I feel miserable because I ______ my best friend at the weekend.

Talking about you

Complete the sentences with one of the phrasal verbs on this page in the correct form.

1. Where did you ______? Do you still live in the same house?
2. How do you ______ your parents?
3. Do you ever ______ your friends and stop speaking to them?
4. Would you like to be a doctor or nurse and ______ people?
5. Are you good at ______ foreign languages?
6. Do you ______ lots of words in your dictionary?

T 5.13 Listen and check. Ask and answer the questions about you with a partner.

EVERYDAY ENGLISH

Expressing doubt and certainty

1 Read the questions and the possible answers. Which are ...?

- 100% certain
- 75% certain
- 50% certain

1 **Q** Do you think Tom will pass his exams?

A – Of course he will.
– He might do.
– Mmm ... maybe.
– I doubt it.
– No chance.

2 **Q** Does Martin earn a lot of money?

A – Yes, absolutely.
– I think so.
– Mmm ... I'm not sure.
– I don't think so.
– Definitely not.

3 **Q** Are England going to win the World Cup?

A – Definitely!
– Perhaps.
– They might do.
– Anything's possible.
– Not a chance.

2 **T 5.14** Listen to the conversations. Underline the answers the two people give. Do they agree with each other?

3 **T 5.14** Listen again. Pay attention to the stress and intonation. Practise in groups of three. Choose your own replies.

4 Complete these conversations with a word or phrase from exercise 1.

1 A Kelly's job is really stressful, isn't it?
B ________. She's a paramedic.
A Is she having a holiday soon?
B I ______ so. She says she ______ go to Spain.

2 A Isn't it Rob's birthday next week?
B Yes, ________. It's on the 21st.
A So he's a Capricorn.
B No, I ________. I think he's an Aquarius.

3 A Do you think Anita and Paul are in love?
B ________. They're going to get married next June in Hawaii.
A Hawaii! Are you going to the wedding?
B ________. I can't afford it.

T 5.15 Listen and compare.

5 Work in groups. Ask everyone in the group for their opinion.

1 Did Leo Tolstoy write *War and Peace*?
2 Is Nicole Kidman American?
3 Was Sherlock Holmes a real person?
4 Is the population of China more than 2 billion?
5 Do some vegetarians eat fish?
6 Is the weather going to be nice next weekend?
7 Are you going to be rich and famous one day?
8 Is your school the best in town?

T 5.16 Listen and compare.

6 The way I see it

What … like? • Comparatives and superlatives • Synonyms and antonyms • *What's on?*

STARTER

Look at the pictureof Mia. Describe her. *She's about 25. She's got … She's quite …*

TELL ME ABOUT HER

What's she like?

1 **T 6.1** Listen to four conversations about Mia. Which question …?

- asks about her health
- asks for a physical description
- uses *like* as a verb
- means *Tell me about her in general.*

1 **'Do you like Mia?'**
'Yes, I do. I like her a lot.'

2 **'How's Mia?'**
'She's fine, thanks. Very well.'

3 **'What's Mia like?'**
'She's really nice. Very friendly.'

4 **'What does Mia look like?'**
'She's tall, and she's got brown eyes and black hair.'

2 Think of more answers to the questions.

Do you like Mia?
Yes, she's my best friend.
No, I can't stand her!
She's all right.

3 Match a question in **A** with an answer in **B**.

A	B
1 What's your teacher like?	__ a Lovely! Warm and sunny.
2 What sports do you like?	__ b She's great! She helps us a lot.
3 What does your brother look like?	__ c They're OK. Busy as usual.
4 Do you like pizza?	__ d He's got blond hair and blue eyes.
5 What's the weather like today?	__ e Mmm, I love it!
6 How are your parents?	__ f Cycling and skiing.

T 6.2 Listen and check. Ask and answer the questions about you.

PRACTICE
What's it like?

1 Mia often travels in her job. She's talking to her friend, Tom, about Shanghai. Complete Tom's questions.

T What _'s Shanghai_________ like?
M It's very big and noisy, but it's very exciting.
T What ____________ like?
M It's the best in the world! I just love Chinese food!
T What ____________ like?
M They're very friendly, and they really want to do business.
T What ____________ like?
M When I was there, it was hot and humid.
T What ____________ like?
M There are new buildings everywhere, but if you look hard, you can still find some older ones, too.

2 **T 6.3** Listen and check. Practise the conversation with a partner.

3 Ask and answer the same questions about the town or city you are in now.

SINGAPORE, SHANGHAI, AND DUBAI
Comparatives and superlatives

1 **T 6.4** Mia also went to Singapore and Dubai. Listen and complete some of the things she says.

THE CITY Singapore is older than Shanghai, but it's ________ smaller. Shanghai is ________ bigger than Singapore and __________ noisier too.

BUSINESS They're both top financial centres, but Singapore is ________ important. It's better for investment.

BUILDINGS AND PEOPLE Shanghai is more ________ than Singapore, but it isn't as cosmopolitan. Dubai is ________ newest and ________ city, and it's the most ________.

CLIMATE Singapore is __________ than Shanghai. But it isn't ________ hot ________ Dubai. Dubai is the ________ place. Singapore is very humid, so it's ________ than Shanghai. But Dubai is the ________. It only rains for a few days a year.

WHICH IS BEST? For me Shanghai is the ________ because it's the ________ and the ________ exciting.

2 **T 6.4** Listen again and check. What extra information do you hear?

3 What questions was Mia asked about each topic in exercise 1? Ask and answer them with a partner.

GRAMMAR SPOT

1 What are the comparative and superlative forms of these adjectives?

old	busy	big	important
small	noisy	wet	modern
new	dry	hot	exciting

When do we use *-er* and *-est*? When do we use *more* and *the most*?

2 These adjectives are irregular. What are the comparative and superlative forms?

good bad

3 Look at these patterns.

It **a bit/a little** bigger. It's **a lot/much** smaller.
It's **isn't as** hot **as** Dubai.

▶▶ **Grammar Reference 6.1–6.2 p141**

PRACTICE

Pronunciation

1 **T 6.5** Listen and practise the sentences.

/ə/ / ə/	/ə/ /ə/	/ɪ/
I'm older than Jane.	But I'm not as old as John.	He's the oldest.

2 **T 6.6** Listen and practise the conversation with a partner.

Clever
A WHO's cleverer, YOU or BEN?
B ME, of course! I'm MUCH cleverer than Ben! He isn't NEARLY as clever as ME!

Practise again using these adjectives.

kind funny good-looking ambitious

T 6.7 Listen and compare.

Comparing people

3 Read the profiles of the four people. Complete the sentences comparing them.

1 Agnes has the *largest* family. She has ______ children. Kevin doesn't have ______ children ______ Agnes. He has just two.

2 Marilou is ______. She's 41. Marcel is ______. He's only 25. Agnes is a little bit ______ Kevin. She's 34, and he's 32.

3 Kevin works the ______ hours – 60 hours a week. Agnes doesn't work as ______ hours as Kevin, but she still works hard. She works ______ than Marcel, who only works 35 hours a week.

4 Kevin earns the ______. He has the ______ salary. Marilou has the ______ salary. Marcel doesn't earn anything like ______ Agnes. She earns nearly twice ______ as him.

5 Agnes has ______ house than Marilou, but it isn't ______ Kevin's. He has a huge house – six bedrooms! Marcel has ______ house.

4 Compare the two women. Then compare the two men.

Agnes is younger than Marilou.

5 Make sentences about their personalities. Compare two or three of them.

Marilou isn't as … , but she's more …

6 Work in small groups. Who do you think …?

- has the most important job
- is the most creative
- is the busiest

Why do you think Agnes is the happiest?
Why is Marilou the unhappiest?

AGNES from Sweden

LIFE DATA

Age: 34

Family: Married, 3 children

Job: Interior designer

Works hours/week: 50

Salary: $75,000 a year

House: 4 bedrooms

PERSONALITY

Intelligent: ★★★★★

Ambitious: ★★★

Happy: ☺☺☺☺☺

KEVIN from Chicago

LIFE DATA

Age: 32

Family: Married, two sons

Job: Financial advisor

Works hours/week: 60

Salary: $100,000 a year

House: 6 bedrooms

PERSONALITY

Intelligent: ★★

Ambitious: ★★★★★

Happy: ☺☺☺

MARCEL
from France

LIFE DATA

Age: 25

Family:
Single

Job:
Cheese maker

Works hours/week:
35

Salary:
$40,000 a year

House:
2 bedrooms

PERSONALITY

Intelligent:
★★★

Ambitious:
★★

Happy:
☺☺☺☺

MARILOU
from the Philippines

LIFE DATA

Age: 41

Family:
Married, 1 daughter

Job:
Nurse

Works hours/week:
55

Salary:
$25,000 a year

House:
3 bedrooms

PERSONALITY

Intelligent:
★★★★

Ambitious:
★

Happy:
☺☺

LISTENING AND SPEAKING
My family

1 What are you like as a person?
Do any of these adjectives describe you?

messy	tidy	lazy	moody	noisy
kind	selfish	shy	ambitious	cheerful

2 **T 6.8** Listen to three people talking about their family. Complete the chart.

Sally 20
Who is she like? ____________
In what ways? ____________
____
____

Jamie 16
Who is he like? ____________
In what ways? ____________
____
____

Rachel 28
Who is she like? ____________
In what ways? ____________
____
____

3 How are these people different from each other?

- Sally and her sister, Lena
- Jamie and his twin brother, Rob
- Rachel and her father
- Rachel and her sister, Jenny

4 **T 6.8** Listen again. Complete the sentences.

Sally
1 We ____________ films …
2 And she's ____________ size as me.

Jamie
3 We're ____________ character.
4 We ____________ art.

Rachel
5 I hope I'm ____________ him.

5 Who are *you* like in *your* family? Who do you look like?

READING AND SPEAKING

Multicultural London

1 What do you want from the country you live in? Put these qualities in order of importance for you (1 = most important).

- ☐ a safe and honest society
- ☐ a good education for children and adults
- ☐ the opportunity to find work and have a career
- ☐ a good place to bring up your children
- ☐ a society where people are free to say and do what they want

Talk with a partner, then in small groups. Discuss your answers as a class.

2 Read the introduction to the article. What is special about London? What is special about Stroud Green Road?

3 Look at the pictures and profiles of the people in the article. Where are they from? What are they doing in London?

4 Work in small groups. Choose two of the people. Read about them and answer the questions.

1. When and why did she/he come to England?
2. How did he/she find it at first?
3. What does she/he say about her/his business?
4. How does England compare to his/her own country?
5. What family does she/he talk about?
6. What does he/she think of living in England?
7. Does she/he intend to stay or go back home?

5 Find a student from another group. Compare and swap information.

6 Which of the qualities of a country in exercise 1 are important to the four people? Did they find these qualities in England?

What do you think?

- When people go to live in a foreign country, they can experience culture shock. What do you understand by this?
- Why do people leave their own country? What are they looking for? What are they escaping from?

Project

Find someone living in your country who is from a different country. What do they do? What do they think of living in your country? Bring the information to class and tell the other students.

▶▶ **WRITING** **Describing my hometown** *p110*

The world in

London is the most multicultural city in the world. On an ordinary street in north London, people from across the globe live and work side by side. Here on Stroud Green Road there are Turks, Chinese, Afghanis, Pakistanis, Vietnamese, Colombians, Polish, Kenyans, and French.

What are the thoughts of the people who live here? What do they think of the land they now call home?

PROFILE

Name	Burkan Mehmet, 41
Born	Istanbul, Turkey
Business	The Sunflower Gallery

“This area is very cosmopolitan, and that's why I love it. When I first came to England in 1986, I thought it would be like New York, but it was much quieter. I didn't know anybody, and I wanted to go home.

I came here to study business at college. First I had a restaurant. Now I run this florist's shop. My customers come from so many different cultures – I learn something new every day.

What I like about England is that there's a system that works. Things are more organized here. I'm a British citizen now. When I go back to Turkey, I see how I've changed. Life in Turkey is faster, and more hectic than here.

I would like to go back to Istanbul one day. But for now, I love London. I'm married, and I have a daughter, Ceren. I wouldn't think of living anywhere else.”

one street

STROUD GREEN ROAD N4

PROFILE

Name	Ming Liang Chen, 50
Born	Qingdao, **China**
Business	The Chinese Medical Centre

"I was a doctor in China. My daughter wanted to study in England, so we moved here in 2000.

Life for us here was impossible for the first few years. It was hard to find work. It was also difficult to talk to people. But things got easier as my English improved. People in the West are now more interested in herbal medicine.

My daughter is married and has a son and lives here. I see her every day. That is Chinese culture – children and parents stay together.

This is the big difference for us. In China we are surrounded by family. Here I feel like a foreigner. I miss my friends and colleagues, and my wife is very close to her family back home.

My daughter is settled here, but I think my wife and I will return to China. We'll see."

PROFILE

Name	Luz-Elena Lamprea, 41
Born	Tuluá, **Colombia**
Business	Los Guadales restaurant

"My parents divorced, and my mother came to England to make a new start. I was 19.

For me it was an enormous shock. When you are in Colombia, you think everything in Europe is wonderful. I arrived in September, the weather was awful and the skies were grey. London wasn't nearly as exciting as I thought.

I spent a year studying English, then fell in love. The marriage didn't work, but I had two children, Jennifer and Julian.

I bought this restaurant. It's becoming more and more popular, especially with Europeans. I love my work. It's the most interesting job in the world. I'm not just serving food, I'm giving people an experience of my culture.

I'm so thankful now that I came here. There is more opportunity. I go to Colombia every year, but when I'm there I miss England. I really love being here."

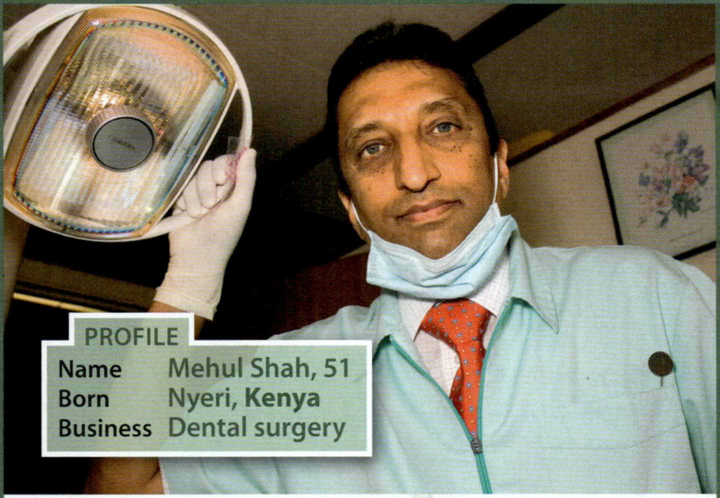

PROFILE

Name	Mehul Shah, 51
Born	Nyeri, **Kenya**
Business	Dental surgery

"I always wanted to study medicine. I had an uncle in London, so when I was 16, I came here.

It was very hard. I remember the drive from the airport. The roads were so much bigger and busier than in Kenya. It was summer, and the weather was lovely. But then of course the first winter came. It was the coldest winter for years!

My patients are of all nationalities, all religions, all colours. I love it. I'm seeing the third generation of the same families.

This is a democratic country. You're free here, you can say and think, and do what you like.

England is a welcoming society. My children were born here. All their friends are English. I feel British now. I became a British citizen 24 years ago. Britain gave me an education and the opportunity to better myself. This is my country, my home."

VOCABULARY
Synonyms and antonyms

1 Look at the extract from the text on page 51.

> "It was hard to find work. It was also difficult to talk to people. But things got easier ..."

Which words are synonyms?
Which words are antonyms (opposites)?

2 We use synonyms and antonyms because we don't want to repeat words. What's wrong with this conversation?

Try the conversation again using the words *beautiful*, *nice*, and *horrible*.

Synonyms

3 Complete the conversations with a synonym in the box.

tiny	clever	annoyed	wealthy	fed up	pleased

1 'Jane comes from a very rich family.'
'Really? I knew her uncle was very ______.'

2 'Was Sophie angry when you were late?'
'Yeah. She was pretty ______, it's true.'

3 'Jack's such an intelligent boy!'
'Mm. He's very ______ for a ten-year old.'

4 'I've had enough of winter now.'
'I know. I'm ______ with all these dark nights.'

5 'Dave and Sarah's flat is small, isn't it?'
'Mm. It's ______. I don't know how they live there.'

6 'Are you happy with your new car?'
'Yes, I'm very ______ with it. It goes really well.'

T 6.9 Listen and check. What's the extra line of each conversation?

4 Think of another word for these adjectives.

good-looking	amazing	crazy	big
new	old	awful	cold

5 Work in pairs. Write sentences using an adjective in exercise 4. Read them to another group. They must reply using a synonym.

George is good-looking, isn't he?
You bet! He's really handsome!

Antonyms

6 We can agree with people by using *not very* + an antonym.

7 Think of a word that means the opposite of these adjectives.

easy	difficult	naughty	______
noisy	______	exciting	______
miserable	______	clever	______
polite	______	clean	______

8 Agree with these sentences using antonyms.

1 That man was so rude to me!

Yes, he wasn't very polite, was he?

2 Some people are so stupid!
3 Dave's flat is always so dirty!
4 His wife always looks so miserable!
5 Their children are so naughty!
6 This lesson is boring!

T 6.10 Listen and compare. Practise the conversations.

EVERYDAY ENGLISH

What's on?

1 Read the listings and find the answers to these questions.

- How much is it to go in the British Museum?
- Is the Van Gogh exhibition open on Sunday?
- How many nights is the concert on at the Royal Festival Hall?
- What film is suitable for young children?
- Is *The Phantom of the Opera* popular? How do you know?

2 **T 6.11** Listen and complete the conversations.

1 **A** What shall we do today?
B I'm not sure. How about __________ ?
A Mmm ... I don't really feel like __________ .

2 **B** OK. Would you like to go to an exhibition?
A That sounds interesting! __________ ?
B Well, there's a Van Gogh exhibition.
A Is it __________ ?
B I think it __________ really good!

3 **A** __________ ?
B It's on at the Royal Academy.
A What's the __________ ?
B Piccadilly Circus.
A How much is it?
B It's __________ students.
A What time is it open?
B From ten till six.
A Right! __________ !

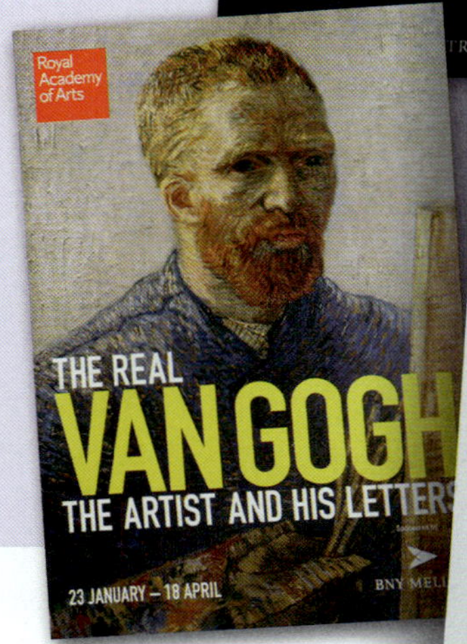

3 **T 6.11** Listen again. Practise the conversations in pairs.

4 Work with a partner. Have similar conversations about other things to do.

5 Imagine you are in London for a weekend. You and your partner have £50 each to spend on going out. Talk together and decide what you want to do.

Time Out London

Listings

British Museum
44 Great Russell Street, WC1B 3DG
Russell Sq
10am–5.30pm
FREE
Exhibitions
Chinese Vases Pottery from the Ming Dynasty 1368–1644
South American Indians The gold and silver of the Incas
Ancient Egypt Statues of kings, pharaohs, and gods

Peruvian Inca gold

Royal Academy Of Arts
Burlington House, Piccadilly, W1J 0BD
020 7300 8000
Piccadilly Circus
Exhibition
The Real Van Gogh: the Artist and his Letters
10am–6pm daily
£12; £10 seniors; £8 students; under 7s free.
Booking 0844 209 1919
Van Gogh's artistic development is revealed in his private letters.

Royal Festival Hall
Southbank Centre, Belvedere Road, SE11 8XX
0844 875 0073
Waterloo
Concert
Beethoven's Pastoral Symphony
Thurs 4th only; 7.30pm
£6–£20
The Paddington Symphony orchestra perform one of the world's most popular symphonies.

Odeon Cinema Piccadilly Circus
19 Regent St, SW1Y 4LR
0871220 6000
Piccadilly Circus
before 5pm £10; after 5pm £13
Films
The Survivors (15)
10.40am, 1.50, 4.00, 6.10, 8.20, 10.30
Family fights to live after nuclear war destroys world.
My Favourite Fairy (U)
10.00am, 12.15pm, 3.00, 5.30
Dolls and toys come alive in a girl's bedroom.
Final Solution (18)
12.40pm, 3.50, 6.15, 8.30, 11.10
Drugs, murder, violence in New York crime gang.

Her Majesty's Theatre
Haymarket and Charles II St, SW1Y 4QL
0844 579 1940
Piccadilly Circus
Musical
The Phantom of the Opera
Mon–Sat 7.30pm; Tues and Sat matinee 2.30pm. £20–£55. Runs 2hrs 30 mins. Booking recommended.
Andrew Lloyd Webber's musical in its 24th year. A heart-breaking story of love.

TIME OUT London

7 Living history

Present Perfect • *for* and *since* • *ever* and *never*
Word formation • *Agree with me!*

STARTER

What's the Past Simple and the past participle of these verbs? Which are regular? Which irregular?

live	have	be	give	go	eat
know	meet	move	work	write	

A HOUSE WITH HISTORY

Present Perfect, *for* and *since*

1 **T 7.1** Look at the pictures. Listen and read about **John**. Answer the questions.

1 Where does he live?
2 What's his job?
3 Where did he meet his wife?
4 Does he have any children?

2 Read about **John's flat**. Why is it famous? Who lived there? When? What tense are the verbs in **bold**? Why?

3 Work with a partner. Read the questions. Are they about **John** (J) or **Karl Marx** (KM)?

1 How long has he lived in the flat? J
2 How long did he live in the flat? ____
3 Where does he work? ____
4 How long has he worked there? ____
5 What was his job in London? ____
6 Which newspaper did he write for? ____
7 How long has he been married? ____
8 How long was he married? ____

John

"Hi! I'm John. I live in London. I have a flat in Dean Street, Soho. I**'ve lived** here for three years. I'm a press photographer. I**'ve worked** for *The London Gazette* since 2010. My wife's name is Fay. We**'ve been** married for two years. We met at university. Fay's a receptionist at the Ritz Hotel. I get around town on a motorbike. I**'ve had** it since I was 25. Fay goes by bus. We don't have any children yet."

John's flat today

4 Ask and answer the questions in exercise 3 with your partner.

T 7.2 Listen and check. Practise again.

GRAMMAR SPOT

1 What are the tenses in these sentences? Why are they used?

Karl Marx **lived** there for five years.
John **has lived** there for three years.

Find more examples in the texts.

2 How do we form the Present Perfect?

3 Look at the examples. When do we use *for*? When do we use *since*?

for three years/two hours/a long time
since six o'clock/Monday/2009/July

▶▶ **Grammar Reference 7.1 p141**

5 Read the texts again. What differences and similarities are there between John and Karl Marx?

John's flat

John's flat is famous. Karl Marx, the German philosopher and historian, **lived** there for five years in the 19th century. He **moved** to London in 1849 and **worked** as a foreign correspondent for an American newspaper. He **wrote** for *The New York Daily Tribune*. He **was** married to Jenny von Westphalen for 38 years. They **had** seven children.

John's flat in the 19th century

PRACTICE

for or *since*?

1 Complete the time expressions with *for* or *since*.

_____ half an hour	_____ a long time	_____ October
_____ 2001	_____ ten o'clock	_____ last Tuesday
_____ I was 14	_____ three months	_____ a couple of weeks

2 Match the lines in **A** and **B** with a sentence in **C**. There is more than one possible answer. Read them aloud to a partner.

A	B	C
1 I've known John	from 2005 to 2007.	We went to Spain.
2 I last went to the cinema	for over an hour.	We met at university.
3 I've had this watch	two weeks ago.	I really need a coffee.
4 I lived in New York	since 2008.	My Grandpa gave it to me.
5 I've lived in this house	since I was a child.	I had a great time there.
6 We last had a holiday	for ages.	What have you been up to?
7 I haven't seen you	for three years.	The film was really boring.
8 We haven't had a break	two years ago.	It's got a beautiful garden.

T 7.3 Listen, compare, and practise. Make similar sentences about you.

Asking questions

3 Complete the conversations. What tense is used in each question?

A Where *do you* live, Susan?
B In a flat near the town centre.
A How long _________ there?
B For three years.
A Why _________ move there?
B Because we wanted to be in a nicer area.

T 7.4 Listen and check. Practise the conversation with a partner.

4 With your partner, make more conversations using these prompts.

1	2
A What ... do?	**A** ... know Dave Brown?
B I work ...	**B** Yes, I ...
A How long ... ?	**A** How long ... ?
B For ...	**B** For ...
A What ... do before that?	**A** Where ... meet him?
B I worked ...	**B** We ...

T 7.5 Listen and compare.

5 Work with a partner. Ask and answer questions with *How long ...?* Then ask for more information.

How long have you lived/worked/had/known ...?

Where did you ...? What ...? Why ...?

AN ARCHAEOLOGIST

Present Perfect – *ever* and *never*

1 Look at the photos of Frieda Hoffmann and read the introduction. What's her nationality? Which countries has she been to? What are her passions?

2 Read the interview with Frieda and write the questions on the correct line.

Have you always been interested ...?
~~When did you first go abroad?~~
Why did you move there?
Have you ever discovered anything?
How many times have you been to Egypt?
~~Which countries have you been to?~~
How many books have you written?
... have you ever been in any dangerous situations?
How did you travel?

T 7.6 Listen and check.

3 Work with a partner. Ask and answer questions about Frieda.

- Which countries ... been to?

Which countries has she been to?

She's been to Egypt, Algeria, Kenya, South Africa, China, ...

- ... ever / South America?
- When / move / England?
- Where / her father get a job?
- When / see / the Tutankhamun Exhibition?
- How many times / to Egypt?
- How many books ...?

GRAMMAR SPOT

1 What are the tenses in these sentences?

You**'ve travelled** a lot in your lifetime.
Which countries **have** you **been** to?
When I **was** six, my family **moved** to England.

Which tense refers to a definite time in the past?
Which tense refers to an experience some time in your life?

2 The adverbs *ever* and *never* are often used with the Present Perfect.

Have you **ever** been in danger?
I've **never** been to South America.

▶▶ **Grammar Reference 7.2 p142**

Frieda Hoffmann – archaeologist and writer

Frieda Hoffmann was born in Germany, but she has lived most of her life abroad. She has a passion for history and ancient civilizations. Her greatest love is Africa, and she has written several books about ancient Egypt.

Driving in South Africa

Walking the Great Wall of China

Crossing the Sahara, Algeria

The River Nile, Kenya

Archaeological site, Egypt

I Frieda, you've travelled a lot in your lifetime.
[1] ***Which countries have you been to?***

F Well, I've been to a lot of countries in Africa and Asia, but I've never been to South America.

I [2] ***When did you first go abroad?***

F When I was six, my family moved to England.

I [3] ________________?

F Because my father got a job as Professor of History at Cambridge University.

I [4] ________________ in archaeology?

F Yes, I have. When I was ten, there was an exhibition of Tutankhamun, the Egyptian king, in London. My father took me to see it, and I was fascinated! After that I knew that I wanted to go to Egypt and be an archaeologist.

I [5] ________________?

F Twenty times at least! I go as often as I can.

I [6] ________________?

F Yes, I've made some very important discoveries. I was the leader of a team that discovered some ancient tombs near Cairo.

I You've written books about Egypt, haven't you?
[7] ________________?

F I've written three about the pharaohs. And I've written a book about a journey I made from Cairo to Cape Town.

I [8] ________________? By train? By car?

F In a Land Rover, of course!

I In all your travels, [9] ________________?

F Oh, goodness, yes! I've often been in danger. But in situations like that you learn so much about yourself.

PRACTICE

Present Perfect or Past Simple?

1 **T 7.7** Listen and complete some lines from an interview with Frieda.

1 **Do you go back to Germany much?**
"No, I don't. I _____ back a few times, but I've _____ there again."

2 **What _____ you _____ at university?**
"I _____ Ancient History at Cambridge."

3 **_____ you _____ an ordinary job?**
"Of course I _____! I _____ all sorts of things! After university I _____ any money."
So what _____ you _____?
"I _____ in a restaurant! I _____ it!"

4 **What's the most dangerous situation you _____ in?**
"Well, I _____ a very bad car crash in Cairo. I _____ seriously injured, and _____ several bones."

What extra information did you hear? With a partner, practise the questions and answers.

2 Ask and answer more questions about Frieda. When did she do these things?

Has she ever ...
Yes, she has.
When did she do that?

1 ... cross/the Sahara? (in her early thirties)
2 ... walk/the Great Wall of China? (in 1995)
3 ... travel/up the Nile? (a student)
4 ... work/in a restaurant? (left university)

Talking about you

3 Choose one of the questions in the box. Stand up and ask everyone in the class.

Have you ever ...?	
done anything dangerous?	slept in a tent?
broken your arm or your leg?	worked in a restaurant?
lost something important?	been to hospital?
been to Africa?	written a story?

When you find someone who says *Yes*, ask more questions.

Have you ever done anything dangerous?
Yes, I have.
What / When / How / Why ...?

VOCABULARY AND PRONUNCIATION

Word endings and word stress

1 What are the endings of the nouns in *italics*?

Karl Marx was a *philosoph**er***, *histor**ian***, and an *econom**ist***.

2 Use these endings to make jobs from words in the box.

-er -or -ist -ian -ant

'photograph	re'ception	'science	farm	art
'politics	'music	ac'count	'decorate	act
in'terpret	'library	e'lectric	law	

T 7.8 Listen, check, and repeat the jobs. Pay attention to changes in word stress.

3 Suffixes show the part of speech. Look at the suffixes in the box and complete the chart.

nouns	-tion -sion -ment -ness -ence/-ance -ility
adjectives	-y -ly -ous -ful -less -al

Noun	Verb
_____	com'pete
_____	ex'plain
be'haviour	_____
_____	in'vite
'visitor	_____
'student	_____
_____	de'cide
dis'cussion	_____
_____	em'ploy
_____	in'herit
co'llection	_____

Noun	Adjective
fame	_____
_____	'different
'critic	_____
_____	am'bitious
suc'cess	_____
help	_____
_____	kind
friend	_____
'danger	_____
health	_____
_____	res'ponsible

Word stress

4 **T 7.9** Listen and repeat the words. Where is the stress?

Two-syllabled nouns and adjectives

nouns	danger	kindness	critic	artist	difference
adjectives	dangerous	healthy	friendly	famous	different

Two-syllabled verbs

invite explain discuss employ decide compete

Nouns ending in *-tion* and *-sion*

invitation explanation competition ambition decision

READING

Living in a stately home

1 Look at the pictures and read the introduction. What is the house called? Who lives there? Who visits it? Where do you think the money comes from to run it?

2 You are going to read about the house and its owner. What do you want to know?

Write some questions on the board.

Where ...? How old ...? Who ...? When ...?
How many ...? How much ...? Which ...?

3 Read the article quickly. Which of your questions are answered?

4 Read the article again. Answer the questions.

1 How long has the Cavendish family lived in Chatsworth?
2 Why does the Duke feel lucky?
3 What do these numbers refer to?

300	35,000	500	£500m	£5m	600,000

4 How long has the house been open to the public?
5 How does the estate raise money?
6 Why was the house built so big?
7 Which members of the royal family have visited the house?

Language work

Underline the correct tense.

1 The 12th Duke *lived / has lived* in Chatsworth since 2006.
2 His father *died / has died* in 2004.
3 The Cavendish family *owned / has owned* the house for over 450 years.
4 In 2010 around 600,000 people *visited / have visited* the house.
5 William and Mary *didn't visit / haven't visited* in 1686.
6 William Cavendish *was / has been* Prime Minister for a year.

What do you think?

- Are there houses like Chatsworth in your country? Who owns them? Are they open to the public?
- Is there an aristocracy in your country? Which schools do they go to? Which professions do they often have? What kind of pastimes do they like?
- Is it fair that so much wealth can be inherited?

Living History

Chatsworth House has been home to the same family since 1549. In that time the house has welcomed kings and queens, prime ministers and politicians, and more recently bands and film crews.

The 12th Duke of Devonshire, Peregrine Cavendish, and his wife Amanda have lived at Chatsworth since 2006.

The Duke inherited the house on the death of his father in 2004. He says:

'My family has lived here for over 450 years. The estate has been passed down the Cavendish family for 15 generations, and I now have the pleasure and responsibility to look after it for the next generation.'

Visitors often see him walking through the house and garden when it is open to the public. He says, 'Chatsworth is a magical place, and I feel lucky to be able to share it with all of our visitors.'

The most beautiful house in England

Chatsworth is situated in the hills of Derbyshire, in the Midlands. Many people say it is the most beautiful house in England. It has nearly 300 rooms (with 17 staircases and 26 baths) and is set in 35,000 acres of land. It needs 500 staff to run. The art collection includes paintings by Raphael, van Dyck, and Rembrandt. The whole estate is worth about £500 million.

It costs approximately £5m a year to run Chatsworth, so the house has been open to the paying public since 1949, and in 2010 there were around 600,000 visitors. There are often art exhibitions, flower shows, horse trials, and sometimes concerts in the grounds.

£5m a year to run

The house also earns money from the film industry. It is a favourite location for period films. Chatsworth was used as Mr Darcy's house in the 2005 film of Jane Austen's *Pride and Prejudice*, and Keira Knightley also starred in *The Duchess* here in 2008.

A house fit for a king!

Most English country houses were built during the 17th and 18th centuries by the aristocracy. The Duke likes to explain the historical background to Chatsworth. 'Visitors arrive, see this huge building in this vast parkland, and wonder why it is so big. The reason is that my ancestors built a house fit for a king. It was designed to impress, and to persuade royalty to visit.'

In 1686 the first Duke built a magnificent suite for a royal visit from King William and Queen Mary. Unfortunately they didn't come. However, much later Edward VII was a frequent visitor between 1901 and 1910. George V and Queen Mary visited in 1913.

Many of the Cavendish family were politicians. One, William Cavendish, was Prime Minister from 1756–1757. Today, families like the Cavendish's no longer have the same political influence, but their estates are still huge.

LISTENING AND SPEAKING

A family history

1 What do you know about the lives of your grandparents? Talk about them in small groups.

2 **T 7.10** Listen to David Taylor Bews (33). He comes from England, but now lives in Perth, Australia. He has started to research his family history. Answer the questions.

1 How long has David lived in Perth?
2 Who are the two 'Alices' in his life?
3 Where does his grandmother live?
4 Where were her brothers and sisters born?
5 What did her parents do for a living?
6 What happened in the 9th century?
7 Why do so many people in the family have blonde hair?
8 Why did the family leave the Orkney Islands?

3 **T 7.11** Listen to David talking to his grandmother on 'Skype' about his family history. Answer the questions.

1 '… *she* married when she was just 17.' Who is *she*?
2 'I can't remember *him* at all.' Who is *him*?
3 'She had *two jobs* and a *big family*.' What were her *two jobs*? How *big* was the *family*?
4 '*They* got work in the shipyards.' Who are *they*?
5 '*It* wasn't unusual in those days.' *What* wasn't unusual?
6 '*They* live all over the world.' Who are *they*? Where do *they* live?
7 '*He* helps me keep in touch with you all.' Who is *he*?
8 '*It's all* really wonderful, isn't it?' What is *it all*?

4 In your groups tell the story of David's family in chronological order. Use the maps to help.

David's ancestors came over to Scotland from …

What do you think?

- Is David's family history typical of many families?
- How far back can you go in your family history?
- You can explore your family history online. Has anyone in your family ever done that?

▶▶ **WRITING** A biography *p111*

EVERYDAY ENGLISH

Agree with me!

1 **T 7.12** Read and listen to the sentences.
Does the intonation go up or down at the end?

> The underlined words are question tags.
> They aren't the same as questions.
> When we use these tags, they mean ... *I want you to agree with me.*

It's really wonderful, isn't it?

You come from Scotland, don't you?

Life wasn't easy then, was it?

You've lived in England for years, haven't you?

2 **T 7.13** Read these conversations. How are the question tags formed?
Listen and note the intonation. Practise with a partner after each one.

1 **A** It's a lovely day, **isn't it?**
B Yes, it is! Beautiful!
A We all love days like this, **don't we?**
B We certainly do!

2 **A** Mummy! Our cat isn't very big, **is she?**
B No, she isn't. She's just a kitten.
A And she loves fish, **doesn't she?**
B She does! It's her favourite food.

3 **A** We had such a good holiday, **didn't we?**
B We did. We had a great time.
A And it wasn't too expensive, **was it?**
B No, it wasn't. It wasn't expensive at all.

4 **A** The baby looks just like her mother, **doesn't she?**
B Uh huh. Same blue eyes, same nose.
A But she's got her father's blonde hair, **hasn't she?**
B Yes, she's very fair.

3 Complete the sentences with a question tag.

1. It was a great party last night, __________?
2. Dave knows everything about computers, __________?
3. You went to school with my brother, __________?
4. Learning a language isn't easy, __________?
5. Our English has improved a lot, __________?
6. We haven't had a break for ages, __________?

4 We need to say more than just *Yes* or *No* when we answer these questions. Match these answers with a sentence in exercise 3.

a. Yes, I did. We were really good friends.
b. Yes, it was. I really enjoyed it.
c. No, we haven't. It's time for one right now.
d. No, it isn't. It needs a lot of practice and patience.
e. Yes, it has. We're all much better now.
f. Yes, he does. He can fix them *and* program them.

T 7.14 Listen and check. Practise the conversations with your partner.

5 With your partner look at p156.
Choose two of the conversations and decide where question tags can be added.
Act them to the class.

T 7.15 Listen and compare.

8 Girls and boys

have to/don't have to • *should/must* • Things to wear • At the doctor's

STARTER

Which of these things do you think boys do better than girls, and vice versa?

I think boys are better at ... than girls.

- cooking
- maths
- sports
- driving
- making conversation
- learning foreign languages
- playing computer games
- talking about feelings

YOU HAVE TO CLING ON!

have to/don't have to

1 Look at the photo. Can you find a tiny figure? Is it a man or a woman? What's happening?

2 **T 8.1** The tiny figure is **Tilly Parkins** from Sydney, Australia. She's one of the world's greatest climbers. Listen to the interview and answer the questions.

- Where does Tilly train in the week?
- What's her job?
- Was it difficult to climb Moon Hill Crag?
- Who is Adam Pretty?
- Why does Tilly go rock climbing?

Moon Hill Crag, Yangshuo Mountains, China

3 Work with a partner. Complete the lines from the interview with words in the box.

have to	don't have to	do you have to	had to	didn't have to	can't

1 'I'm sure you __have to__ be very fit and strong to go climbing.'
2 'How often ________ train?'
3 'I ________ train every day, just two or three times a week, that's enough.'
4 'Sometimes I ________ work at the hospital at the weekend.'
5 'I ________ climb very early in the morning.'
6 'You ________ climb later in the day, it's too hot.'
7 'He ________ climb with me. He took the photo from a nearby tourist spot.'

T 8.1 Listen again and check.

4 Complete the questions and answers about Tilly.

1 'How often __does__ she have to ________?'
'Two or three times a week.'
2 ________ she ________ work at weekends?'
'Yes, she does sometimes.'
3 'Why ________ she ________ climb Moon Hill Crag just after dawn?'
'Because later it gets too hot and you ________ climb in the heat.'
4 ________ Adam have to ________ the rock?'
'No, he ________. He took the photo from a tourist spot.'

T 8.2 Listen and check. Practise the questions and answers with your partner.

GRAMMAR SPOT

1 *have to* + infinitive expresses obligation.
She **has to train** hard.
Do you **have to work** at weekends?

2 Write the question, negative, and past tense of *have to*.
________ you ________ work late in your job?
No, I ________ work late usually.
But I ________ work late yesterday.

3 Write *have to, don't have to, can,* or *can't*.
possible __can__ not possible ______
necessary ______ not necessary ______

▶▶ **Grammar Reference 8.1–8.2 p142**

PRACTICE

Pronunciation

1 **T 8.3** Listen to these sentences. What are the different pronunciations of *have/has/had*?

1 I have /hæv/ a good job.
I have /hæf/ to work hard.
2 He has /hæz/ a nice camera.
She has /hæs/ to train a lot.
3 We had /hæd/ a good time.
We had /hæt/ to get up early.

T 8.3 Listen again and repeat.

Talking about sports

2 Work with a partner. Choose a sport from the box, but don't tell your partner. Ask and answer *Yes/No* questions to find out what it is. Use these questions to help you.

sailing
golf
squash
baseball
surfing
athletics
swimming
boxing
car racing
football
tennis
gymnastics
cycling
skiing
skydiving

Do you ...?
- do it inside/outside
- play it with a ball
- play in a team
- do it on water

Do you have to ...?
- wear special clothes
- use special equipment
- train hard for it
- be very strong
- run fast
- have a special place to do it

Can you ...?
- do it anywhere
- do it with friends
- do it on your own
- earn a lot of money

Do you have to wear special clothes?

Yes, you do.

Can you ...?

3 Which sports do both boys and girls do? Are there any sports where girls and boys compete against each other?

4 Which sports do you do? Describe one to a partner. Use the ideas in exercise 2.

WHAT'S YOUR ADVICE?

should/must

1 Do you ever read problem pages in newspapers? What sort of things do people ask about?

2 Work with a partner. Read the problems in *Dear Annie*. Explain the headings. What advice would you give?

3 Read *Advice from Annie*. Match her advice with a problem. Write in the names.

GRAMMAR SPOT

1 Look at these sentences. Which sentence expresses stronger advice?

He **must** get professional help.
You **should** show him this letter.

2 *Should* and *must* are modal verbs. Read the examples.

What **should** I do?
You **shouldn't** worry about this.
He **must** get help.

- How do we make the question and negative?
- Do we add *-s* with *he/she/it*?

▶▶ **Grammar Reference 8.3–8.4 p143**

4 Complete the sentences using the words in the box. Who is the advice to?

shouldn't	should	must	don't think you should

1 You ____________ explain how you feel to your coach and your mother. However, in the end, the decision is yours and yours alone. You __________ decide your own future.

2 Tell him firmly that he ____________ change his ways or he'll lose his wife and family. Talk to all your friends and family about the problem – you ____________ suffer alone.

3 You ____________ write your speech down but I ____________ read it aloud to the group. Just make notes to help you remember it. For more help, you ____________ visit **speechtips.com**.

4 You ____________ talk to your parents about how you feel. And you ____________ feel jealous of your brother! He's older than you, that's all!

T 8.4 Listen and check.

Problems

Dear Annie!

annie@problemforum.com

1 No time for fun!

I'm 14 and I do gymnastics. I have to train 30 hours a week because my mum and my coach want me to try for the next Olympics. I like gymnastics but I have no time for anything else in my life. My school friends tell me that I am missing all the fun. What should I do? **Tracy**

2 I've lost my husband to a game

My husband started playing online computer games last year. Since then he has lost all interest in everything else, even me and our baby. He starts playing as soon as he gets up, and begins again when he gets back from work. He gets angry if I talk to him about it. What should I do? **Paula**

3 I get so nervous

I'm in the army, and in my job I have to give talks to large groups of people. The last time was a disaster because I was so nervous. My hands shook and I spoke too fast. How can I control my nerves? What should I do? **Mark**

4 I hate him!

I'm 11 and my brother is 15. I think my mum and dad love him more than me. They've just bought him the best computer – they say he has to have it for his exams. I don't even have my own mobile phone, AND I have to wear all his old clothes! **Billy**

Advice from Annie!

a Dear ____________
Good preparation is the answer. You must prepare well and practise a lot. The first 30 seconds are the most important. You should begin with a personal story. It will relax you and the audience.

b Dear ____________
More and more people worldwide have become addicted to this. He must get professional help, but this is difficult because he won't accept that he has a problem. I think you should show him this letter, and visit the website **olganon.org**.

c Dear ____________
These feelings are very common between brothers and sisters. I'm sure your parents love you and your brother just the same, so you shouldn't worry about this. When you're older, you'll get your own phone – and your own clothes!

d Dear ____________
The fact is, that to get to the top in sport you have to train very hard indeed. You should talk to someone else about your doubts. I don't think you should listen to just your friends.

PRACTICE
Giving advice

1 Work in small groups. Give advice to people with these problems.

1 I can't sleep at night.
You must do more exercise.
You shouldn't drink so much coffee.
2 I don't like my brother's new girlfriend.
3 I've got an important exam tomorrow, and I'm really nervous.
4 A boy in my class is bullying me.
5 I'm hopeless at all sports.
6 I fell over and I think I've twisted my ankle.
7 My computer's behaving very strangely.
8 My car's making a funny noise.

T 8.5 Listen and compare your answers.

What do you think?

2 Make sentences from the chart to express your opinion.

If you want to …

… learn English,
… be successful,
… keep fit,

you have to
you don't have to
you should
you shouldn't
you must

… work hard.
… do some sport.
… learn the grammar.
… go to university.
… buy a dictionary.
… smoke.
… translate every word.

Tell a partner.

▶▶ **WRITING Letters and emails** *p112*

LISTENING AND SPEAKING
Heptathlon champion

1 The word *Heptathlon* comes from the Greek *hepta* (seven) and *athlon* (contest). It is an athletic competition where there are seven events over two days. These are …

- 100 m hurdles
- 200 metres
- 800 metres
- long jump
- high jump
- javelin throw
- shot put

Match the events with the pictures.

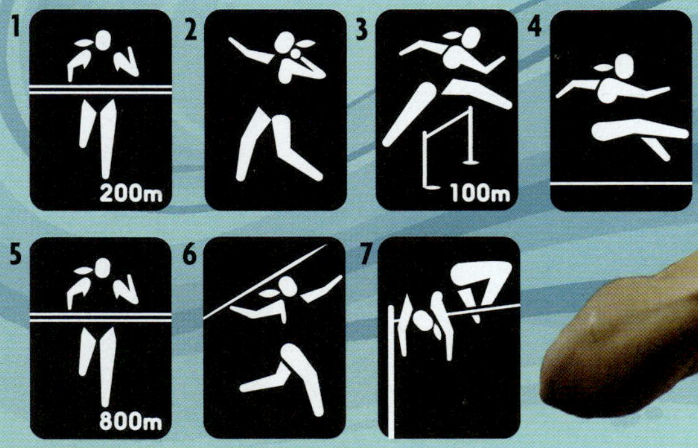

Jessica Ennis –
Britain's first world heptathlon champion!

2 **T 8.6** Listen to an interview with Jessica Ennis. She is Britain's first women's heptathlon champion. Underline the correct answer.

1 The World Athletic Championships were in *Brighton / Berlin / Brussels*.
2 Jessica missed the Olympics because she injured her *ankle / knee / wrist*.
3 She had to work with physiotherapists for *five / nine / ten* months to recover.
4 Her mum works for *a chemist's / a charity / a painter*.
5 Jessica's coach says that she must be more *patient / determined / aggressive*.
6 He told her that she shouldn't *eat chocolate / get a dog / see her boyfriend*.
7 Her boyfriend is *always / sometimes / never* with her when she competes.
8 She keeps her *gold medal / dog / javelin* by her bed.

3 **T 8.6** Listen again. Answer the questions.

1 Why did Jessica miss the Olympics in China?
2 Why does her mum have to have a lot of patience?
3 What nationality is her dad? What does he do?
4 What do Jessica and her coach fight about?
5 What are Jessica's interests other than athletics?
6 Which sports does she have to improve?

What do you think?

Work in groups. Think of some successful people. What do they do? How and why did they become successful? Tell the class.

READING AND SPEAKING

Families with all boys or all girls

1 Do a class survey. Which girls have sisters and no brothers? Which boys have brothers and no sisters? How does this affect their family?

2 Look at the adjectives in the box. Which do you think usually describe boys, and which girls? Use your dictionary if necessary.

sporty	gentle	boisterous	loud	quiet
chatty	untidy	competitive	sensitive	polite

3 Read the introduction to *Sons and Daughters*. What was the aim of the TV programme? Who were the two families? What did they have to do?

4 Work in two groups. Answer the questions.

Group A Read about the Cafearo family and the swap.
Group B Read about the Tibbett family and the swap.

THE FAMILY
1 What jobs do the parents do?
2 How long have they been married?
3 Why did they want a big family?
4 Why are the husbands happy with their families?
5 How do the children behave? Do they get on well?

THE SWAP
6 What were the parents' first impressions when they swapped families?
7 What differences did they find?
8 Do they think boys or girls are harder to bring up?

5 Find a partner from the other group. Go through the questions together and compare your families.

What do you think?

- What are the pros and cons of all-girl or all-boy families?
- What is the ideal family? How many children is the ideal? Why?
- Are/Were there many house rules in your family? What do/did you have to do? Write a list of house rules for the ideal family.

Listening – Brothers and sisters

6 T 8.7 Listen to three people talking about their families. After each one answer these questions. Who do you think is the happiest?
1 How many brothers and sisters do they have?
2 Where do they come in the family? First? Second? etc.
3 What do they like about their situation?
4 What don't they like?
5 Do they think their parents have a favourite child?
6 How many children do they want?

SONS

THE CAFEARO FAMILY

THE TIBBETT FAMILY

AND DAUGHTERS

Is an all-boy family very different from having an all-girl family? What is it like to be totally outnumbered by the opposite sex in your own home? To find the answer, TV's Channel 4 asked Marianne and Jon Tibbett, the parents of four daughters to swap homes with Karen and Steve Cafearo, who have four sons.

Karen talks about her family

Karen Cafearo, 43, lives with husband, Steve, 49, a manager at Jaguar Cars, and their sons Francis (17), Alex (15), Joseph (11), and Samuel (9). Karen is an accountant. She says:

'I married Steve when I was 21. I'm the oldest of four children and I always wanted a big family. Also, I wanted a son for Steve, he's very sporty, loves his football, so he's delighted to have four sons. The boys love kicking balls and racing around on their bikes. They don't see danger. Steve says I mustn't worry. He says boys will be boys. Sometimes I feel left out of all their sport, but I'm pleased that I don't have to watch football in the pouring rain. The boys see everything in black and white. I should learn not to ask them about their lives and feelings. 'Dunno' is their usual answer. I have often wondered what a family of girls would be like.'

THE SWAP
Karen and Steve Cafearo go to the TIBBETT HOME

When Karen and Steve arrived at the Tibbett family home, she had to laugh. There were piles of pink ballet shoes and riding boots all over the floor. Karen says:

'The four girls are as passionate about dancing and horse-riding as my boys are about football and rugby, but I was shocked by the mess. I have strict rules for my boys. They can't wear their shoes upstairs and they have to tidy their rooms. The girls were so excited to see us, they wanted to chat and ask us questions. It was fantastic, but exhausting. They came to help me cook in the kitchen, they didn't want to play in the garden. I think girls need more attention than boys. Another shock for me was how nice the girls were to each other. The boys love each other but they fight and fall out endlessly.

The thing I loved most was shopping with the girls. We had great fun. I miss that with boys. Poor Steve had to carry the bags. I saw a big change in him. With girls he was so sensitive and gentle.

I loved the chats with the girls, but I also like my own space. I think girls are harder work.'

Marianne talks about her family

Marianne Tibbett, 38, lives with husband, Jon, 45, and their daughters Annabelle (14), Francesca (11), Genevieve (9), and Catherine (8). They run a haulage business together. Marianne says:

'Jon and I met and married within sixteen months. He was 29. People often ask us if we have so many children because we were trying for a boy. But this isn't true. I'm an only child and it was my dream to have a big family. We were delighted when Annabelle arrived and equally delighted when Francesca arrived three years later, followed by Genevieve and Catherine. Jon loves having four girls, he is their superhero dad! Our daughters are fabulous. Most of the time they get on really well together. They're a chatty group! But we were fascinated to try living with boys.'

THE SWAP
Marianne and Jon Tibbett go to the CAFEARO HOME

Marianne expected the Cafearo boys to be loud and boisterous. In fact on the first day they were very quiet and polite. Marianne says:

'They even took their shoes off before going upstairs. However, I soon realised why Karen and Steve had to have such strict house rules. The boys were constantly on the go and wildly competitive. They raced around the garden and dived into the pool. There was a fight between one of the little boys and his big brother. I tried to make them apologize, which is what I do with my girls, but it just made them more angry. The little one went away by himself, cried, then forgot all about it.

But the biggest shock for me was the change in my gentle husband. He became more and more competitive. We all went go-karting. We've never done this with our family. Jon joined in with the boys and it was clear he wanted to win as much as they did. He had great fun and I loved seeing him so happy. I know he would love to have had a son to continue the business. But now we've seen the reality of having boys! They're exhausting. I honestly think they are much harder work than girls.'

VOCABULARY AND SPEAKING

Things to wear

1 What things to wear can you see on this page?

2 Work with a partner. Read the words in **Things to wear**. Where do they go on Person X? Label the parts of the body you mention as you work.

Things to wear

a belt, a jumper, shorts, a skirt, a cap, make-up, socks, boots, pyjamas, a suit, a watch, a blouse, a ring, a dress, aftershave, sunglasses, earrings, sandals, tights, a jacket, trainers, a scarf, bikini, jeans, a shirt and tie, a T-shirt

3 Answer the questions about the **Things to wear**.

1 Which are usually for boys? Which for girls? Which both?
2 Which are *not* clothes?
3 Which are for casual wear? Which for smart? Which both?
4 Which do you usually wear in winter? Which in summer?
5 What can the things be made of? Match these materials with them.

leather	wool	denim	cotton	silk	gold	silver

Dress Person X

4 Choose the clothes to dress Person X for one of the situations below. Describe the outfit to the class. Can they guess the sex and the situation?

- a job interview
- a party
- a skiing holiday
- a beach holiday
- going to school

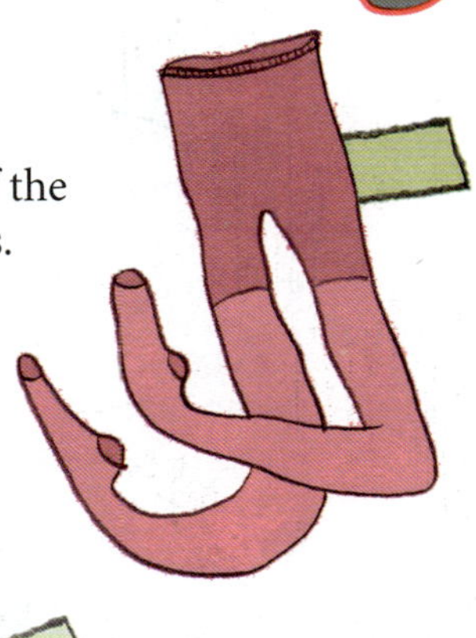

EVERYDAY ENGLISH

At the doctor's

1 Match the pictures with an illness from the box.

a sore throat	diarrhoea /daɪə'rɪə/	flu	an allergy	a twisted ankle	food poisoning	a cold

2 Read the symptoms and complete the diagnosis with an illness.

Patient's symptoms	Doctor's diagnosis
1 I can't stop coughing and blowing my nose.	You've got ________.
2 I've got a fever and my whole body aches.	You've got ________.
3 It hurts when I walk on it.	You've got ________.
4 I keep going to the toilet.	You've got ________.
5 My glands are swollen, and it hurts when I swallow.	You've got ________.
6 I keep being sick, and I've got terrible diarrhoea.	You've got ________.
7 I start sneezing and itching when I'm near a cat.	You've got ________.

T 8.8 Listen and check. Practise saying the lines with a partner.

3 **T 8.9** Listen to a conversation between a doctor (**D**) and Edsom (**E**), a student from Brazil. Answer the questions.

1. What are Edsom's symptoms?
2. What questions does the doctor ask?
3. What does the doctor think is the matter with Edsom?
4. What does she prescribe?
5. What advice does she give him?
6. Does he have to pay for anything?

4 Read and complete Edsom's conversation with the doctor.

T 8.9 Listen again and check.

5 Act the scene with your partner. Make similar conversations with other symptoms.

Seeing the doctor

D What seems to be the ________?

E Well, I haven't felt ________ for a few days. I've had a bad ________ and now I've got a ________.

D Any sickness or diarrhoea?

E Well, I haven't been ________.

D Do you feel hot?

E Yes, especially at night. I feel hot and I start ________ when I lie down.

D OK, I'll just ________ your temperature. Ah, yes. You do have a bit of a ________. Now, let me see your throat. Open your ________ wide, please.

E Can you see anything?

D Yes, your throat looks very red. Does this ________?

E Ow!

D And your glands are ________. You just have a bit of an infection. You need antibiotics. Are you allergic to penicillin?

E No, I'm not.

D Good. Now, you ________ take things easy for a couple of days and you ________ drink plenty of liquids. I'll write you a prescription.

E Thank you. Do I have to pay you?

D No, no. But you'll have to pay for the ________. It's £7.20.

E Right. Thanks very much. Goodbye.

9 Time for a story

Past Perfect and narrative tenses • Joining sentences • Feelings • Exclamations

STARTER

1 Work in small groups. Who are these characters from English literature?

2 What do you know about the stories they are from?

AESOP'S FABLES

Past Perfect and narrative tenses

1 Aesop was a story teller who lived in Greece in around 600 BC. Look at the picture of one of his fables, *The Bear and the Travellers*. What can you see?

2 Read the story. What is the moral?

TRUE FRIENDS ARE HARD TO FIND.

CHOOSE YOUR FRIENDS CAREFULLY.

DON'T RUN AWAY FROM DANGER.

The Bear and the Travellers

Two travellers were walking slowly along a country road. They were going to the city because they were looking for work. They were tired (...) and they were hungry (...)

Suddenly, in the woods in front of them, they saw a huge bear. The men were terrified. One of them ran away, climbed a tree, and hid.

The other man fell to the ground and pretended to be dead. (...) The bear came towards him. It bent down, sniffed him, and whispered something in his ear. Then it wandered away.

(...) The other man came down from his tree and went to see how his friend was. (...)

"The bear gave me some advice," said his companion. "He said, 'Next time you go on a journey, travel with someone who won't leave you at the first sign of danger.'"

THE MORAL OF THIS STORY IS ...

____

The bear whispered in his ear.

3 Complete the questions and the answers.

1 Where ________ the travellers ____________?
Along a country road.

2 Why __________________ to the city?
Because they were looking for work.

3 What ______________ in the woods?
They saw a huge bear.

4 What ________ the men do?
One ________ in a tree, the other ________ to be dead.

5 What ________ the bear ________?
It bent down, sniffed, then wandered away.

T 9.1 Listen and check.

4 Put these lines in one of the places (…) in the story.

1 … because they had walked twenty miles.
2 He wanted to know what the bear had said to him.
3 … because they hadn't eaten all day.
4 After the bear had gone, …
5 He had heard that bears don't like eating dead meat.

T 9.2 Listen to the complete story and check your answers. Do you agree with the moral?

GRAMMAR SPOT

1 What tense are the verbs in **bold**?
They **were looking** for work.
They **saw** a bear.
They **had walked** twenty miles.

2 *They didn't eat all day. They were hungry.* How is this expressed in the story?

3 The Past Perfect expresses an action before another time in the past. How do we form this tense?
had + the ______________ ______________

▶▶ **Grammar Reference 9.1 p144**

5 Ask and answer the questions with a partner. Use the Past Perfect.

1 Why were the travellers tired?
2 Why were they hungry?
3 Why did one of them pretend to be dead?
4 When did the other man come down from the tree?
5 What did he want to know?

T 9.3 Listen and check. Practise them again.

PRACTICE

Pronunciation

1 **T 9.4** The contraction *'d* can be difficult to hear. Listen to the sentences. Put a tick (✓) if you hear *'d* = ***had***.

1 ________ 2 ________ 3 ________
4 ________ 5 ________

Discussing grammar

2 What is the difference in meaning between these sentences?

1 When I arrived,
… she cooked dinner.
… she was cooking dinner.
… she'd cooked dinner.

2 She spoke good French because
… she lived in France.
… she had lived in France.

3 I listened to music
… while I did my homework.
… when I'd done my homework.

4 When I got home,
… the children went to bed.
… the children had gone to bed.

5 She gave me a book,
… so I read it.
… but I'd read it.

3 Match a line in **A** with a line in **B**.

A

1 I was nervous on the plane because
2 When I'd had breakfast,
3 I met a girl at a party. Her face was familiar.
4 I felt tired all day yesterday because
5 My wife was angry with me because
6 The little girl was crying because

B

___ I was sure I'd seen her somewhere before.
___ I'd never flown before.
___ I'd forgotten our anniversary.
___ she'd fallen over and hurt herself.
___ I went to work.
___ I hadn't slept the night before.

T 9.5 Listen and check.

THE SHEPHERD BOY

Joining sentences

1 Here is another of Aesop's fables. Work with a partner. Tell the story from the pictures.

2 Read the story. Choose the correct word or phrase to join the sentences.

What do you think is the moral of this story?

T 9.6 Listen and check.

3 Answer the questions.

When did the boy have his idea? *While …*
When did the villagers race to the hills? *As soon as …*
When did the shepherd boy smile? *After …*
When did the wolf appear? *As …*

GRAMMAR SPOT

1 Conjunctions are used to join sentences.

He wanted to have some fun **because** he was bored.
Although they were all busy, they stopped work.
No one believed the boy, **so** he climbed back up the hill.

2 *When, while, before, after, as, until,* and *as soon as* are conjunctions of time.

As soon as the villagers heard the boy, they went to help.
While the boy was in the village, the wolf killed all the sheep.

▶▶ **Grammar Reference 9.2 p144**

4 Complete the sentences with *although*, *so*, or *because*.

1 They didn't find the wolf, ________ they went back to work.
2 They helped the boy ________ they were worried about their sheep.
3 ________ they heard his cries, they didn't do anything to help.

5 Look at the pictures, not the text. Tell the story again. Use these prompts.

Once … there was … shepherd boy who …
One day … bored … idea.
… ran … village … shouted …
As soon as the men … but … nothing.
… smiled …
A few days later … again.
The men … angry … laughed.
Next day … wolf …
… raced … shouted …
This time … didn't believe …
… climbed back … wolf … killed …
… ashamed … cried.

The boy who cried wolf

ONCE upon a time there was a shepherd boy who looked after the sheep in the hills near his village. He thought his job was very boring. One day, (1) *while / because* he was sitting under a tree, he had an idea. He decided to have some fun, (2) *so / but* he went down to the village and shouted 'Wolf! Wolf!' at the top of his voice. (3) *As soon as / Until* the villagers heard the boy, they stopped work and raced to the hills to help him. But (4) *when / while* they got there, they saw nothing. They returned to their work. (5) *Before / After* they'd gone, the shepherd boy smiled to himself.

A few days later, the boy did the same thing again. He ran into the village and shouted 'Wolf! Wolf!' The villagers didn't know whether to believe him or not, but they were worried about their sheep (6) *because / so* they had to help him. They went back to the hills. Again, there was no wolf. They were angry (7) *because / so* the shepherd boy had lied again, but he just laughed.

THEN, the next day, just (8) *as / before* the sun was setting, a wolf really did appear, and it began attacking the sheep. In terror, the boy raced down the hill to the village, shouting 'Wolf! Wolf!' (9) *But / Although* the villagers heard his cries, they did nothing to help. This time they really didn't believe him.

THE shepherd boy climbed back up the hill to look for the sheep, but the wolf had killed them all. He was so ashamed of himself that he sat down in the moonlight and cried.

PRACTICE

Discussing grammar

1 Join the sentences using the conjunction. Put one verb in the Past Perfect.

1 I did my homework. I went to bed.	WHEN
2 I drove two hundred miles. I stopped for a coffee.	AFTER
3 She passed her driving test. She bought a car.	AS SOON AS
4 I didn't go to Italy. I learned Italian.	UNTIL
5 I read the book. I didn't understand the film.	ALTHOUGH
6 His mother sent him to bed. He was naughty.	BECAUSE
7 She burnt the food. We went out to eat.	SO
8 She cooked a lovely supper. Unfortunately I ate a large lunch.	BUT

T 9.7 Listen and compare your answers.

2 Choose the correct words to join the sentences.

1 *When / While* I got home, I checked my emails.
2 I cut myself *before / while* I was shaving.
3 He worked for the same company *until / as* he retired.
4 I got out of bed *before / as soon as* I woke up.
5 She was thinking about her father *as / until* she was going to work.
6 *After / Before* I went to bed, I locked all the doors.
7 *After / Before* I left school, I lived abroad for a year.

Your ideas

3 Complete the sentences with your own ideas.

1 We enjoyed the holiday although …
2 As I sat on the plane, I felt nervous because …
3 I lived in Sweden for a year, but I …
4 I met my wife while I …
5 I wanted to get fit, so I …
6 My phone rang just as I …
7 Although I didn't feel well, I …
8 We watched TV until …

Compare your sentences with a partner.

LISTENING AND SPEAKING

My favourite writer

1 What do you know about the writer Charles Dickens?

1 He was *American / Scottish / English.*
2 He wrote in the *18th / 19th / 20th* century.
3 He wrote about *the aristocracy / adventurers / ordinary people.*

2 **T 9.8** Listen to *Part one* of a radio programme. Check your answers to exercise 1 and read the information about Dickens in the chart. Some of it is wrong. Correct it.

	Charles Dickens	Robert Louis Stevenson
When?	twentieth century	
Kind of books	novels and poetry	
Reasons for success	wrote about rich and famous people	
Best-known books	*Peter Copperfield* *Oliver Twist* *A Summer Carol*	
Best-known character	Scrooge – a happy man who becomes miserable	
Personal life	married and divorced six children – happy life	

3 Work with a partner. Compare your answers.

4 **T 9.9** Listen to *Part two* of the radio programme. Fill in some information about Robert Louis Stevenson. Compare your answers.

Speaking

What was the last book you read? What was it about?

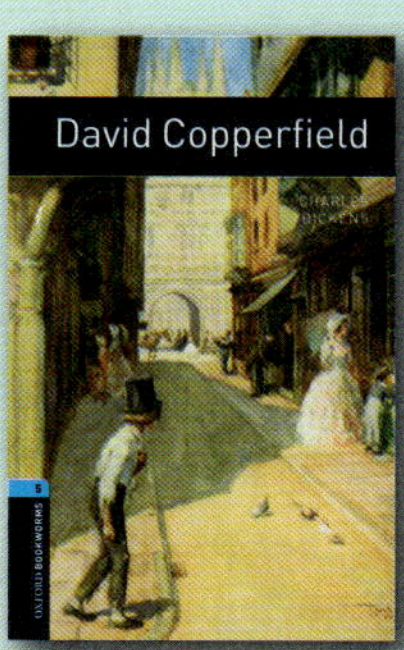

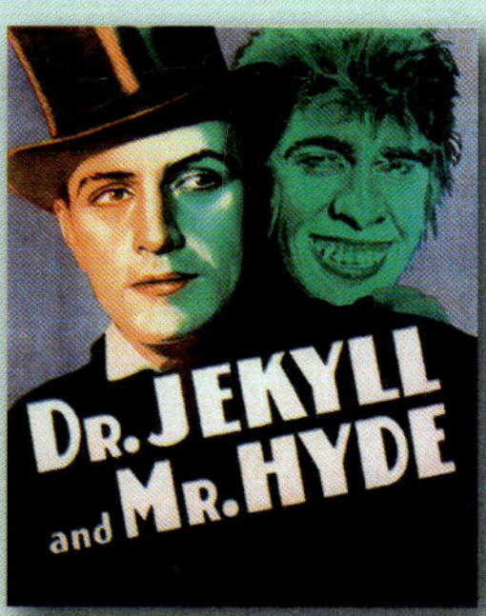

READING AND SPEAKING
Good and evil

1 Look at the pictures in the story of *The Strange Case of Dr Jekyll and Mr Hyde*.

1 When and where is it set?
2 Is it a romance, a horror story, or a crime story?
3 Is it fact or fiction?

2 Read the story quickly. Label these characters.

3 T 9.10 Read and listen to the story. Answer the questions.

Frames 1–3
1 Describe the attack and the attacker.
2 How did Mr Hyde react when he was caught?
3 What was strange about the cheque?
4 Why was Dr Jekyll angry? Why was Utterson confused?

Frames 4–7
1 Describe the murder.
2 What did Utterson suspect?
3 What did Dr Jekyll say about Mr Hyde?
4 Why were the servants worried?
5 What did they see when they broke down the door?

Frames 8–12
1 What was Jekyll's theory about personality?
2 What happened when he took the first potion?
3 Why did Dr Jekyll like being Mr Hyde?
4 How was Mr Hyde cruel?
5 In what way did Dr Jekyll lose control?
6 Why did Dr Jekyll have to die?

4 With a partner look at the pictures and retell the story.

What do you think?

- *The Strange Case of Dr Jekyll and Mr Hyde* was published in 1886. It was an immediate best-seller. Why, do you think?
- We sometimes describe a person as being 'a Jekyll and Hyde character'. What do you think this means? Is it a compliment?
- What stories can you remember from your childhood? Who are the good characters? Who are the bad ones? Who usually wins?

1 Late one night, a lawyer, Gabriel Utterson, was walking home through dark, silent streets when he saw a man attacking a woman. Utterson ran after him and caught him. The man's name was Mr Hyde, and he looked ugly and evil.

4 A year passed. One night an old man was murdered as he was walking home. A maid witnessed the crime and recognized the killer. Mr Hyde had struck again! The police went looking for Hyde, but he had disappeared.

7 Utterson and the servants broke down the door. Mr Hyde was lying dead on the floor. He had taken poison. But why was he wearing Dr Jekyll's clothes? And where was the doctor? Were Dr Jekyll and Mr Hyde one and the same person?

10 But after a time Jekyll found that he liked changing into Mr Hyde. He enjoyed being bad. He became more and more violent and cruel. He took pleasure in hurting innocent people.

# of Dr Jekyll and Mr Hyde

by Robert Louis Stevenson

2 Mr Hyde showed no regret for what he had done. To buy the woman's silence, he wrote her a cheque. Utterson noticed that the cheque was signed in the name of Dr Jekyll, a well-known and well-respected man.

3 Utterson was worried. He was Dr Jekyll's lawyer and also his friend. He went to visit him. As soon as he mentioned Mr Hyde, Dr Jekyll turned pale and became angry. Utterson was confused. Who *was* Mr Hyde?

5 Again, Utterson went to visit his friend Dr Jekyll. He suspected that Dr Jekyll had helped Mr Hyde to escape. When questioned, the doctor replied in a strange, wild voice that Mr Hyde had gone forever.

6 Over the next few weeks Dr Jekyll's behaviour became more and more unusual. He locked himself in his laboratory and refused to open the door. His servants were worried. When they heard his voice, it sounded different. They asked Utterson for help.

8 On the desk was a letter addressed to Mr Utterson. In it, Dr Jekyll tried to explain himself. He said he believed that inside every human being there was a good side and an evil side.

9 Jekyll had created a potion. When he drank it, his whole body changed. The good, kind doctor became cruel, ugly, and evil. He called this other man Mr Hyde. To change back, he had to drink another potion.

11 Finally Dr Jekyll couldn't control Mr Hyde anymore. He began to change into this monster even without taking the potion. Jekyll hoped and prayed that Hyde would disappear. But Hyde always returned.

12 The potion to turn Hyde back into Dr Jekyll no longer worked. It had lost its strength. Dr Jekyll could no longer get rid of the evil Mr Hyde. He had to kill this monster. But to kill Mr Hyde, Dr Jekyll also had to die.

VOCABULARY AND SPEAKING

Feelings

1 Look at the adjectives in the box that describe feelings. Which are positive? Which are negative?

angry	nervous	delighted	stressed	upset	homesick	jealous	proud	scared	amazed	lonely	disappointed

2 How would you feel in these situations?

1 It's the day before an exam.

2 You've got your exam results. You've failed.

3 Your son or daughter comes first in a race.

4 You have no friends.

5 You're a long way from home and you miss everyone.

6 You get a parking ticket.

7 It's night, you're alone in the house. Suddenly there's a noise.

8 People are saying horrible things about you.

9 Your boyfriend is getting very close to another girl.

3 Complete the sentences with your own ideas. Tell a partner.

1 I was delighted because *I'd won £1,000 in a competition*.
2 I was stressed because ______________.
3 I was proud because ______________.
4 I was amazed because ______________.
5 I was upset because ______________.

T 9.11 Listen and compare.

4 Match a line in **A** with a line in **B**.

A	B
1 Sometimes I feel really lonely.	__ Yes, but people can be really nice as well.
2 I've got so much to do! And the baby's crying! Help!	__ Cheer up! You've got me! I'm your best friend!
3 Guess what? I've just won £10,000!	__ Calm down! You're so stressed! Chill out!
4 When I watch the news on TV, I get scared.	__ I know what you mean. The world's a scary place.
5 I get upset when people are so horrible.	__ That's fabulous! I'm delighted for you! Can *I* have some?

T 9.12 Listen and check. Work with a partner. Practise the conversations. Continue one or two.

EVERYDAY ENGLISH

Exclamations with *so* and *such*

1 **T 9.13** Read and listen to the sentences.

What an amazing film!

I was scared!

I was really scared!

I was SO scared!

Do you think this use of *so* is more spoken or written?

2 Look at the sentences. When do we use *so*, *such*, *so many* …?

I was **so** surprised! It was **such a** shock!
It was **such an** awful day! You have **such** crazy ideas!
We had **such** terrible weather!
There were **so many** problems! I've got **so much** work!

▶▶ Grammar Reference 9.3 p144

T 9.14 Listen and practise the sentences. Copy the stress and intonation.

3 Complete the sentences with words from the box.

so	such	such a(n)	so many	so much

1 That was ________ good book! You must read it!
2 The film was ________ scary that I couldn't watch it!
3 Jane and Pete are ________ nice people!
4 But their children are ________ badly-behaved!
5 There were ________ people at the party!
6 They made ________ mess!
7 I've spent ________ money this week!
8 I've had ________ awful day!

4 Match these sentences with lines in exercise 3.

__ I'm glad I didn't have to tidy up.
__ I'll lend it to you. You'll really like it.
__ They're always so welcoming and pleased to see you.
__ I hate the sight of blood and people killing each other.
__ The parents have no control at all!
__ I haven't got a penny left!
__ I didn't manage to talk to everyone.
__ I need a drink to cheer me up!

T 9.15 Listen and check. Cover exercise 3. Try to remember the lines. Then cover exercise 4 and do the same.

5 Work with a partner. Write a conversation on one or two of these topics. Include some exclamations.

- a great party
- a tiring journey
- a lot of problems
- a scary experience
- a disgusting meal
- an amazing flat
- an annoying girlfriend/boyfriend

▶▶ **WRITING** **Writing about a book or a film** *p114*

10 Our interactive world

Passives • Compound nouns • Words that go together • On the phone

STARTER

1 Look at the public notices. Where might you find them?

English is spoken here	Mobile phones must be switched off	Travel cards are sold here

2 Underline the past participles in the notices. Which is regular? Which are irregular?

THE MOBILE PHONE

Passives

1 What is the mobile phone called in your country? What is it called in American English? Do you always have yours with you? When do you switch it off?

2 Read the introduction to *A phone call that changed the world*. Answer the questions.

1 Who made the first mobile phone call?
2 When and where did he make it?
3 How was the phone different from mobiles today?

3 **T 10.1** Read and listen to the *Fact File*. Correct the false information in these sentences.

1 30 million phones are sold worldwide every year.
2 The first text message was sent in the 1990s.
3 Smartphones have been sold since 2002.
4 Apple's iPhone now has over a million apps.
5 The most expensive phone costs £6,000.
6 We throw away nearly a million mobile phones a year.

A phone call that

Once the mobile phone was an oversized luxury item, now it's a pocket-sized mini-computer.

The first mobile phone call **was made** on April 3, 1973, by Martin Cooper, an American engineer, while he was walking along a street in New York City. People stopped and stared in amazement. Martin's phone was like a brick. It was over 20 cm long and weighed 1.3 kilograms. The battery lasted only thirty-six minutes.

GRAMMAR SPOT

1 Many of the verb forms in the text are in the passive.

Mobile phones **are owned** by almost 6 billion people.
The first mobile phone call **was made** in 1973.

How do we make passive forms?

2 Read the text again. Write the passive verb forms in the chart.

Present Simple	Past Simple	Present Perfect	*will* future
are sold		have been sold	

▶▶ Grammar Reference 10.1 p144

Active to passive

4 Read the text again. How are these verbs expressed in the passive?

1 Martin Cooper **made** the first mobile phone call in 1973.
2 Almost six billion people worldwide **own** mobile phones.
3 Shops in the UK **sell** 30 million phones every year.
4 They **have sold** camera phones since 2002.
5 Engineers **have added** a lot of amazing features.
6 They **decorate** the Goldstriker phone with over 550 diamonds.
7 We **throw away** 100 million mobile phones every year.
8 Some people believe that mobile phones **will** eventually **replace** all landline phones.

T 10.2 Listen and check.

5 What can you do on *your* mobile phone? What do you think they will be used for in the future?

I can play Scrabble on mine!
Maybe they'll be used as credit cards.
They might be used as passports.

changed the world

FACT FILE

- Today, mobile phones **are owned** by almost six billion people worldwide. In the UK, 30 million **are sold** every year.
- The first text message **was sent** in 1989. Last year 6.1 trillion texts **were sent** worldwide.
- Camera phones **have been sold** since 2002.
- 'Smartphones' **were introduced** in 2007. The mobile phone had become a multimedia gadget.
- Over the years a multitude of amazing features **have been added**, including Internet browsing, email, MP3 players, video, and camera.
- In 2008 Apple's iPhone had 500 applications (apps). Now there are over 500,000 apps.
- The most expensive mobile is the Goldstriker iPhone 4S Elite Gold. It **is made** of 24ct gold and **decorated** with over 550 diamonds. It costs £6 million.
- 100 million mobile phones **are thrown** away every year.
- Some people believe that before long all landline telephones **will be replaced** by mobile phones.

Goldstriker iPhone 4S Elite Gold

PRACTICE

Inventions that changed the world

1 Work with a partner. Look at the list of inventions. Which is the oldest? Which is the newest? Match them with the dates.

> I think the telephone was invented in 1901. What do you think?

> I'm not sure. I think it was invented in . . .

the telephone	105 AD
the printing press	1440
paper	1876
the ballpoint pen	1901
the personal computer (PC)	1924
television	1938
radio	1976

T 10.3 Listen and check. What nationality were the inventors? What were their jobs?

Speaking

2 Which inventions do you think are most important? Why? Order them 1–7 (1 = most important). Discuss your ideas as a class.

Passive forms

3 Read *All things online!* Complete the sentences with the correct passive form. Which numbers and dates do you think are correct?

T 10.4 Listen and check.

4 Make questions about the information in exercise 3. Ask and answer them with a partner.

1 How many emails/every year?

> How many emails are sent every year?

> Over 90 . . .

2 How many questions/by Google/every day?
3 When/eBay? Who/by?
4 How many items/on eBay/it began?
5 How many films/YouTube every week?
6 When/the first Twitter message/sent? Who/by?
7 How many languages/Facebook/translated into?
8 When/Amazon.com/founded? Who/by?

T 10.5 Listen and check.

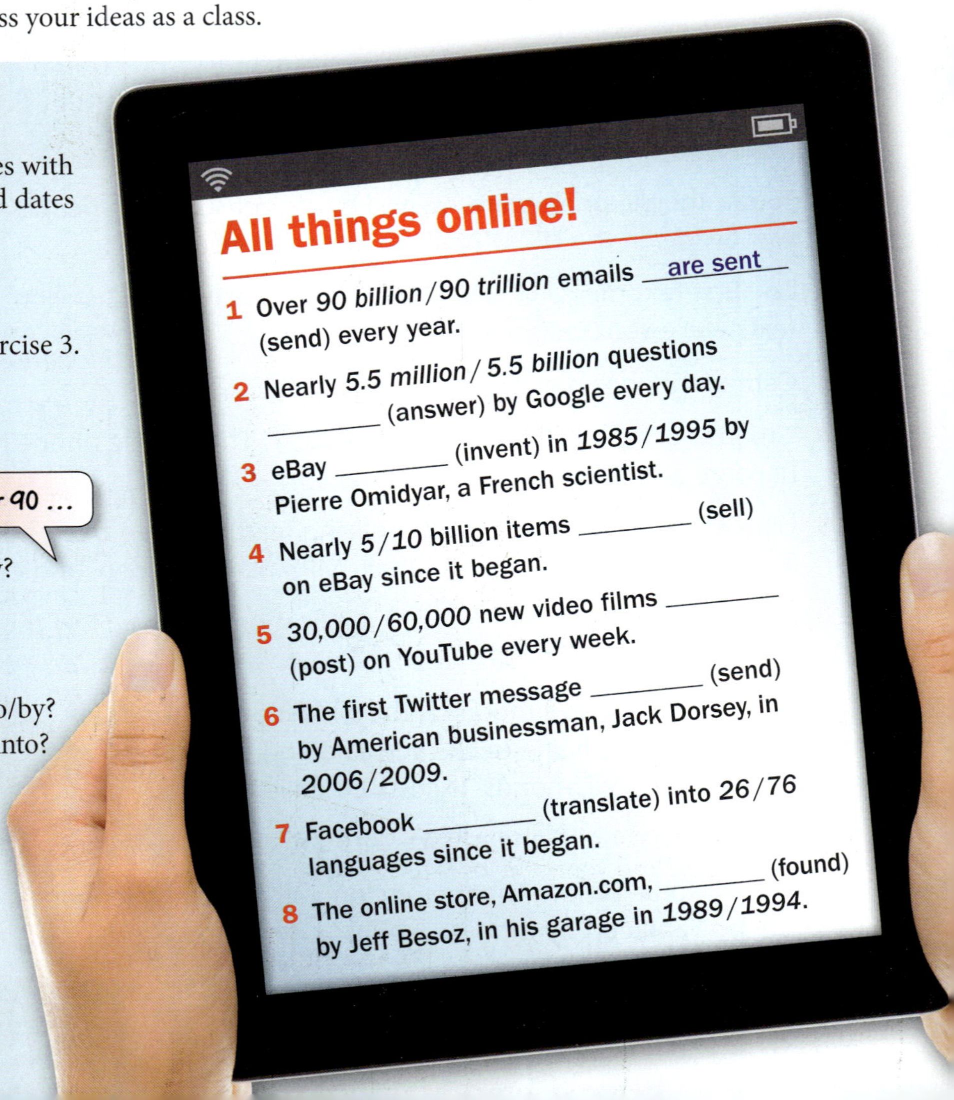

All things online!

1 Over *90 billion/90 trillion* emails __are sent__ (send) every year.
2 Nearly *5.5 million/5.5 billion* questions ________ (answer) by Google every day.
3 eBay ________ (invent) in *1985/1995* by Pierre Omidyar, a French scientist.
4 Nearly *5/10* billion items ________ (sell) on eBay since it began.
5 *30,000/60,000* new video films ________ (post) on YouTube every week.
6 The first Twitter message ________ (send) by American businessman, Jack Dorsey, in *2006/2009*.
7 Facebook ________ (translate) into *26/76* languages since it began.
8 The online store, Amazon.com, ________ (found) by Jeff Besoz, in his garage in *1989/1994*.

VOCABULARY AND SPEAKING

Words that go together

Noun + noun

Two nouns can go together to make a compound noun.
text + message = **text message**
business + man = **businessman**
news + agent = **newsagent**
cell + phone = **cellphone**

1 **T 10.6** Listen to the compound nouns. Which word is stressed? Practise them.

2 Work with a partner. How many compound nouns can you make from these lists? Use your dictionary to help.

business **computer** **lap** **phone** **radio** **web**	+	**call** **number** **card** **site** **deal** **top** **games** **waves** **man** **virus** **news** **program(me)**

T 10.7 Listen and check. Read the words aloud.

Verb + noun

3 In each box below, *one* noun does not go with the verb. Which one?

1 send	a text message an email a phone call a present a postcard
2 start	a business a car a family work an idea
3 make	a complaint a discovery a phone call the housework a lot of money
4 do	research the shopping a photo exercises the housework
5 take	notes a photo a coffee a long time size 41
6 play	games the piano yoga a part baseball

4 Choose a noun from each group and write a sentence using the verb. Read your sentences to the class.

I've just sent you a text message.
Are you taking notes in this lesson?

Adverb + adjective

The adverbs *well-* and *badly-* can combine with past participles to form adjectives.
well-known **badly-behaved**

5 Complete the sentences with an adjective formed with *well-* or *badly-* and a past participle from the box.

done	paid	written	equipped
behaved	dressed	known	

1 She has a wonderful job. She's very ___________ .
2 I didn't enjoy that novel. It was really ___________ .
3 You don't need to spend a lot of money on clothes to look ___________ .
4 Our office is really ___________ . We have all the latest machines.
5 I hope their children don't come. They're so ________ .

6 Can I have my steak very ___________ , please? I don't like it rare.
7 Surely you've heard of Elizabeth Taylor? She was really ___________ .

T 10.8 Listen and check. Practise the sentences.

Talking about you

6 Ask and answer these questions with your partner.

1 Do you ever play computer games? Which ones?
2 Which websites do you visit most often?
3 Do you send a lot of text messages? How many per day?
4 Who does the most housework in your home?
5 What size shoes do you take?
6 How do you like your steak?
7 Is your school well-equipped?

T 10.9 Listen and compare.

READING AND SPEAKING

There's a first time for everything

1 Work in groups. What do you use the Internet for? Make a list. Read the introduction and compare your ideas.

2 Match the headings in *Five Internet firsts* with these lines.

A He built a single, easily searchable database for students to access information.

B But soon his main topic became his personal life. He wrote openly about his relationships, his passions, his plans and fears.

C They are simply computer programs that replicate themselves again and again.

D It quickly became the place for fashionable people to be seen.

E People loved exchanging life stories with old schoolmates, and school romances were reignited.

3 You're going to read some of the articles. Divide them amongst your group. Read and take notes about …

- names and nationalities of the people
- what and where was the first
- important dates and events in its history

4 Use your notes to report back to your group. Do any of the *Five Internet Firsts* play a part in your life? How?

5 Read *all* the articles. Answer the questions.

1 What is there less need for these days? Why?
2 What is PCBang?
3 What was 'Archie'? How did it get its name?
4 How did 'blogging' get its name? Who named it?
5 Which virus broke hearts? How?
6 Which has more users, *MySpace* or *Facebook*? How many do they have?

Listening

6 T 10.10 Listen to five people. Which of the Internet firsts are they talking about? What do they say that helped you work it out?

7 All these words are connected with the Internet. What do you understand by them? Discuss in your groups.

bookmark	download	inbox	mouse	log in	spam

▶▶ **WRITING Discussing pros and cons** *p115*

http://www...

No technology has evolved so much in so little time as the Internet. We not only shop, bank, work, and meet people online, but we share what we are doing at any given moment with such sites as Facebook and Twitter. So how did all this begin?

The first Internet café 1

A café with full Internet access (sometimes called a Cybercafé) was designed in early 1994 by Ivan Pope. He was asked to develop an Internet event for an arts weekend in London. Pope created a café with Internet access from the tables.

Inspired by this, the first commercial Internet café, called *Cyberia*, was opened later that year in central London. It quickly became the fashionable place to be seen.

Internet cafés soon extended across the world under a variety of names, for example, the *Binary Café* in Canada, *CompuCafé* in Finland, *PCBang* in South Korea, and the *@Café* in New York.

Cafés have always been places to exchange information, chat to friends, read newspapers, and play games. Internet cafés were a natural evolution of this. Now, people can connect to the Internet in any café using their own laptops and iPhones. There is less need for the Internet café.

Five Internet firsts

The first search engine

2

For many people, using search engines has become a routine part of their lives. But how did they begin?

In 1989 a young computer scientist from Barbados, Alan Emtage, was studying at Montreal's McGill University in Canada. He built a single, easily searchable database for students to access information. This created a lot of interest and Alan was joined by two colleagues, Mike Parker and Bill Heelan, who helped develop the system. They called it 'Archie'. Why was it named Archie? Simply the word 'archive' without the 'v'.

Emtage found himself at the heart of an Internet revolution. It didn't take long for search engines to become big business. Many more followed such as *Excite* in 1993, created by six Stanford University students, *Yahoo* in 1994, and *Lycos* also in 1994. With 60 million documents this was the largest of its time until *Google* was launched in 1997. *Google* now has 620 million visitors every day.

The first blog

3

The first ever blogger may never be identified, but the most likely candidate is an American journalist, Justin Hall. He began blogging in 1994 (before the word 'blog' existed) with a website called 'Justin's Links from the Underground'. At first his website just gave rather boring information about the Internet. But soon his main topic became his personal life. He wrote openly about his relationships, his passions, his plans and fears. More and more readers were attracted to his site, fascinated by his daily blogs. They began to share their lives with his.

The word 'blog' wasn't used until 1997. It is short for 'WebLog' (web log), a name invented by Jorn Barger in December of that year. Now the number of active bloggers is estimated to be about 100 million worldwide, and Justin Hall has been named 'the founding father of personal blogging' by the *New York Times*.

The first virus

4

What exactly are computer viruses? They are simply computer programs that replicate themselves again and again. This ability was predicted as early as 1949 by a German mathematician, John von Neumann. It is generally believed that the very first was a virus called *Creeper*. It was detected on ARPANET (the forerunner of the Internet) in the early 1970s. It was written by an engineer called Bob Thomas from Cambridge, Massachusetts in 1971. However, the *Creeper* was not a bad virus, it did not damage computers. When a machine was infected a message simply appeared on the screen saying 'I'm the Creeper, catch me if you can!' More damaging viruses appeared in the 1980s with the spread of personal computers.

In 1986, *Brain* was the first virus to infect PCs; in 1991, *Michelangelo* was the first to make international news; in 2000, *Love Letter* broke hearts by sending emails saying 'I love you' to tens of millions of computers, and in 2007, *Storm Worm* spread with a message saying '230 dead as storm batters Europe!'

The first social networking site

5

In the 1990s more and more homes had Internet access. People could connect easily with each other. Would they also like to reconnect with old friends? In 1995 *Classmates.com*, the first social networking site, began life in the basement of Randy Conrads, a Boeing employee in the US. It was immediately popular. People loved exchanging life stories with old schoolmates and school romances were reignited. In one year this led to 100 marriages.

The idea was copied in many countries, including *Friends Reunited* in the UK. In 2003 the business networking site *LinkedIn* began. This has over 60 million members. In the same year and with three times that number is *MySpace*. However, one name leads all other global social networking sites, *Facebook*. Created in 2004 by students at Harvard University, it went worldwide in 2006 and has more than 750 million users. There has even been a film, *The Social Network*, made about it.

It seems people love talking about themselves. On the micro-blogging site, *Twitter*, users inform their followers about tiny details of their lives: 'I'm having honey with my toast this morning!'

LISTENING AND SPEAKING

Modern life drives me crazy!

1 What things annoy you in a typical day? Write down one or two and give them to your teacher.

Jack's stressful day

2 Look at the photos of Jack. What do you think is annoying him?

3 **T 10.11** Alan is meeting Jack at the railway station. Jack has not had a good journey. Listen and tick (✓) what he complains about.

- the train is late
- the girl behind him
- the train is overcrowded
- the little boy
- parking
- booking a ticket
- the food
- traffic
- coffee bars

4 **T 10.11** Work in small groups. Listen again. What exactly are his complaints?

5 Have you ever had similar complaints to Jack's? Tell the class.

What do you think?

6 What do the different generations complain about? Think of typical complaints for these people. Share ideas as a class.

- very young children
- teenagers
- parents
- the middle-aged
- old people

7 Your teacher will read out some of the things that annoy you. Can you guess who wrote it?

Roleplay

It's the end of a difficult day and you've just arrived home to your flatmate/husband/wife/parents. Work with a partner and write a conversation about all the problems you've had that day. Begin like this:

A I've had a really terrible day!
B Why? What happened?
A Well, I …

Act your conversations to the class.

EVERYDAY ENGLISH

On the phone

1 T 10.12 Listen and practise saying these telephone numbers.

07700 900333
0049 021 37474
0115 496 0499
0800 142 2466

How were these numbers expressed?

0 00 99 0800

2 T 10.13 Listen and write the numbers. Compare your answers with a partner.

3 In your country what are the telephone numbers for …?

- your house • your mobile • the emergency services • directory enquiries

How many telephone numbers do you know by heart? Give examples. Whose are they?

4 T 10.14 Listen to four phone conversations. Answer these questions after each one.

1 Who is speaking to who?
2 Are they on a landline or a mobile?
3 Where are they?
4 What they are talking about?
5 How well do they know each other?

5 T 10.14 Listen again and complete the expressions from the telephone conversations.

1 **A** Sorry Brian, you're ________ up. I couldn't hear that.
B I know Adam, it's not a good ________. But, listen, I'm calling because I can't ________ it on Thursday. Are you free on Friday?
A Friday? I'm not sure. Can I get ________ to you?
B Sure. That's fine. Text me. Speak ________!

2 **A** Hello, Carol? It's Adam. I'm trying to get ________ of Brian.
C I'm afraid he's not in. Have you ________ his mobile?
A Yeah. I tried that first but he's not ________.
C It's probably ________ off.
A Oh, OK. Can you give him a ________ then?
C Of course.

3 **D** I'm afraid Brian's line's ________. Would you like to ________?
E Yes, please.
D It's ________ for you now.
E Thank you.
F Hello. Brian Doyle's office. Flora ________.
E ________ is Emma Smith from Digby and Moss Associates.
F Oh, good morning Ms Smith. I'll put you ________ immediately.

4 **C** Hi Flora. Can I speak to Brian, please?
F Oh, I'm ________, he has ________ with him at the moment. Is it ________?
C Just tell him Carol ________ and I'll see him this evening.
F Will ________. I hope there isn't a problem.

T 10.14 Listen again and check.

6 Work with a partner. Learn one of the conversations by heart. Act it to the class.

Roleplay

Work in pairs. You are going to have three telephone conversations.

Student A Look at p152.

Student B Look at p154.

Hi, Maria. I'm calling because I can't make it on Tuesday.

Sorry, you're breaking up …

11 Life's what you make it!

Present Perfect Continuous • Tense review
Birth, marriage, and death • Good news, bad news

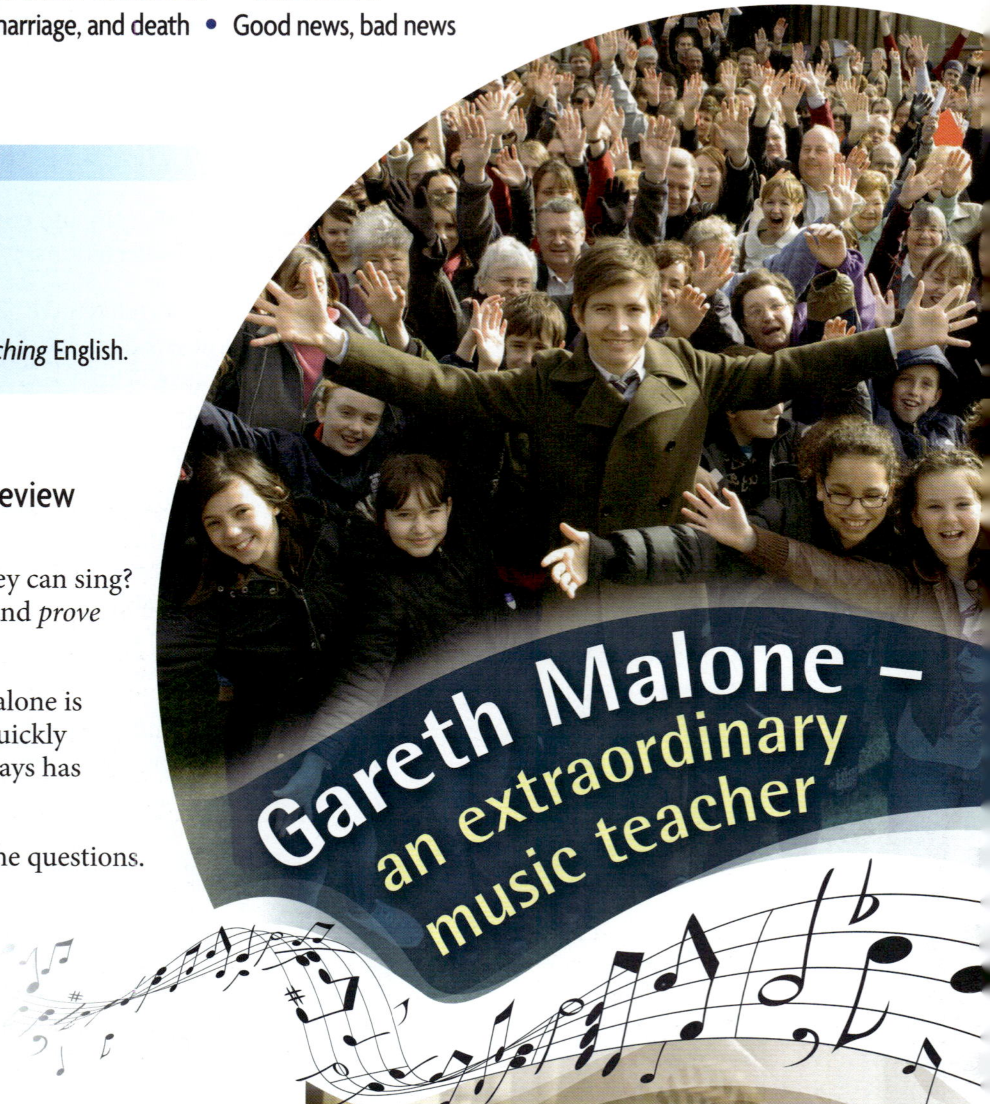

STARTER

1 Ask and answer these questions with a partner.

- How long have you been learning English?
- When did you start?

2 Ask your teacher the same questions about *teaching* English.

ANYONE CAN SING!

Present Perfect Continuous and tense review

1 How many students in your class think they can sing? How many think they can't? Do a survey and *prove* your answers.

2 Choirmaster and TV Presenter, Gareth Malone is passionate about teaching singing. Look quickly through the chart about his life. In what ways has music been part of his life?

3 Study the chart more closely and answer the questions.

1. Where and when was Gareth born?
2. When did he move to London?
3. What did he study at university?
4. How long did he work for the LSO?
5. How many awards has he won?
6. How long has he been married?
7. Does he have any children?
8. What is he doing now?

4 Match a question about Gareth with an answer.

1 When did he start playing the piano?	___ Three.
2 How long has he been playing the piano?	___ For about 30 years.
3 When did he start teaching singing?	___ When he was three.
4 How long has he been teaching singing?	___ Since he was three.
5 When did he make his first TV programme?	___ When he was 23.
6 How long has he been making TV programmes?	___ Since he was 23.
7 How many programmes has he made?	___ In 2007.
8 How long has he been living in London?	___ Since 2007.

T 11.1 Listen and check. Ask and answer the questions with a partner.

Age	Life event
0	Born in Bournemouth, England, 1975.
3	Started playing the piano.
5 to 10	Bournemouth Grammar School. Started singing in the choir.
10	Moved with family to London.
18 to 21	Studied Drama at the University of East Anglia.
23	Started teaching singing in schools.
26	Started working for the London Symphony Orchestra (LSO). He ran their Youth Choir.
27 to 30	Did a postgraduate course at the Royal Academy of Music in London.
32 to now	Started making programmes for BBC TV. Has made three: The Choir, Boys Don't Sing, Unsung Town.
33	Married Becky, an English teacher.
34	Won two TV (BAFTA) awards for The Choir. Stopped working for the LSO.
35	Daughter Esther born.
now	Still teaching music and making more radio and TV programmes. Still living in London.

GRAMMAR SPOT

1 Read the sentences. What tenses are used?

He **made** his first TV programme in 2007 and he still **makes** them.

He**'s been making** programmes since 2007.

He**'s made** three so far.

The Present Perfect Continuous expresses an activity that began in the past and still continues.

2 Complete the questions. Answer them.

How long ________ he ____________ TV programmes?

How many programmes ________ he ________ so far?

3 Remember! State verbs such as *be*, *have* (possession), *know*, *love* are rarely used in continuous tenses.

I**'ve known** him for a long time.

▶▶ **Grammar Reference 11.1 p145**

PRACTICE

Discussing grammar

1 Choose the correct tense.

1 How long *have you been waiting / are you waiting* here?
2 I *bought / have bought* a computer a few weeks ago.
3 Alice *has been looking / has looked* for a new job for ages.
4 How long *have you had / have you been having* your car?
5 Sue *has been talking / has talked* on her phone for ages.
6 She*'s been speaking / has spoken* to at least six friends.

Asking questions

2 Work with a partner. Read the sentences aloud and reply using a question with *How long ...?* Think of an answer.

How long has she been working there?

Only a couple of months.

1 My sister's working in New York.
2 I'm training to run the marathon.
3 My boss is on holiday.
4 I'm learning how to drive.
5 I know Maria very well.
6 I have the new iPad.

T 11.2 Listen and compare.

Talking about you

3 Put the verbs in the Present Perfect Simple or Continuous or the Past Simple. Then ask and answer with a partner.

1 How long ______ you ______ (come) to this school?
2 How long ______ you ______ (use) this book?
3 Which book ______ you ______ (use) before this one?
4 How long ______ you ______ (know) your teacher?

What have they been doing?

4 Work with a partner. Ask questions with *Why?* about the people in the pictures. Reply with *because* and a reason.

> Why are the students bored?
>
> Because the teacher's been talking for hours.

1 bored

2 sore throat

3 tired and dirty

4 backache

5 covered in paint

6 no money left

5 Complete these sentences in the Present Perfect Simple about the people in exercise 4.

1 They ***haven't understood*** (not understand) a word.
2 He __________ (sing) every night for the last three weeks.
3 They're happy because they __________ (win) the match.
4 He __________ (plant) six rows of cabbages.
5 She __________ (paint) two walls already.
6 They __________ (spend) over £200.

T 11.3 Listen and check.

SPEAKING

Tense review

1 Look at the pictures of Charlotte Church and read what she says. What kind of music do you think she sings? What do you learn about her family?

Charlotte Church: the girl with 'the voice of an angel'!

"Everyone in my family sings. It's just a natural thing that I haven't thought about much. There was never a time when I wasn't singing. Mum and dad loved classical music and my nan used to sing show tunes."

2 Work with a partner.

Student A Look at p152.
Student B Look at p154.

You have different information about Charlotte Church's life and career. Ask and answer questions.

> Where was Charlotte Church born?
>
> In Cardiff, in Wales. When was she born?

LISTENING AND SPEAKING

I haven't seen you for ages!

1 Write down the names of some friends you had when you were small. Talk to a partner about them.

- Why were you friends?
- Do you still see them?
- What do you know about their lives now?

Friends

+ Add friend

From: **SHansson6@chatchat.com** MESSAGE
Subject: **Hi**

Are you **Mike Elliot** from Grange School, Bedford, 1996 – 2002? I hope so. I'm Sophie Simpson – yes – 'Silly Sophie'! (Now **Sophie Hansson**). I've been trying to find information about you for a while. How's life? I'd love to hear your news. My email address is: SHansson6@chatchat.com

From: **Mikeyell@gargle.co.uk** MESSAGE
Subject: **What a surprise!**

Dear **Sophie**,
Great to hear from you! It's been ages since we spoke – our last day at school I believe. What happened to all those promises about keeping in touch? How long have you been Mrs Hansson? I'm not married but I've been going out with a very nice girl for a while, so who knows? I'm working in Madrid at the moment. What have you been doing with your life? We must meet when I'm back in the UK and catch up. **Mike**

2 Two old friends have just made contact again via a social networking site. Read their first messages.

- Who are they?
- When were they friends?
- What do you learn about their lives now?

3 **T 11.4** Sophie and Mike finally meet and catch up. Listen to the first part of their conversation. Are these statements about Mike true (✓) or false (✗)? Correct the false ones.

1 Mike thinks Sophie looks older.
2 He's been working in Madrid for eight months.
3 The headquarters of his company are in Germany.
4 His Spanish girlfriend speaks no English.
5 He's been learning Spanish for six months.
6 Now he's going to learn Swedish.

4 Look at the second part of the conversation. Read what **Sophie** says. Answer the questions.

1 Who did she marry?
2 What and where was her first job?
3 Where does she work now?
4 What have they been trying to do?
5 Why do they need a place of their own?

5 **T 11.5** Complete **Mike's** questions. Listen and compare. How does the coversation end?

Sophie I got married a year ago to a Swedish guy. Ragnar, Ragnar Hansson.

Mike ____________________?

S We met while I was working in Stockholm.

M ____________________?

S Well, after university I studied fashion design and my first job was in Sweden, as a buyer for H&M Fashion.

M ____________________?

S I worked there for over three years. Ragnar was my boss.

M ____________________?

S Yes, we did. My parents came over for the wedding.

M ____________________?

S No, we don't. We've both got new jobs in the UK.

M ____________________?

S About ten months. We've been trying to buy a flat since we got back.

M ____________________?

S With my parents. They're lovely, but it's not great and we're expecting a baby next April, so we really need a place of our own.

M Oh, congratulations!

Roleplay

6 Have a similar conversation with your partner. Pretend you have met again after a few years. Begin like this:

How great to see you! It's been ages, what have you been doing?

▶▶ **WRITING Filling in forms** *p116*

READING AND SPEAKING

Four generations of Gettys

1 Who are the richest families in your country? How did they get their wealth? Describe their lifestyle.

2 Look at the pictures and read the introduction. What did you learn about the Getty family?

3 Work with a partner. Read about **Jean Paul Getty I**. Correct the information below about him.

1 Jean Paul Getty I made his money from art and antiques.
2 He was one of the world's first millionaires.
3 He built the J. Paul Getty Museum in Guildford, England.
4 He used his house in England to entertain British and American oil friends.
5 He was famous for his generosity.
6 He had five wives and four sons.

4 Read about **Jean Paul Getty II**. Answer the questions.

1 Which adjectives best describe his relationship with his father. Give reasons.

close	distant	loving	cold	cruel	caring

2 How many wives did he have? Who were they? How did each marriage end?
3 What did he have in common with his father?
4 Who was kidnapped? Where and why?
5 Why did Paul I refuse to pay the ransom?
6 Why did he change his mind?
7 How much money did Paul II inherit? What did he do with it?
8 Where was he living when he died? Where is he buried?

5 Read about **Jean Paul Getty III**. Make a list of the tragic events in his life. Who do you blame? Discuss as a class.

6 Read about **Balthazar Getty**. Complete the questions about him. Ask and answer them with a partner.

1 Where/born?
2 What/do?
3 How long/working in films?
4 … made a lot of films?
5 Which TV series/appearing in?
6 How many children/got?
7 Why/marriage nearly end?

What do you think?

1 Which Gettys do you think are the most tragic? Which the least? Why?
2 What do you predict for Balthazar? Will he break the cycle of tragedy?

Project

Research the history of a famous family. Tell the class about it.

A Tragic Dynasty

The Getty family is one of the richest families in the world, yet it has been plagued by tragedy for generations. The family are proof that money cannot buy happiness.

Jean Paul Getty I (1892–1976)

Jean Paul Getty I was an American businessman. He founded the *Getty Oil Company*, and in 1957 was named the richest living American. He was one of the world's first billionaires.

A keen collector of art and antiques, he built the J. Paul Getty Museum in Los Angeles, California. He left over $661 million to the museum when he died.

> In 1957 he was named the richest living American

He moved to England in the 1950s and bought a 16th-century Tudor estate, Sutton Place, near Guildford. This house became the centre of the Getty Oil Company and he used it to entertain his British and Arabian oil friends. Paul I was famous for his meanness. He installed a pay phone in Sutton Place for his guests' use. He died there on June 6th, 1976, aged 83.

Getty married and divorced five times in his life. He had five sons with four of his wives.

Jean Paul Getty II (1932–2003)

Jean Paul Getty II was the son of Paul I's fourth wife, Ann Rork. His parents divorced when he was three. The young Paul II rarely saw his father, but he wrote to him. His father never answered the letters. He just returned them with the spelling mistakes underlined.

In 1956 he married his childhood sweetheart, Gail Harris and had four children. They moved to Rome where Paul II ran *Getty Oil Italiana*. They were a popular, party-loving couple, but alcohol and drugs took control of their lives. They divorced in 1964. Two years later Paul II married the Dutch model Talitha Pol (pictured). This also ended in disaster. She died of a drug overdose in 1971.

Paul II and Paul I had one thing in common – they were very bad fathers. In 1973 Paul II's eldest son, Jean Paul III, was kidnapped in Rome, and a ransom of $17 million demanded. His grandfather refused to pay, saying 'I have 14 other grandchildren.' An envelope arrived from the kidnappers. Inside was Paul III's ear and a note:

This is Paul's ear. If we don't get some money within ten days, then the other ear will arrive.

Paul I finally paid $3 million and his grandson was released.

Paul II moved back to England and in 1997 became a British citizen. He had inherited $2.5 billion from his father. He donated over $2.25 million of this to the arts. In 1994, he married his third wife, Victoria Holdsworth. It was Victoria who helped him finally beat his drug addiction. He died in 2003 and is buried in Westminster Abbey.

Jean Paul Getty III (1956–2011)

Jean Paul Getty III spent his childhood in Italy. His parents divorced when he was nine and after that he saw very little of his father. By the age of fifteen he had been expelled from seven schools and he was already taking drugs. Then in July, 1973, when he was sixteen, came the kidnapping. He was imprisoned in a cave in the mountains for five months, until his ear was cut off and his grandfather finally paid a ransom. Paul III never recovered. He returned to a lifestyle of parties and drugs. In 1974, aged eighteen, he married Gisela Zacher, a German model, and moved to Los Angeles. He was just nineteen when his son Balthazar was born.

Paul III was now an alcoholic and drug addict and in 1981, at just twenty-four years old, he took a drug overdose and had a stroke. He was in a coma for six weeks and afterwards he was paralysed, nearly blind and unable to speak. His father, Paul II, like his grandfather before, refused to help. Paul III and Gisela divorced in 1993 and he was looked after by his mother, Gail, until his death on February 5th, 2011. He was fifty-four.

Balthazar Getty (1975–)

Balthazar Getty, the great-grandson of Jean Paul Getty I, was born in California in 1975. He is an actor and a musician. When he was eleven he was sent to Gordonstoun School, an elite boarding school in Scotland which has educated three generations of the British royal family.

Balthazar has been working in films since he was twelve years old, when he was given the leading role of the schoolboy, Ralph, in the film *Lord of the Flies*. He's made many films since then, including *Young Guns II* and *Natural Born Killers*. He has also been in TV shows. Recently he has been appearing in the hit ABC series, *Brothers and Sisters*.

Balthazar has also worked as a fashion model and in 2000, he married fashion designer Rosetta Millington. They have a son, Cassius Paul, and three daughters. The marriage almost ended in 2008 when Balthazar was photographed kissing the actress Sienna Miller. He has since returned to his wife.

So far Balthazar's life has been more successful than his father's and grandfather's. He says: ***'As a child, I really didn't know what it was to be a Getty. I had a pretty modest upbringing.'***

VOCABULARY AND LISTENING

Birth, marriage, and death

BIRTH

1 Work in small groups. When were you born? Do you know the exact time of your birth?

I was born on March 21st, 1991 at 2.40 in the morning.

2 Look at the pictures and complete the sentences with a word from the box.

birth	pregnant	expecting
weighed	born	due

Sophie's [1] *pregnant* . She's [2] ________ a baby. The baby is [3] ________ in four weeks.

She gave [4] ________ to a baby boy. He was [5] ________ at 3.00 a.m. last night. He [6] ________ 3.4 kilos

MARRIAGE

3 When did you last go to a wedding? Whose was it? What was it like? Complete the sentences with a word from the box.

married	widowed	single	divorced	engaged

1 He's ________ .

2 They're ________ .

3 They're ________ .

4 They're ________ .

5 She's ________ .

4 These sentences describe the events in **Nina's** life. Put them in the correct order. Read them aloud round the class. What is a *honeymoon*?

Nina and Ted in 2002

__ They got married in 2002 in a registry office.
__ They went to Venice on honeymoon.
__ The marriage started to go wrong.
__ In 2004 they had a son, **Sam**.
__ They split up and got divorced in 2008.
9 It's their anniversary today! They've been married since 2010.
__ **Nina** remarried. She married **Robert**, a colleague from work.
__ They got engaged two years later.
1 **Nina** and **Ted** started going out when they were both 17.

5 **T 11.6** Listen to **Alison** talking about her life. In what ways is her story different from Nina's? Who are Ben, Mark, Ellen, Tessa, and Tom?

DEATH

6 Complete the sentences with words on the right.

1 'Are your grandparents still ________ ?'
'My grandmother is. My grandfather ________ before I was born.'
2 The ________ of his uncle came as a great shock. It was totally unexpected.
3 He ________ a heart attack. The ________ is next Thursday.
4 'Do you still have your dog?' 'No. He's been ________ a long time. I ________ him terribly.'

EVERYDAY ENGLISH

Good news, bad news

1 Look at the pictures. What is the good news? What is the bad news?

2 **T 11.7** Work with a partner. Complete the conversations with words in the box. After each one listen and check.

1

A My wife [1]________ a baby last night.
B [2]____________! Was it a boy or girl?
A A boy! William James.
B How much did he [3]________?
A 4.1 kilos.
B Ooh! A big boy. How are mother and baby [4]________?
A They're fine.
B That's wonderful. [5]____________ when you see her.

2

A Alfie and I have got [1]________.
B That's [2]____________! Congratulations!
A Do you like my [3]________?
B Wow! Diamonds! It's [4]________. When's the [5]________?
A We're thinking of getting married next spring.
B I hope I'm invited.
A Of course you are. I want you to be a [6]____________.
B Really? I'd love that. I've never been one before.

3

A Have you heard about Bill and Josie?
B No! [1]____________?
A Well, they've been having a [2]________ recently.
B I know, they haven't been [3]____________ at all.
A Mm. Well, they've finally decided to [4]________.
B I'm so [5]____________ that. What a [6]________!
A Yes, I always thought they were so good together.

4

A We lost Grandpa last week.
B I know. Your dad told me. I'm [1]________. He was a [2]____________. Everyone was really [3]____________.
A He and Grandma were [4]________ nearly sixty years.
B That's incredible! How old was he?
A Eighty-eight.
B And how's your Grandma [5]________?
A She's OK. She's got her family around her.
B Well, I'm sure you all have wonderful [6]________ of him.

3 Choose two of the conversations and practise them with your partner. Act them out to the class.

12 Just wondering ...

If + *will*/*might*/*would* conditionals • Prepositions • Thank you and goodbye!

STARTER

What's the weather forecast where you are for . . .?

- today
- tomorrow
- the weekend

REAL POSSIBILITIES

First conditional + *will* and *might*

1 **T 12.1** Read and listen to the conversation.

A What are you doing this weekend?
B Mmm ... if the weather's nice, we'll go for a picnic.
A Ooh! Sounds nice. Where to?
B Not sure. We might go to the park, or we might go to the country.
A Well, I'm sure you'll have fun!

What's the difference between . . .?

We'**ll go** for a picnic. We **might go** to the park.

Practise the conversation with a partner.

2 Have similar conversations with your partner.

- sunny – go swimming – the outdoor pool / the river
- it rains – go shopping – the High Street / a shopping centre
- have time – see some friends – a restaurant / the pub

T 12.2 Listen and compare.

3 What do you think you'll do at the weekend?

If it's a nice day on Saturday, I'll go to the beach.
If it rains, I won't go to the beach.
I might see some friends.

GRAMMAR SPOT

1 In first conditional sentences what tense comes after *if*? What is the other verb form?

If it's sunny, we**'ll go** for a picnic.
We **won't** go out **if** it **rains**.

2 The first conditional refers to real time and real future situations.

If we have time, **we'll see** some friends.

3 *Might* + infinitive expresses a future possibility.
Might = *will perhaps*.

I **might go out**, or I **might stay** at home. I'm not sure.

▶▶ Grammar Reference 12.1 and 12.2 p146

PRACTICE

Discussing grammar

1 Work with a partner. Choose the correct answer.

1 If I see Pete, *I might tell* / *I'll tell* him I saw you.
2 I'll come and see you if *I have* / *I'll have* time.
3 *I might see* / *I'll see* you later. I'm not sure.
4 *I might collect* / *I'll collect* the kids from school if you want.
5 If *you'll arrive* / *you arrive* there before me, wait by the door.
6 If you tell me, *I won't say* / *I'll say* a word to anyone else. I promise.

going to and *might*

2 Work with a partner. Make conversations about these future possibilities.

What are you going to do after school?

I don't know. I might go home, or I might go into town.

1 What/going/do/after school?
don't know – go home/go into town

2 Where/going on your next holiday?
not sure – Spain/Turkey

3 What/study at university?
haven't decided – languages/business

4 What/buy Jane/birthday?
not sure – a T-shirt/make-up

5 When/see your boyfriend again?
don't know – Friday night/Saturday afternoon

T 12.3 Listen and check.

When I leave school …

3 **T 12.4** Listen to Tara and Ben talking about when they leave school. Who knows what they want to do? Who isn't sure?

Talk to a partner about Tara and Ben.

First Tara's going to …

Ben might …

4 Ben has decided to go travelling with James. Tara sees a lot of problems. Use the prompts to continue his conversation with Tara.

Tara	What will you do if you don't have any money?
Ben	I'll get a job, of course!
Tara	But what will you do if you …?

- don't like the food
- are ill
- miss your family
- get lonely
- don't get on with James
- can't speak the language

Advice, warnings, threats

5 Who is speaking? Complete their sentences.

1

If ________ these pills, ________ feel better.

2

If ________ junk food, ________ fat.

3

You ________ fail ________ exams if ________ (not do) your homework.

4

Careful! If ________ touch ________, ________ an electric shock!

5

If ________ (not do) what I say, ________ kill ________.

T 12.5 Listen and check.

DREAMS AND WISHES

Second conditional *if* + *would*

1 Look at the picture of the genie? What can he do?

2 **T 12.6** Read and listen to Lily. How old do you think she is? What does she wish for?

I'd love a baby brother. If I had a baby brother, I would play with him all the time. We'd have a lot of fun. I'd be so happy! I wouldn't ask my mum and dad for anything else!

3 Answer the questions.

1 Does Lily have a brother?
No, she ...
2 How does she express her wish?
If I had ..., I would ...
3 What would she do with her brother?
They'd ...
4 How would she feel?
She'd ...
5 Why would her mum and dad be pleased?
Because she ...

T 12.6 Listen again and repeat what Lily says.

4 **T 12.7** Listen to Sam and Annie. What do they wish for? Complete their sentences.

I'd like to be taller. If I <u>*were*</u> taller, I ________ in the first team at rugby. And if I ________ really well, I ________ captain. And then if I ________ really hard, maybe one day I ________ for England! My dad ________ so proud of me!

I have two kids. I love them, but I never have any time to myself. If I ________ a free weekend, I ________ in bed all day. I ________ magazines and watch TV. Then I ________ all night and my children ____________ me. Oh, heaven!

5 What is the reality about Sam and Annie? What would they do if they could?

Sam isn't tall. If he were taller, he'd ...

GRAMMAR SPOT

1 What verb forms do we use in second conditional sentences?
If I **had** a brother, I **would play** with him.

2 The second conditional describes an improbable/impossible situation. Which sentence is more probable?
If he trains hard, **he'll be** in the team.
If he trained hard, **he'd be** in the team.

3 Notice that *was* can change to *were* in the *if* clause.
If Sam **were** taller, he'd ...
If I **were** you, I'd stop smoking.

▶▶ **Grammar Reference 12.3 p146**

My wishes

6 Write down three wishes for you. Show a partner. Say what you would do.

I'd like to be rich. If I were rich, I'd ...

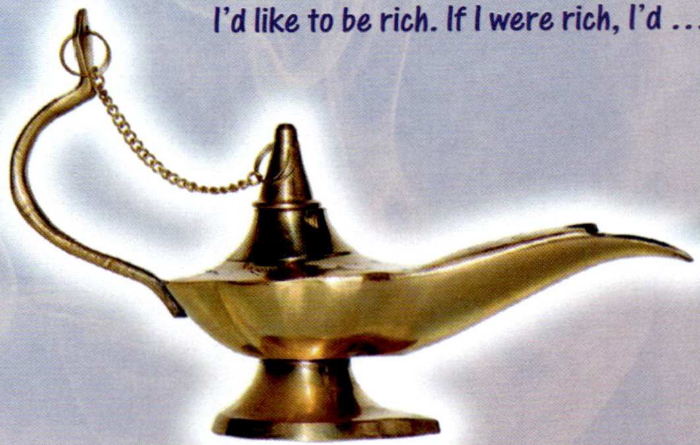

PRACTICE

Discussing grammar

1 Put the verbs in the correct first or second conditional form.

1 If I ________ (win) the lottery, I ________ (give) all the money to you.
2 If you ________ (go) out, ________ you ________ (get) me a newspaper?
3 If I ________ (find) a wallet in the street, I ________ (not keep) it.
4 If I ________ (find) your book, I ________ (give) it back to you.
5 'I'm going to bet £1,000 on a horse.'
'I ________ (not do) that if I ________ (be) you. You might lose the lot.'

2 Work with a partner. How many sentences can you make from the chart? Read them aloud.

If I ...	were had knew didn't know	the answer, the president, you, a millionaire, the time,	I'd I wouldn't	tell you. travel the world. work for world peace. tell the truth. accept the job. help you. ask the teacher.

He's not much good at anything!

3 **T 12.8** Tony's dad is fed up with his son. Listen to him talking about Tony's life. Take some notes.

Tony and his dad

Money
____
Clothes
____
Work
____
Lazy
____
Girlfriend
____

4 Make sentences about Tony using these ideas.

- If / job / have money
- If / money / buy / new clothes
- If / nice clothes / look smarter
- If / a bit more ambitious / apply for more jobs
- If / so lazy / up before midday
- If / shave / shower / look better
- If / look better / get girlfriend

T 12.9 Listen and check.

LISTENING AND SPEAKING

At a crossroads

1 If you are at a crossroads in life, what does it mean? Give an example from your life.

2 **T 12.10** Jimmy and Fiona are at a crossroads in their lives. Listen to them talking to a friend and answer the questions after each one.

1 What is the problem?
2 Who are the people involved?
3 What are the possible options?
4 What are the pros and cons of each option?
5 What might happen as a result?
6 What does the friend advise?

What do you think?

3 What would you do if you were Jimmy or Fiona? What would you advise?

> If I were Jimmy, I'd ...

4 **T 12.11** Listen to the same two people talking a year later. Did they make the right decision?

Discussion

5 Work in small groups. Look at the situations on p157. They all describe dilemmas that people find themselves in, and that require decisions!

Talk together. What would you do?

READING AND SPEAKING

Life, the Universe, and everything

1 Close your eyes. Do nothing for one minute. Did that seem a long time? What *is* a long time?

2 What do you know about the Universe? Do the quiz.

Time and the Universe

1. The Universe is **13.7 billion / 13.7 million** years old.
2. Our solar system was formed **5 billion / 1 billion** years ago.
3. The Earth was formed **4.5 billion / 500,000** years ago.
4. Homo sapiens appeared in East Africa **2 million / 200,000** years ago.

The answers are at the bottom of this page.

3 Read the introduction to *The Wonders of our Universe*. Answer the questions.

1 Why is it hard for us to understand the size of the Universe?
2 Why are the time scales involved difficult?

4 Read the rest of the article. Answer the questions after each part.

Part 1

1 What is it about these features of the Earth that make it suitable for life?

- distance from the sun
- rotation
- angle
- water
- atmosphere
- size

2 What would happen if these features were different?

Part 2

3 What are the main objects in our solar system? What holds them all together?
4 What are the planets made of?
5 How would you give an alien directions to our solar system?
6 How many stars are there in the Milky Way?
7 How many galaxies are there in the Universe?

Part 3

8 Look at the diagram *The Life Cycle of the Sun*. Explain it. Where are we now? How will the Universe end? When?
9 What are the wonders of it all?

What do you think?

How does it make you feel to think …

… the Universe is so old? … it is infinite? … one day it will end?

▶▶ **WRITING** T 12.12 T 12.13 **Listening and note-taking** *p117*

Answers:
1 13.7 billion **2** 5 billion
3 4.5 billion **4** 200,000

The Wonders

There are two things that are impossible for us to understand about the Universe.

Part 1 > The Earth

The Earth is the only place in the Universe where life is known to exist. It has all the conditions that are suitable for supporting life.

- It is a **perfect distance** from the sun. If it was closer, there would be too much radiation. The Earth would be too hot, and all the oceans would evaporate. If it was further from the sun, it would be too cold, and the planet would be covered in ice.
- The Earth **rotates** on its axis, so the whole surface is warmed and cooled once a day every day. If it didn't rotate, one side would be permanently hot, and the other cold.
- It is at an **angle** (23.5°) to the sun, which gives us our seasons. At different times of year, the northern hemisphere gets more or less sunlight than the southern hemisphere. Without seasons, our weather would be too extreme.
- 70% of the Earth is covered in **water**. If there was no water, there would be no life.
- Our **atmosphere** blocks harmful solar radiation, but allows enough heat from the sun to warm us.
- The earth is the right **size**. If it was bigger, gravity would be much stronger, and we wouldn't be able to move. If it was smaller and gravity was weaker, it wouldn't hold our oceans.

# of our Universe

> One is its ... sIZE

It is probably **infinite**.
Which means it goes on for ever ...
and ever ... and ever ... and ever ... and ever ...

> Another is its ... TIME

If you think a year lasts a long time ...
If you think 20 is old ...
If you think 2,000 years ago is ancient history ...
think again. The Universe is
13.7 billion years old.

Part 2 > Our Solar System

The Earth is part of our solar system. At the centre of this is the sun, which is the solar system's star.

Our solar system consists of the sun and objects connected to it by gravity – eight planets and some moons. The four smaller planets, Mercury, Venus, Earth, and Mars, are made of rock and metal. The two largest, Jupiter and Saturn, are called the gas giants. They consist mainly of hydrogen and helium. The two furthest from the Sun, Uranus and Neptune, consist of ice.

> Our Galaxy

Our solar system is part of the galaxy known as the Milky Way. It is about half way out from the centre.

Our sun is just one of the stars in the Milky Way. One of between 100 and 400 billion stars.

Our solar system goes round the centre of the Milky Way once every 250 million earth years.

> The Universe

Our galaxy is just one of more than 170 billion galaxies in the observable Universe. The Universe is probably infinite. There is no end to it.

Part 3 > The End

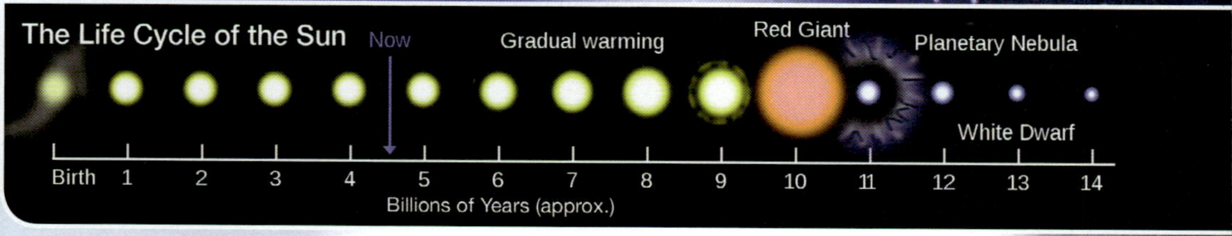

Our sun is getting hotter. In one billion years' time, the Earth will become too hot for water to exist, and all life will end. Our sun will continue to burn until it uses all its supply of hydrogen. In five billion years' time it will expand, then explode and become a red giant. After that it will collapse and become smaller than the Earth.

Some scientists believe that the Universe will continue to expand. All the stars, every single one, will burn out and it will go dark. The temperature will drop to zero. This will happen when the Universe is 100 trillion years old. After that, there will be nothing. Forever.

> The wonder of it all

There is a short period of time in the early years of the Universe when life is possible. This period, in the history of time, lasts just a second, a flash, a click of the fingers.

That miraculous time is **now**.
We are in the **most precious place**
at the **most precious time**.

And it's now!

VOCABULARY
Prepositions

Prepositions are little words, but they're everywhere!

*We are connected **to** the sun **by** gravity.*
*I'm going out **on** a date **with** Alice.*

1 It's easy to make mistakes with prepositions. Correct these sentences. Sometimes no preposition is necessary.

1 Are you interested of art? ✗
2 I phoned to Peter, but he didn't answer. ✗
3 I arrived at London last week. ✗
4 It depends of the weather. ✗
5 She's married with James. ✗
6 I'm looking at a pair of jeans size 34. ✗
7 Did you pay the meal? ✗
8 I'm reading a novel of Dickens. ✗
9 I worked like a waiter. ✗
10 If you have a problem, ask to the teacher. ✗

0/10

2 Complete each sentences with a preposition and a noun.

in	by	strike	purpose	touch
for	on	dinner	myself	business

1 It wasn't an accident. She broke it ______ ___________.
2 What's ______ ___________ ? I'm starving!
3 He isn't in the office this week. He's away ______ ___________.
4 When you go, keep ______ ___________ with me via email.
5 Transport workers are ______ ___________ for better pay.
6 I don't need other people. I like being ______ ___________.

T 12.14 Listen and check.

3 What prepositions go with these nouns?

- **some information** ________ **Prague**
- a recipe ________ paella
- **be in love** ________ **the girl next door**
- **a book** ________ **butterflies**
- **a problem** ________ **my central heating**
- a lot of damage ________ a building
- a meeting ________ your boss
- a cheque ________ £100
- **a cure** ________ **cancer**
- the difference ________ two cultures

4 Complete the sentences with an adjective in the box and a preposition.

good	used	afraid	angry	famous	worried	different

1 I'm ______ ______ spiders. I can't even look at them.
2 Dave is very ______ ______ cooking. He makes amazing cakes.
3 Why are you ______ ______ me? What have I done to annoy you?
4 I found the city noisy at first, but I'm ______ ______ it now.
5 New York is ______ ______ its skyscrapers.
6 They're late. Where are they? I'm ______ ______ them.
7 I'm very ______ ______ my sister. She's clever, I'm not.

5 What prepositions go with these verbs? Sometimes there is more than one.

listen look talk ask wait worry belong laugh think agree believe

Write sentences with the verbs and a preposition.

I like listening to the radio. *What are you thinking about?*

EVERYDAY ENGLISH

Thank you and goodbye!

1 Look at the pictures. Where are the people? Who are they? Complete the conversations with the words in the boxes.

1

pleasure	be going	glad	so much

A Well, it's late. I must ________ now. Thank you ________ for a lovely evening.
B My ________!
A And the food was delicious!
B I'm ________ you liked it. I hope you get home all right. Bye!
A Bye! And thanks again!

2

mention	kind	grateful	mind

A Thank you so much! It was so ________ of you.
B That's all right!
A I'm so ________ for all your help.
B Don't ________ it!
A Er ... Would you ________ helping me with just one more thing?
B Of course not! No problem!

3

love	boarding	yourself	flight

A I hope you have a good ________! Who's meeting you?
B My sister, Sarah.
A Remember to give her my ________.
B Will do. OK, it's ________. I have to go now. Bye!
A Right. Look after ________! Bye!

4

pleasure	kind	having	welcome

A Thanks for ________ me. I really enjoyed staying with you.
B You're ________. It was a ________. Come back and see us again sometime!
A That's very ________. Maybe next year!
C That would be lovely!

5

hello	I'll text	care	journey

A Have a safe ________!
B Thanks. ________ you when I arrive.
A Say ________ to your parents from me.
B I will. Oh! The train's leaving!
A OK! Bye! Take ________!
B See you soon! Bye!

6

everything	luck	fun	will

A Goodbye! And thanks for ________! It was great ________!
B I really enjoyed being your teacher.
C We learned such a lot with you!
B Thank you! Good ________ with your English. Keep practising!
A We ________!

2 **T 12.15** Listen and check.

3 Work with a partner. Learn two of the conversations. Act them to the class.

Writing and reference materials

Writing contents

1 Look at the symbols often used to correct mistakes in writing. Correct the underlined mistakes in the sentences. Compare your answers with a partner.

Sp	Spelling	1 I'm enjoing [Sp] the party.
WW	Wrong word	2 They went in [WW] Italy on holiday.
WO	Word order	3 I have two brothers younger [WO].
Gr	Grammar	4 She's got some new reds [Gr] shoes.
T	Tense	5 He arrive [T] yesterday.
P	Punctuation	6 They arent [P] coming.
ʎ	Word missing	7 She's [ʎ] doctor.

2 Work in two groups. In each of the sentences below there is one mistake.

Group A Find the mistakes in **A**. Use the symbols to mark them, but don't correct them.

Group B Find the mistakes in **B**. Use the symbols to mark them, but don't correct them.

A

1 I like Rome because is a beautiful city.
2 She studied for three years psychology.
3 There aren't any milk.
4 He's speaking French, German, and Spanish.
5 I watched TV, than I went to bed.
6 Did you by any bread at the supermarket?

B

1 I lost my all money.
2 What did you last night?
3 He always wear jeans.
4 My town is quite at the weekend.
5 I want that I pass the exam.
6 She's married with Peter.

3 Find a partner from the other group. Correct each other's sentences.

4 Correct this piece of student writing.

My best friend

My best friend was my best man when I get [T] married two year [Gr] ago. He's [Gr] name is Antonio and we met in [WW] university in Bologna. In fact we met on our very first day their [Sp]. Antonio was [ʎ] first person I spoke with [WW] and we discovered we were both studying Spanish and that we were both football fans. When we left university we went together travelling [WO] for six month [Gr]. We had a fantastic time touring north [P] and south america [P]. When we were in Mexico we met two [P] sisters of [WW] London, Emma and Kate. Now I'm married with [WW] Emma and next year Antonio and Kate [ʎ] going to get married. I like Antonio because he [ʎ] very funny and we has [Gr] really good times together. He live [Gr] in a different town now, but we text or call often each other [WO]. I'm very lucky that he's my friend.

5 Write about your own best friend.

6 Swap with a partner and see if you can find any mistakes. Read your work aloud to the class.

 ◀◀ p16

1 Read the postcard. Where are Gemma and Martin? Are they enjoying their holiday? Why? What is wrong with the style of the writing?

Dear Melanie,

Here we are in New York having a nice time. The weather is very nice. We're staying in quite a nice hotel in a nice part of town, Lower Manhattan. We've got a nice view of the Empire State Building from our bedroom window. We think all the skyscrapers are nice. Yesterday we went on a really nice helicopter tour of the city and then in the evening we saw a nice show on Broadway. Today we are going shopping in Bloomingdales. It's a nice store for buying clothes. This evening we're going to eat at Michael Jordan's 'The Steak House' in Grand Central Station. The restaurants here are nice and the food is really nice, but the portions are so huge that we often can't finish the meal.

See you soon,

Love,

Gemma and Martin

CITY OF NEW YORK

Melanie Baker
10 Wallasey Road
Brentwood,
Essex
CM15 7LE
ENGLAND

2 Gemma and Martin use *nice* eleven times. Complete the sentences below with other adjectives from the box. Sometimes more than one adjective is possible, but not always!

great	warm and sunny	interesting	excellent
delicious	luxurious	spectacular	amazing
exciting	brilliant	wonderful	

1 We're having a/an ______________ time here in New York.
2 The weather is ______________.
3 We're staying in a/an ______________ hotel in a/an ______________ part of town.
4 We have ______________ views of the Empire State Building.
5 We think the skyscrapers are ______________.
6 We went on a/an ______________ helicopter ride.
7 In the evening we saw a/an ______________ show.
8 Bloomingdales is a/an ______________ store for buying clothes.
9 The restaurants here are ______________.
10 The food here is really ______________.

3 Work with a partner. Read the postcard aloud using a variety of adjectives. Use *nice* once only. Discuss where you think is the best place to use it.

4 Think of a holiday you once had. Imagine you are still there. Write a postcard to an English friend about it, but use the adjective *nice* once only! You can write about some of these things:

- the journey
- the weather
- the accommodation
- the food
- some things you did yesterday
- some things you are going to do today

Compare postcards with your partner then read them to the class.

1 Work with a partner. Look at the picture story. What is it about?

The burglar who fell asleep

2 Read the sentences. They tell the story. Put the words in *italics* in a suitable position in the sentence. Change the punctuation if necessary.

1 A burglar broke into a house in Paris.
Last Sunday evening | *large, expensive* | *in the centre of*

Last Sunday evening, a burglar broke into a large, expensive house in the centre of Paris.

2 He went into the living room and he filled his sack with all the silverware and a Chinese vase.
First | *quickly and quietly* | *priceless*

3 He went to the kitchen and found some cheese and two bottles of champagne.
Next | *delicious* | *the best*

4 He was feeling hungry and thirsty. He ate the cheese and drank the champagne.
extremely | *so* | *all*

5 He felt very tired. He went to the bedroom and lay down on a big bed, and fell asleep.
Suddenly | *upstairs* | *comfortable* | *immediately* | *fast*

6 He slept very well. When he woke up, three policemen were standing round his bed.
Unfortunately | *the next morning*

T 3.13 Listen and check.

3 The pictures below illustrate a news story. What is it about? Match notes 1–6 with the pictures.

1 The phone was smelly and dirty. It still worked. Glen called some numbers.

2 Andrew Cheatle, a businessman from Worthing in Sussex, was walking on the beach. He lost his mobile. **(a)**

3 He was preparing the fish for sale. He noticed something metal inside a cod fish. It was a mobile phone.

4 One week later, fisherman, Glen Kerley, was on his boat catching fish to sell in the market.

5 Glen returned the phone to Andrew. He still uses it.

6 Andrew was with his girlfriend, Rita Smith. Her mobile phone rang. She said, 'It's for you! It's a call from your phone.'

A fishy tale

4 Write the news story. Use suitable words to join the ideas and to make the story more interesting. Compare your stories in groups and with the sample answer on p157.

1 You receive an email from an old friend. It is many years since you heard from them. You want to reply and tell them about you and your life. Make some notes.

but, *although*, and *however*

2 Read these sentences. They all mean the same, but how are they different?

- I don't write many letters, **but** I send a lot of emails.
- **Although** I don't write many letters, I send a lot of emails.
- I don't write many letters. **However**, I send a lot of emails.

3 Join these pairs of sentences in different ways.

1 I love ice cream. I don't eat it often.
2 He's a good friend. We don't have a lot in common.
3 She isn't English. She speaks English very well.
4 It rained a lot. We enjoyed the holiday.

so and *because*

4 Read these sentences.

1 He lived in France for many years, **so** he speaks French well.
2 He speaks French well **because** he lived in France for many years.

Which pattern goes with which sentence?

a Result ⟶ Cause
b Cause ⟶ Result

5 Join the pairs of sentences in two different ways using *so* and *because*.

1 I don't eat broccoli. I don't like it.
2 She went home. She was tired.
3 We didn't enjoy our holiday. The weather was bad.
4 He worked hard. He passed all his exams.
5 I enjoy history lessons. I like the teacher.
6 It started to rain. We stopped playing tennis.

6 Read the email. Who is writing to who? Why? What news does she give? Complete the email with these linking words.

but although however so because

Date: Wed, 27 Apr. 20:07:36 +0100 (BST)
From: "Lindy Cameron" <lindy.cam5@donwana.com>
Subject: RE: Do you remember me?
To: "Teresa Tate" <Teresa@Tate174.fsnet.co.uk>

Dear Teresa,

How wonderful to hear from you. Of course I remember you (1) _________ it's nearly seven years since we were neighbours. How did you get my email address? You told me a little about you and your family, (2) _________ now I'd like to know more. You ask how we all are, (3) _________ here's some of our news.

First things first – George and I are now divorced! I know you never liked him much, (4) _________ you are probably not too surprised. (5) _________, we still see each other a lot (6) _________ of the twins. They're nine now and they're good girls, (7) _________, of course, sometimes a bit of a handful. We moved from Birmingham (8) _________ I didn't want them to grow up in a big city. We now live in a beautiful, old farmhouse in Wales. I love country life. We have lots of land, (9) _________ we grow all our own vegetables and keep a few chickens. (10) _________, it's all very expensive to look after and (11) _________ I sell some of our produce to the local shops, we never have enough money for holidays and treats, (12) _________ we're happy and healthy.

I can't wait to hear more of your news. Write very soon.

Please come to stay. I'd love to see you again.

Love
Lindy X

7 Write an email to your old friend. Use your notes from exercise 1 and the phrases below. Compare your email with your partner's.

Dear X
How wonderful/amazing to hear from you.
I was so surprised./What a wonderful surprise.
How did you get my email address?
It was great to get your news.
Let me tell you something about my life.
Please let's keep in touch.
Love/Best wishes/All the best

◀◀ p39

1 Think about your future. How do you see your life …?

- next year
- in ten years' time
- in five years' time
- when you're 40 or 50

Write some notes about your hopes and ambitions at each of these times. Tell the class.

2 **T 5.5** Read and listen to Susannah talking about her future. What are her definite plans? What is she not sure about? What are her hopes, ambitions, and dreams?

3 Read Susannah's talk again carefully. Underline any words or expressions that would be useful when you write a talk about your future. Compare with your partner. Have you chosen the same ones?

4 Rewrite the first paragraph about you. Read it aloud.

5 Write a talk about your future plans and dreams. Mark pauses and words you want to stress. Practise reading it aloud. Give your talk to the class. Answer any questions.

My dreams for the future

Hello everyone. My name's Susannah – Susie for short. I'm 20 years old. At the moment I'm in my second year at art school and I often dream about my future. I have big plans and I'd like to tell you a bit about them.

My most immediate plans are holiday plans. I'm going to visit my brother who's working in Australia. My mother and I are going to spend Christmas with him in the summer sun. I'm very excited about that.

When I return I need to make a final decision about which course to study next year. I'm still not sure – I'm thinking of doing either fashion design or landscape design. It's difficult because I'm interested in both clothes and gardens. If I choose landscape I'd like to work with my friend, Jasper. He's brilliant with gardens and we've already worked on two together. It was great fun and we get on very well.

In five or ten years' time I would like to have my own business and work for myself like my father. He has his own building business. Perhaps I'll do a business course after I finish art school.

Of course, one day I hope to marry and have children. Ideally before I'm 30, but I can't plan when I'll meet the right person and I haven't got a boyfriend at the moment.

In my dreams I see myself at 40 running a successful gardening company with about 20 employees. I'll design beautiful gardens for beautiful people. I'll have a beautiful house, two beautiful children, and of course a husband who's as successful as I am. Who knows, it could even be Jasper!

1 Complete this sentence in any way you can.

The town where I was born is / has ...

Share the information with the class.

GRAMMAR SPOT

1 We use *who*, *that*, *which*, and *where* to join sentences. Look at these sentences.

I met a man. He is from my town.
I met a man ***who*** is from my town.

I bought a house. It's in Market Street.
I bought a house ***which/that*** is in Market Street.

The hotel was very comfortable. We stayed in it.
The hotel ***where*** we stayed was very comfortable.

2 *Who*, *which*, *that*, and *where* are relative pronouns. Complete the rules with a relative pronoun.

- ________ is for people.
- ________ or ________ is for things.
- ________ is for places.

2 Join the sentences with the correct relative pronoun.

1 There's the boy. He broke the window.
2 That's the palace. The Queen lives there.
3 There are the policemen. They caught the thief.
4 I bought a watch. It stopped after two days.
5 Here are the letters. They arrived this morning.
6 That's the hospital. I was born in it.

3 Look at the pictures of Pittsburgh. What do you learn about the town from them? Read the text and complete it with *who*, *which/that*, or *where*. Answer the questions.

1 Where is the town?
2 How many bridges are there?
3 Who is the city named after?
4 What was it like 50 years ago?
5 What is it like now?
6 Which artists come from Pittsburgh?
7 What are the people like?

4 Write a similar description of your hometown in about 200 words. First write some notes about it.

- Where is it? • What's its history? • What's it like now?

Next write some personal opinions.

- Do you like it? • Why?/Why not?

5 Read some descriptions aloud and compare your towns.

PITTSBURGH
THE TOWN WHERE I WAS BORN

I was born in Pittsburgh, the second largest city in Pennsylvania, USA, with a population of about 2.4 million. Pittsburgh lies on the banks of three rivers (1) ___that___ are crossed by over 400 bridges. The city is named after William Pitt, (2) ________ was the Prime Minister of Britain in the 1700s. It is sometimes called 'The City of Bridges'.

Fifty years ago, Pittsburgh was a thriving, industrial town. It had dozens of factories (3) ________ produced iron and steel. However, in the 1970s and 80s the steel mills closed and the city suffered badly. Streets, (4) ________ once people hurried to work, became deserted and dangerous. However, today, a lot of these streets are thriving again with theatres, shops, and restaurants.

Pittsburgh is surrounded by hills from (5) ________ you can enjoy great views of the city, views (6) ________ have inspired many artists, such as Linda Barnicott, who painted *My Home Town*. The museums display the work of many local artists, including Andy Warhol, (7) ________ was born and raised in Pittsburgh.

The city is now named one of the 'World's Most Liveable Cities'. I moved away ten years ago, but I often return. I miss the tough, friendly people, (8) ________ have lived through good times and bad. They make me proud to call Pittsburgh my hometown.

Linda Barnicott's *My Home Town*

◀◀ p60

1 Write down the names of any famous families you know. Share your ideas with the class. Why are they famous?

2 What do you know about John F. Kennedy? Discuss with a partner.

3 Read the seven paragraphs about John F. Kennedy. Work together to put the paragraphs in the correct order. Which words helped you decide the order?

THE LIFE OF A KENNEDY

1 John F. Kennedy 1917–1963

a ☐ This was a huge tragedy for Joseph Sr. who had wanted his first son to become president. He now turned his attention to his second son, John. John wanted to please his father, and in 1952 he was elected to the US Senate.

b 1 US President John Fitzgerald Kennedy ('JFK') was born on May 29, 1917. He was the second of nine children in a wealthy and powerful American family. His father, Joseph, was the US ambassador to Britain, and his grandfather was the mayor of Boston. Despite all the money and fame, John's life was not easy.

c ☐ The following year, John joined the Navy and fought in World War II. He almost died when his boat sank in 1943. Then, in 1944, his older brother, Joseph Jr., was tragically killed in a military plane crash.

d ☐ As a child he was often sick and had to miss months of school. However, he was a clever and popular student. His high school classmates voted him 'Most likely to become President'! He graduated from Harvard University in 1940.

e ☐ However, even as President, tragedy continued to follow JFK. In August, 1963, his son, Patrick, died two days after birth. And on November 22, 1963, John F. Kennedy was assassinated in Dallas, Texas. The nation was shocked, and even today millions of Americans remember what they were doing on that day.

f ☐ Around the time of John Jr.'s birth, JFK became President. He was a popular, young leader during an important time in American history. Events during his presidency included the Cuban Missile Crisis, the building of the Berlin Wall, and the beginning of the Space Race.

g ☐ A year later, in 1953 he married Jacqueline Bouvier. In another tragedy, their first child died at birth in 1956. However, the couple had a daughter, Caroline, in 1957. In 1960, they had a son, John Jr.

4 Read the notes about the life of John F. Kennedy's daughter, Caroline. Use the information to write her biography.

2 Caroline Kennedy/Sclossberg 1957–

- Born: November 27, 1957 … only surviving child of President John F. Kennedy.
- Brother John FK Jr. born 1960.
- Aged just 5 in 1963 her father assassinated in …
- After father's death, moved from Washington to New York City with mother. Grew up there.
- 1968, uncle, Robert F. Kennedy, also assassinated.
- Later in 1968, mother remarried – Greek billionaire Aristotle Onassis.
- Another uncle, Ted Kennedy, almost died in a car crash in 1969.
- 1979 graduated, Harvard University.
- 1980 started work in the film and TV department of The Metropolitan Museum of Art. Met her husband there.
- Married Edwin Schlossberg in 1986.
- Three children. Still lives in New York City.
- Her mother died in 1994, age 64.
- Has had many tragedies in her life. May 19th, 1999, brother John Jr. and his wife, Carolyn, died in a flying accident.
- 2008 worked with Barack Obama in the US presidential election campaign.

5 Research information about a famous person (living or dead) that interests you. Make notes and write a biography.

1 Work with a partner. Discuss which beginnings can go with which endings. More than one is sometimes possible.

Which are formal? Which are informal?

1 Dear Peter,	a Lots and lots of love Harry xxx
2 Dear Mr Smith,	b Love Gianna
3 Hello Cathy,	c Yours George
4 Dear Sir or Madam,	d Bye for now, Sammy
5 Dear mum,	e Yours faithfully, Daniel Miles
6 Hi Steve,	f Yours sincerely, Kay Macey
	g Best wishes, Dave

2 Look at the online advertisement for a school. Where is the school? What can you study there? Who do you contact?

The School | About York | Courses | Fees | Accommodation

YORK HOUSE School of English

Welcome to our school

We are one of the UK's most successful language schools. We welcome students from over 100 countries around the world to one of Britain's most beautiful cities. We offer quality English courses including General English, English for Business, and Examination preparation.

Our contact details

Deborah Knight (Principal)
York House School of English
55–57 Harrogate Road
York, YO1 5NU
United Kingdom

Phone: +44 (0) 1904 973694
Fax: +44 (0) 1904 973253

info@houseofyork.co.uk

We look forward to hearing from you.

A formal letter

3 Read the formal letter. Complete it with words or phrases from the box.

frequently	advertisement	However
interested in	sincerely	to hearing
some information	application form	to improve

Via Morgagni 90,
1-00161 Rome, Italy
Tel: +39 06 44 11 97 08

29th March

Deborah Knight, Principal
York House School of English
55–57 Harrogate Rd
York, YO1 5NU

Dear Ms Knight,

I saw your [1]__________ for English classes on your website and I am [2]__________ coming to your school this summer.

I studied English for six years at school and I have to use English [3]__________ in my job. [4]__________, I now feel that it is necessary to study further. I would especially like [5]__________ my pronunciation. Please could you send me more information about your courses, and an [6]__________? I would also like [7]__________ about accommodation.

I look forward [8]__________ from you as soon as possible.

Yours [9]__________,

Gianna Lombardo

Gianna Lombardo

4 Look at the different parts of the letter. Compare with formal letters in your country.

Are the names, addresses, and the date in the same place? Do you have many different greetings and endings for formal and informal letters and emails?

◀◀ p65

Your address

The date

Name and address of who you are writing to

Greeting

Introduction

Main parts

Conclusion

Ending

Signature

An informal email

5 Match these lines from an informal email and a formal letter.

A	B
It was great to hear from you.	Please find enclosed a photocopy of …
Thanks for …	I apologize for …
I want to ask about …	Thank you for your letter of 1st November.
I'm sorry about …	If you require further assistance, …
I'm sorry to have to tell you that …	I regret to inform you that …
I'm sending you a copy of …	I would like to enquire about …
If you need any more help, …	Thank you for …

6 Read Gianna's email to her English friend, Steve. Compare it with her letter to the school.

1 How does she express the highlighted lines from the email more formally in the letter?

2 What other informal words and phrases are in the email?

View Contact Details

Date: Sat, 21 May 07:50:28 -0700 (PDT)
From: "Gianna Lombardo " <gianna.lomb@aol.com>
To: stevojon@ntlworld.co.uk
Subject: Coming to England

Hi Steve,

Just to let you know that I'm thinking of coming to England this summer. You know I have to use English a lot in my new job, so I want (need!) some extra lessons, especially for my pronunciation – as you are always telling me I should try to improve this! Anyway, I saw an interesting ad on the Internet for a school in York. Isn't that quite near you? I'd love to visit you while I'm there.

Can't wait to hear from you. See you soon I hope.

Love

Gianna

7 Write a similar formal letter about yourself to the school in York. Then write an informal email to an English friend and tell them about it.

◀◀ p77

1 What films are popular at the moment? Which have you seen? Complete these sentences. Then talk to a partner about it.

- The last film I saw was …
- It starred …
- It was about …
- I really enjoyed/didn't enjoy it because …

2 Read the paragraph below. What do the words in **bold** refer to?

> I saw a really good film last week. **It** was a horror movie. I went with two friends. **They** didn't enjoy **it** at all. They said the acting was terrible. **That** surprised me because I thought **it** was excellent. My parents rarely go to the cinema. **This** is because **they** wait until the film comes out on DVD and then they watch **it** at home.

3 Have you heard of *Frankenstein*? Discuss these questions as a class.

1 Is *Frankenstein* a book or a film? Or both?

2 What kind of story is it? Is it …?
- a detective story
- a horror story
- science fiction story
- a romance

3 Who or what is Frankenstein? Is he …?
- a doctor
- a scientist
- a monster
- a student

4 What happens in the story?

5 Does it have a happy ending?

4 Read the review of the novel, *Frankenstein*. Check your answers to exercise 3.

5 Read the review again. What do the words in **bold** refer to?

6 Look at these headings. Find the information in the review of Frankenstein.

- title and author
- characters
- type of book/film
- the plot

Make some notes under the same headings about a book or film that you have read or seen recently. Then write a short review. Read it aloud to the class and answer questions.

FRANKENSTEIN

The story of Frankenstein is famous all over the world. Written in 1818 by Mary Shelley, the wife of the English poet P B Shelley, **it** was immediately very popular. It's a horror story, and many people say it is the original science-fiction novel. However, **they** often think that Frankenstein is the name of the monster in the story, but in fact it is the name of the scientist who created **it**.

From the letters of an English explorer, Captain Robert Walton, we learn about Victor Frankenstein, a scientist from Geneva who has discovered the secret of life and decided to make a human being. So, at night he visits graveyards and collects bones and bodies. With **these** he creates a person who is more monster than man.

The monster is huge and ugly, but also intelligent. Of course when people see it they are terrified and as a result the poor monster has no friends and feels lonely and depressed. Finally, it asks Frankenstein to make **it** a wife. **This** he refuses to do. So the monster attacks and kills not only Frankenstein's bride, Elizabeth, but also his brother, and a friend. The scientist is heartbroken and now wants to kill the monster. He chases it across the world. However, he dies when they meet in the Arctic and the monster then kills **itself**.

There are over 40 movies which tell the story of Frankenstein, **the first** as long ago as 1910. It is a fascinating tale because of the complex character of the monster, **which** is both sad and frightening at the same time.

 ◀◀ p82

1 Do you use any **social networking sites** such as **Facebook**? Write down three things you like and three things you don't like about them. Compare your ideas with the class.

2 Read these notes. How many of your ideas are here? What do you think are the most important pros and cons?

Advantages of Facebook	Disadvantages of Facebook
You can: • keep in touch with friends • keep family up to date • find old friends • communicate with friends at any time you want • share photos • share favourite music and videos • join groups that interest you • advertise yourself and your work	• flooded with requests from unknown or unwanted 'friends' • friends and family find out too much about your private life • hearing about boring events in friends' lives • tagged in pictures that you don't want others to see • wasting time on Facebook – can become addicted

3 Now read the text. What is the purpose of each paragraph?

4 Put the linking words on the right into the correct place on each line. Sometimes you will need to change the punctuation.

5 What ideas can you add to the text?

6 Make notes about the advantages and disadvantages of one of these topics. Then write a text similar to the one below.

- the mobile phone
- Google
- television

The Pros and Cons of Social Networking Sites

Social networking sites, such as **Facebook**, have many advantages. They are an excellent way of keeping in touch with people in your life, friends and family. They are a great way of finding old friends. You can communicate with these people at any time you want and in many ways, you can share your photos, your favourite music and videos with them. You can join groups with similar interests to yourself, sports, hobbies, and your work.	clearly, First of all both, and, Also for example Another advantage is that such as,
Social networking sites have many disadvantages. You are often flooded with requests from unknown or unwanted 'friends'. Friends and family may find out too much about your private life and you may hear about boring events in their lives. You can be tagged in pictures that you don't want others to see. The biggest problem is that you can waste too much time on Facebook. Some people can become addicted to it.	However, also, Firstly, Secondly, what is more, also, Finally, perhaps even
Social networking sites are definitely here to stay. They are now one of the main means of communication worldwide. We can't imagine our lives without them.	Despite the disadvantages, The fact is that

1 When do you fill in forms? Give some examples.

2 Match the expressions and questions.

1 First name	a Are you married or single?
2 Surname	b What do you do in your free time?
3 Date of birth	c What are your home and mobile phone numbers?
4 Place of birth	d What's your first name?
5 Permanent address	e What do you do?
6 Marital status	f Where were you born?
7 Occupation	g When were you born?
8 Qualifications	h What's your family name?
9 Hobbies/Interests	i What degrees, diplomas, certificates, etc. do you have?
10 Tel. nos.	j Where do you live?

3 Follow these instructions. Write about you.

1 Write your name in capital letters.
2 Sex. Circle **F** or **M**.
3 Delete where not applicable. (**Mr/Mrs/Miss/Ms**)
4 Date of birth. (**dd/mm/yyyy**)
5 Phone no. including country code.
6 Write your postcode.
7 Signature.

4 Complete the form.

The Global School of English

PLEASE WRITE IN CAPITAL LETTERS

Mr/Mrs/Ms* Family name ______ First name ______

Sex ______ Date of birth ______ Nationality ______

First language ______ Level of English ______

Address in your country ______ Occupation ______

Email address ______

Emergency contact & relationship to student ______

Type of accommodation required: homestay/hostel/student residence/other* (If other please specify) ______

Dietary requirements (if any) ______

Any medical conditions we should be aware of ______

Where did you hear about the school? ______

Date of arrival ______ Date of departure ______

Reason for learning English: business/pleasure/exams/other* (If other please specify.) ______

How many hours do you want to study? ______

Signature ______

*Delete where not applicable.

1 **T 12.12** Listen to the first part of Professor Igor Petrov's talk about his vision of life in the future. Write down three things you remember. Tell the class.

2 Read the notes taken by two students during his talk. Work with a partner. Use the notes to help you remember more of the talk. Which kind of note-taking do you prefer?

3 **T 12.13** Listen to the second part of his talk. Complete Student 1's notes OR Student 2's notes.

4 **T 12.13** Compare your notes with a partner. Listen again and check.

Student 1

LIFE IN THE FUTURE

OPTIMISTIC

- life expectancy = 50 ➔ 80 USA – improved health care and technology
- last 20 years = DNA, microchips, Internet – in the future computers + Internet for all
- the environment – learning to control weather + natural disasters, no illness – new body parts: livers, etc.
- world population – if people educated and richer = decrease
- world government to manage global resources
- already world language = English + worldwide communication system = the Internet

PESSIMISTIC

____

____

____

____

____

____

Student 2

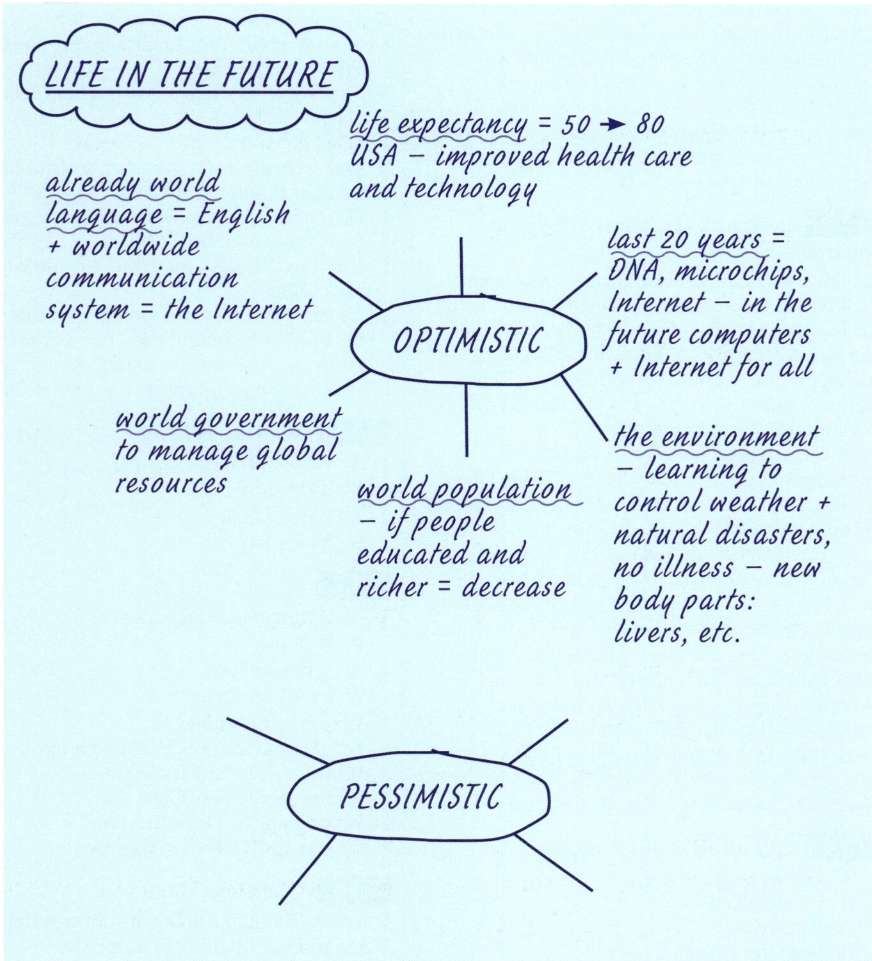

5 Use the notes to write a summary of Professor Petrov's talk.

Tapescripts

UNIT 1

T 1.1

A Where were you born?
B In Scotland.
A What do you do?
B I'm a teacher.
A Are you married?
B No, I'm not.
A Why are you learning English?
B Because I need it for my job.
A When did you start learning English?
B Two years ago.
A How often do you have English classes?
B Twice a week.

T 1.2 Anton Kristoff from Toronto, Canada

Hi! I'm Anton. I come from Canada, but at the moment I'm living here in New York. I'm working as a bike messenger. I really like New York, it's the center of the universe and it's very cosmopolitan. I have friends from all over the world. I earn about $100 a day in this job. That's good money. I'm saving money for my education.
I was born in Toronto, but my parents are from Bulgaria. They moved to Canada thirty years ago. When they first arrived they didn't speak any English. They worry about me. Last month I had a bad accident on my bike, but I'm fine now.
Next September I'm going back home to Toronto, and I'm going to study for a Master's degree and then I hope to get a good job.

T 1.3 Rowenna Lee from Melbourne, Australia

Hi, I'm Rowenna. I'm Australian, I come from Melbourne, but now I live in north London with my husband David. He's English. David and I run an art gallery. It's a gallery for Australian Aboriginal art. I just love Aboriginal art, I love all the colours and shapes. I'm preparing a new exhibition at the moment.
I came to England in 2006 as a student. My parents wanted me to study law, but I didn't like it, -er, I hated it in fact. I left the course after three months and got a job in an art gallery, that's where I met David. Then, we had the idea of opening our own gallery just for Aboriginal art, because most English people don't know anything about it. That was in 2006, and we borrowed £25,000 from the bank to do it. We're lucky because the gallery's really successful and we paid the money back after just five years. I go back to Australia every year. I usually go in the English winter because it's summer in Australia. But I'm not going next year because, you see, I'm going to have a baby in December. It's my first so I'm very excited.

T 1.4 Questions about Rowenna

1 **A** Where does she live?
B In north London.
A Who with?
B With her husband, David.
2 **A** What does she do?
B She runs an art gallery.
3 **A** What is she doing at the moment?
B She's preparing a new art exhibition
4 **A** When and why did she come to England?
B She came to England in 2006 to study law.
5 **A** How long did she study law?
B For three months.
6 **A** How much money did she borrow from the bank?
B £25,000.
7 **A** How many children does she have?
B She doesn't have any at the moment.
8 **A** Why is she excited?
B Because she's going to have a baby.

T 1.5 Questions to Serkan

I Hi, Serkan. Nice to meet you. Can I ask you one or two questions?
S Yes, of course.
I First of all, where do you come from?
S I'm from Istanbul in Turkey.
I And why are you here in England?
S Well, I'm here mainly because I want to improve my English.
I How much English did you know before you came?
S Not a lot. I studied English at school, but I didn't learn much. Now I'm studying in a language school here.
I Which school?
S The Shakespeare School of English.
I A good name! Your English is very good now. Who's your teacher?
S Thank you very much. My teacher's called David. He's great.
I What did you do back in Turkey?
S Well, actually, I was a teacher, a history teacher. I taught children from 14 to 18.
I How many children were in your classes?
S Sometimes as many as 40.
I Goodness! That's a lot. How often do you go back home?
S Usually I go every two months, but this month my brother is coming here. I'm very excited. I'm going to show him round.
I Well, I hope your brother has a great visit.

T 1.6 *Who's* or *Whose*?

1 **A** Whose phone is ringing?
B It's mine.
2 **A** Who's calling?
B It's my brother.

T 1.7

1 **A** Whose phone is ringing?
B It's mine.
2 **A** Who's calling?
B It's my brother.
3 Who's on the phone?
4 I'm going to the pub. Who's coming?
5 Whose coat is this? It's not mine.
6 Whose are all these CDs?
7 Who's going to Tina's wedding?
8 Do you know whose glasses they are?

T 1.8 Questions about you

1 What do you like doing in your free time?
2 Do you like listening to music?
3 What kind of music do you like?
4 What did you do last weekend?
5 What are you doing tonight?
6 What are you going to do after this lesson?
7 How many languages does your teacher speak?
8 What's your teacher wearing today?

T 1.9 Listen and compare

A What do you like doing in your free time?
B I like being with my friends. We go to each other's houses and chat.
A Do you like listening to music?
B Yes, of course. I have an iPod.
A What kind of music do you like?
B I like all kinds, rock, jazz, pop, but the thing I like best is listening to my dad's old *Beatles* albums.
A What did you do last weekend?
B It was my mum's birthday so we all cooked a special meal for her.
A What are you doing tonight?
B Nothing much. I want to get an early night before the weekend.
A What are you going to do after this lesson?
B I have a bit of shopping to do. Then I'm going home.
A How many languages does your teacher speak?
B Only English! She says she's going to learn Italian next year.
A What's your teacher wearing today?
B A very pink jumper and red trousers. Mmm – not a great look!

T 1.10 My oldest friend

1 Kenny talking to Judy

J Kenny, I see you have more than 300 friends on Facebook!
K Amazing, isn't it? I don't know how it happened. I think it's because my job takes me all over the world and I make friends wherever I go.
J I travel too, but I don't have that many friends.
K Come on Judy. I'm your friend, that's one friend at least!
J But what about close friends? How many of the 300 are close?
K I have no idea.
J No idea? More than ten? More than twenty?
K Er, probably no more than ten really close friends.
J So, who's your oldest friend?
K That's easy. Pete's my oldest friend – since we were both 16, and he came to my school. He lives in Canada now. But he was best man at my wedding and I was best man at his.
J How often do you see him?
K Not often. Maybe once or twice a year. I went over to Canada last year when his son was born. Do you know, he named him Ken after me?
J Hey, that's lovely! You and Pete are really good friends, aren't you?
K Yeah!
J Why do you think that is?
K It's our love of football!
J Don't tell me, he supports Liverpool too!
K Of course. Best team in the world. No, seriously the best thing about Pete is that maybe we don't see each other for months, even years, but when we get together immediately we're talking …
J … about football.
K No, about all kinds of things. Our families mainly. He's a great guy.

2 Damian talking to Toby

T Am I your best friend?
D No, silly, you're my brother!
T I'm not silly. Can't I be your best friend?
D No, you can't. No one's best friends with his brother!
T But I don't have many friends.
D That's *your* problem. Look, I'm going to meet Thomas and the gang now.
T Is Thomas your best friend?
D No.
T Is he your oldest friend?
D No. Zac's my oldest friend. You know that – since we sat next to each other in Class 1. Zac and me are going to travel the world together when we finish school.
T Can I come?
D NO,YOU CAN'T! Just shut …
T Well, can Thomas be my friend?
D Toby, be quiet about friends! You are so boring, I'm not surprised you have no friends.
T But can I …?
D No, no, no! I'm off. See you!
T But …

3 Katie talking to Beth

B Katie, you're lucky, you have so many friends!
K Mmm, I suppose so. I do have quite a lot.
B Why do think that is?
K Well, I'm not sure, I think I kind of collect friends. I have friends from all different times in my life. You know school, university, and now at work, and I keep my friends.
B So, who's your oldest friend?
K You are, of course! You and me, Beth, we're the same age, 24, and you could say we met before we were born.
B I suppose you're right …
K Yeah, our mums met when they were …
B I know they met at the hospital when they went for check-ups before we were born.
K Yeah, and we were born on the same day.
B I know, but I'm ten hours older than you!
K That's why you're wiser than me! You're my oldest and my best friend. You're like a sister to me.

T 1.11 A survey – How do couples meet?

A survey of over 10,000 couples asked them how they first met. The top three were: first, with 22%, 'at work'; second, with 20%, 'through friends', and third, with 15%, 'at school or university'. Next, with 12%, was 'meeting online'. Nowadays more and more couples are meeting this way. Just 8% met at a bar or club and 5% through the family, which was quite surprising. Only 4% met on a blind date – perhaps not so surprising. Last of all, just 1% met while shopping – so don't go looking for love in the supermarket. That leaves just 13% who didn't meet in any of these places.

T 1.12 What happened next?

Dominic

I sent Sally a text a couple of days after the date. She played it cool and didn't reply for two days. We met up a week later, went for a walk, and then to the cinema. We're still seeing each other. She's helping me train for the marathon which is next month. She's going to come and watch me. Also, she came to the theatre to watch my play and she said she liked it. I'm going to meet her parents next weekend. I'm a bit worried about that, but I enjoy being with her a lot.

Sally

When Dom texted, I knew I wanted to answer, but I made him wait. I'm not sure why, silly really because I really do like him. I enjoyed seeing him act. I think he's a very good actor, but I didn't really understand the play. He's coming to meet my family next weekend. I don't usually take my boyfriends home so soon, but with Dom it's different. I have a good feeling about this relationship. Will it last? Ask me again a year from now!

T 1.13 Words with two meanings

1 Turn **left** in the High Street and my house is first on the right.
She **left** hurriedly to catch her bus.
2 I love travelling by **train**.
He's going to **train** for the marathon.
3 I'm going to **run** a marathon next month.
They **run** the art gallery together.
4 I'm working at home for the **rest** of the week.
I need a **rest**! I'm so tired.
5 What **kind** of books do you like reading?
How **kind** of you to bring me some flowers!
6 Our **flat**'s on the fourth floor of a big apartment block.
Holland is a very **flat** country.
7 What do you **mean**? I don't understand you.
He never even buys me a coffee. He's very **mean**.

T 1.14 Listen and repeat

1 **A** Hi, Anna. How are you?
B I'm fine, thanks. How are you?
2 **A** Thank you so much.
B My pleasure.
3 **A** Can I help you?
B No, thank you. I'm just looking.
4 **A** Excuse me! Is that seat free?
B No, sorry. I'm afraid it isn't.

T 1.15 Social expressions

1 **A** Good morning!
B Good morning! Lovely day again!
2 **A** See you tomorrow!
B Yeah! About 9.00, in the coffee bar.
3 **A** How do you do?
B How do you do? Pleased to meet you.
4 **A** Thank you very much indeed.
B My pleasure. Don't mention it.
5 **A** I'm sorry. I can't come tonight.
B Never mind. Perhaps another time.
6 **A** Can you help me with this exercise?
B Of course. What's the problem?
7 **A** Bye!
B Bye! See you later!
8 **A** Bye! Have a good weekend!
B Thanks! Same to you.
9 **A** Sorry I'm late.
B It doesn't matter. You're here now.
10 **A** Cheers!
B Cheers! Here's to your new job!

T 1.16 Conversations

1 **A** Good morning!
B Good morning! Lovely day again.
A Yes, it's really warm for the time of year.
2 **A** See you tomorrow!
B Yeah! About 9.00, in the coffee bar.
A Fine. 9.00 is good for me, too.
3 **A** How do you do?
B How do you do? Pleased to meet you.
A Pleased to meet you, too.
4 **A** Thank you very much indeed.
B My pleasure. Don't mention it.
A It was so kind of you.
5 **A** I'm sorry. I can't come tonight.
B Never mind. Perhaps another time.
A I'm free tomorrow night. What about that?
6 **A** Can you help me with this exercise?
B Of course. What's the problem?
A I don't know what this word means.
7 **A** Bye!
B Bye! See you later!
A Yes. Let's meet after class.
8 **A** Bye! Have a good weekend!
B Thanks! Same to you.
A Thanks. Are you doing anything special?
9 **A** Sorry I'm late.
B It doesn't matter. You're here now.
A Yeah, I missed the bus.
10 **A** Cheers!
B Cheers! Here's to your new job!
A Thanks a lot. I'm excited, but a bit nervous.

UNIT 2

T 2.1 Mamy Rock, The Granny DJ

Ruth Flowers is not an ordinary grandmother. She's in her 70s, and has silver hair and bright-red lipstick. She's a DJ and works in clubs in Europe and tours festivals.
She lives alone in Bristol. She says, 'I've got a son and a grandson. They think what I'm doing is very cool!'
She likes rock bands such as Queen and the Rolling Stones, but she also plays electro and dance music. 'I love being with young people,' she says. 'They've got so much energy and enthusiasm!'
She's planning another European tour, and is currently making a new single. 'I'm having a lot of fun,' she says. 'I don't want it to stop.'

T 2.2 The SuperJam millionaire

Fraser Doherty is an extraordinary young man. He has his own company, SuperJam, which he started when he was just 16. 'I earn more money than my parents,' he says. His company makes jam – 500,000 jars every year – using a secret recipe from his grandmother.
All the major supermarkets sell his products. The business is growing fast – four flavours at the moment, but more on the way. And he has a charity that organizes huge tea parties for old people with live music and dancing.
'At the moment I'm very busy. I'm writing a cookbook. I've got an idea for a TV programme. And we're trying to get into the American market.'

T 2.3

Ruth Flowers

A What does Ruth do?
B She's a DJ.
A Where does she work?
B She works in clubs in Europe.
A How many children does she have?
B She has one son, and she also has a grandson.

A What sort of music does she like?
B She likes Queen and the Rolling Stones, and she also likes electro and dance music.
A Why does she like young people so much?
B Because they're so energetic and enthusiastic.
A What's she doing at the moment?
B She's planning another European tour, and she's making a new single.

Fraser Doherty

A What does Fraser do?
B He has his own company that makes jam.
A How much does he earn?
B He earns more than his parents.
A How many jars of jam does he make every year?
B He makes half a million jars a year.
A Whose recipe does he use?
B His grandmother's. It's a secret recipe.
A What's he writing?
B He's writing a cookbook.
A What's he trying to do?
B He's trying to get into the American market.

T 2.4 An interview with Ruth

I = Interviewer, R = Ruth

I Do you like being famous?
R Don't be silly. I'm not really famous. I'm just an old lady who's having fun.
I But it is unusual for someone your age, if you don't mind me saying, to be DJing in clubs for young people.
R Well, I just like the music. And I don't want to be an old woman in an old people's home watching television all day long and going to church once a week.
I Why do you do it?
R I DJ because the energy is fantastic! Because I love to see young people enjoying themselves. Because it makes me happy!
I Does your family agree with you?
R My family thinks it's great. Some of my friends say that it's not right for a woman my age to be wearing these clothes and staying out all night.
I And what do you say to them?
R I say it's none of their business. It doesn't matter how old you are. If you want to do something, you can.

T 2.5 An interview with Fraser

I = Interviewer, F = Fraser

I Do you like being a businessman?
F Oh, yes, I love it! I like the planning, the marketing, the selling. I like meeting people and talking about my business and everything about it!
I It seems to me you really love what you're doing!
F It's true! I do!
I Do you have any free time?
F Er … a bit, but not a lot.
I What do you do in your free time?
F I go out with my friends. I go to clubs. I love walking.
I Have you got a girlfriend?
F Well, er … that's none of your business!
I Sorry. Er … Who do you live with?
F I live with a group of friends in a flat in Edinburgh. It's not far from my parents' house.
I Do you see much of your parents?
F I see them all the time. We're very close.

T 2.6

A Do you have a car?
B Yes, I do.
C No, I don't.
A Have you got a bike?
B Yes, I have.
C No, I haven't.
D I don't have a camera.
E I haven't got an iPod.

T 2.7 Things I like doing

play games on my PlayStation
go out with my friends
download music and films
send emails and texts
shop for clothes online
have a lie-in
relax in front of the TV
meet friends for a drink
listen to music
go out for a meal
get a takeaway pizza
do nothing
read magazines
chat to friends online
go to the gym
watch a football match live on TV

T 2.8 Listen, check, and practise

1 I like shopping in the High Street, but mainly I shop online.
2 When I hear a band I like, I download their music from the Internet.
3 I listen to music on my iPod when I go jogging.
4 I spend hours chatting to friends online, even though I'm with them all day at school!
5 Sometimes I like to chill out at home and do nothing.
6 I'm always so tired after work I just want to relax in front of the TV.
7 On Saturdays, I have a lie-in, and don't get up till midday.
8 Do you want to cook tonight, or shall we get a takeaway pizza?
9 It's Pete's birthday tonight, so we're going out for a meal. Indian, I think.
10 I like keeping fit. I go to the gym three times a week.

T 2.9 Money

The best things in life are free
But you can give them to the birds and bees
I want money
That's what I want
That's what I want
You love gives me such a thrill
But your love don't pay my bills
I want money

T 2.10 Two neighbours

Mrs Crumble

I have the flat above that young man. I think his name is Alfie Smith, because I see the postman delivering his letters. He never says hello.
He hasn't got a job, well he doesn't go out to work at 8.00 in the morning, and that's for sure! He doesn't get up till the afternoon, and he wears jeans and a T-shirt all the time. He never looks smart. He certainly never wears a suit. Goodness knows where he gets his money from! It's funny! I never hear him in the evening. I've no idea what he does in the evening.
There are people coming and going in and out of his flat all day long. I have no idea how many people are staying. Four? Five? Have none of them got jobs?
He's got a girlfriend. She's very … pretty. Blond hair, dyed. She's living with him. I know a lot of young people live together these days, but I don't like it, living together and not married. It's not right.
He always makes such a noise! Listen! There he is now! Music! He's listening to music! Why can't he turn it down? It's so loud!
Young people these days have no manners, they live in their own world, and they just don't care about other people. They don't even notice old people like me. He probably doesn't know who I am.

T 2.11 Two neighbours

Alfie

I've got this new flat. It's so nice! I really love it. I'm having such a good time. The only thing is it's below an old lady, and that's a bit difficult. Her name's Mrs Crumble. I always say hello when I see her, 'How are you, Mrs Crumble?', 'Nice day, Mrs Crumble!' and all that, but she never replies. She just looks at me. I think she's deaf.
She probably thinks I'm unemployed because I don't go out to work in the morning and I don't wear a suit. I think I wear really cool clothes. Well, I'm a musician. I play the saxophone, and at the moment I'm playing in a jazz club. I don't start till 8.00 at night, and I don't finish till 2.00 in the morning, so I sleep from 3.00 till 11.00.
There's only me living here, but my flat's a bit busy at the moment because some of the other guys in the band are using it to keep their instruments in, so they're always coming in and out.
I've got a lovely girlfriend, she's the singer in the band. She's so beautiful! She lives the other side of town, but obviously I see her every day because we work together. She comes to my place sometimes.
I know I make a bit of noise, because I practise my saxophone. See what I mean? What can I do? I have to practise somewhere!
I know that old Mrs Crumble is always watching me. It's sad because she has nothing to do. I feel sorry for her, and I'm always really kind to her like I am to my own grandmother, but she's so suspicious of young people. She thinks we're all no good and take drugs. It's just not true! I work really hard!

T 2.12 Making conversation

1: John and Maria

J Hello. My name's John. What's your name?
M Maria.
J Hi, Maria. Where are you from?
M Italy.
J Ah, OK. Where in Italy are you from?
M Roma.
J Ah, Rome. I love Rome. It's beautiful. And what do you do in Rome?
M I'm a student.
J I see. And are you enjoying being in London?
M Yes.
J Well, I've got a class now, Maria. Bye! See you again!
M Bye.
J Not in my class, I hope.

2: Maggie and Jean-Jacques

M Hello. My name's Maggie. What's your name?
JJ My name is Jean-Jacques. Nice to meet you, Maggie.
M And you. Where are you from, Jean-Jacques?
JJ I'm French. I live in Paris – Paris, as you say in English – but I'm from the south, from Provence. Do you know the south of France?
M Yes, I do. It's beautiful!

JJ It's true! It is! And you, Maggie, where are you from?
M I'm from Scotland.
JJ Oh, really! I've never been there, but I'd like to. It's a beautiful country, isn't it?
M Very! Lots of mountains and lakes. What do you do in France, Jean-Jacques?
JJ I'm an architect. I design very expensive houses for very rich people.
M Wow! That's an interesting job! Are you enjoying being in London?
JJ Yes, I am. Very much. I'm having a really good time. I think London's a really interesting city, and there's so much to do! And you, Maggie? What do you do?
M Well, I'm a teacher. I work here.
JJ Oh, really! What class are you teaching?
M 3B.
JJ Oh, great! That's my class! You're my teacher!
M Oh, how lovely! Well, it's 9.00. Let's go to class!
JJ What a good idea! I'll follow you …

T 2.13 Making conversation

1 **A** What a lovely day it is today!
B Yes, beautiful, isn't it! Much nicer than yesterday.
2 **A** Are you having a good time in London?
B Yes, I am. It's a very interesting city. There's so much to do. I love the shops.
3 **A** Have a good weekend!
B Thanks. Same to you. Are you doing anything interesting?
4 **A** Did you have a nice weekend?
B Yes, I did. It was really good. I saw some old friends. What did you do?
5 **A** What are you doing tonight?
B Nothing special. Just at home. What about you?
6 **A** How's your mother these days?
B She's OK, thanks. She's feeling a lot better. Thank you for asking.
7 **A** Did you watch the football last night?
B No, I didn't. I missed it. Was it a good game?
8 **A** I like your shoes.
B Thank you! They're new. I got them last week in the sales. They're nice, aren't they?
9 **A** If you have a problem, just ask me.
B Thank you very much. That's very kind of you. I will.

T 2.14 Keeping a conversation going

A I was on holiday last month.
B Oh, really? Did you go away?
A Yes, I went to Italy.
B How wonderful! Italy's beautiful, isn't it?
A I think it's fabulous. I love all the history.
B Yes, and the buildings, and all the art! Where did you go?
A Well, first I went to Florence and I spent a few days going round the museums.
B Oh, fantastic! Did you see the statue of David?
A Oh, yes! Amazing! And then I went to see some friends who live in the countryside around Siena.
B Wow! Lucky you! Did you have good weather?
A Well, actually …

UNIT 3

T 3.1 Walking the Amazon

Amazing journey ends after 6,000 miles

Ed Stafford became the first man in history to walk the length of the Amazon River from the source to the sea. He walked for 860 days.
The journey began in April 2008 when Ed left the town of Camana on the Pacific coast of Peru. It ended in August 2010 when he arrived in Maruda, on the Atlantic coast of Brazil.
He went through three countries, Peru, Colombia, and Brazil. The journey took nearly two and a half years. 'I did it for the adventure,' says Ed.

T 3.2 Questions and answers

1 **A** How far did Ed walk?
B He walked six thousand miles.
2 **A** When did the journey begin?
B It began in April 2008.
3 **A** Where did the journey end?
B It ended in Maruda on the Atlantic coast of Brazil.
4 **A** Which countries did he go through?
B He went through Peru, Colombia, and Brazil.
5 **A** How long did the journey take?
B It took nearly two and a half years.
6 **A** Why did he do it?
B He did it for the adventure.

T 3.3

A What was Cho doing when he met Ed?
B He was working in the forest.
A Where were they walking when they saw the tribe?
B They were walking in a very dangerous part of the forest.
A Why did the tribe think Ed was crazy?
B Because he was walking the Amazon for an adventure.

T 3.4 Ed's blog

12 July

The day I nearly died

Today I was walking next to the river when I nearly stood on a snake. I stopped immediately. The snake's fangs were going in and out. I was terrified. I didn't move. One bite and you're dead in three hours.

10 September

Knives and guns!

Early this morning we were crossing the river by boat when we saw five canoes. The tribesmen were carrying knives and guns. They were angry because we didn't have permission to be on their land. We left as fast as we could.

24 November

The jungle at night

I was lying in my hammock last night trying to sleep, but it was impossible because the noise of the jungle was so loud. Monkeys were screaming in the trees, and millions of mosquitos were buzzing round my head. I took a sleeping pill and finally fell asleep at 3.00 a.m.

T 3.5 Pronunciation /d/ /t/ /ɪd/

/d/ stayed, played, phoned, answered
/t/ stopped, worked, laughed, looked
/ɪd/ decided, studied, wanted, mended

T 3.6 Pronunciation

We stayed in a hotel.
They played on the beach.
She phoned a friend.
I answered all the questions.
They stopped at lunch time.
I worked in a bank.
We laughed and laughed.
I looked at the photo.
We decided immediately.
I studied at university.
She wanted a cup of tea.
I mended it.

T 3.7

I was having dinner.
What was she wearing?
They were playing football.
Where were you going?
He wasn't listening.
They weren't enjoying the party.

T 3.8 The news

Here are the news headlines.
A car bomb in Moscow kills three people.
Thieves steal paintings worth $80 million from a New York museum.
A national strike in France brings the country to a stop.
The 71-year-old actor James Robertson dies at his home in California.
And in the European Cup, Arsenal beat Real Madrid.

T 3.9

A car bomb exploded in central Moscow yesterday morning, killing three people who were shopping in a market and injuring many more. Most of those injured were women who were out shopping for food in the early morning, and children who were on holiday. Terrorists say they planted the bomb.
Last night thieves in New York broke into the Museum of Modern Art, and escaped with three paintings by Picasso, valued at $80 million. Cameras were recording the rooms all the time, but the guard who was watching the screens saw nothing. Museum officials didn't discover the theft until the next morning.
A national strike in France yesterday brought the country to a complete stop. Offices, banks, schools, and shops all closed, and there were no trains or buses throughout the whole country. Workers were protesting for higher pay, longer holidays, and a shorter working week.
The actor James Robertson died last night at his home in Hollywood, California. He was suffering from cancer. With him were his five children, his ex-wife, and his second wife, Cherie. The 71-year-old actor is best known for his role as the cowboy Dexter in *Mad Men of the West*.
And finally sport. Arsenal last night beat Real Madrid 2–1. At half-time the Spanish side were winning one nil, but then two goals by Johansson gave the London team a win.

T 3.10 A dictation

Last night thieves in New York broke into the Museum of Modern Art and escaped with three paintings by Picasso, valued at $80 million. Cameras were recording the rooms all the time, but the guard who was watching the screens saw nothing. Museum officials didn't discover the theft until the next morning.

T 3.11 Adverbs

1 Please drive carefully through our village.
2 Romeo loved Juliet passionately.
3 My mother speaks three languages fluently.
4 It rained heavily every day last week.
5 He waited patiently for his girlfriend, but she didn't turn up.
6 The soldiers fought bravely, but many of them lost their lives.

T 3.12 Word order

1 My grandma is nearly 75, and she still goes swimming regularly.
2 'Do you really love me?'
'Of course I do. I'll always love you.'
3 I was just relaxing with a really good book when someone knocked loudly on the door.
4 My sister is only three, but she can already read, and she can write, too.
5 First, break the eggs into a bowl with some milk and butter. Then heat it gently. When it's ready, serve the scrambled eggs immediately with toast.
6 Almost all my friends have a mobile phone. They're on Facebook as well. Even my dad's on Facebook.

T 3.13 The burglar who fell asleep

Last Sunday evening, a burglar broke into a large, expensive house in the centre of Paris. First he went into the living room, and he quickly and quietly filled his sack with all the silverware and a priceless Chinese vase. Next he went to the kitchen and found some delicious cheese and two bottles of the best champagne. He was feeling extremely hungry and thirsty so he ate all the cheese and drank all the champagne. Suddenly he felt very tired. He went upstairs to the bedroom and lay down on a big, comfortable bed and immediately fell fast asleep. He slept very well. Unfortunately when he woke up the next morning, three policemen were standing round his bed.

T 3.14 Dates

A What's the date today?
B March the eighteenth. Tomorrow's the nineteenth. The day after tomorrow's the twentieth.
A When's your birthday?
B November the eighth.
A Oooh! That's next week.
A What's your date of birth?
B 12 – 9 – 87
A Sorry? What was that?
B The twelfth of the ninth, eighty-seven.
A What year were you born?
B 1982.
A Oh. You're the same age as me.

T 3.15

the third of February
February the third
the sixth of April
April the sixth
the twelfth of July
July the twelfth
the twenty-fifth of December
December the twenty-fifth
the first of May
May the first
the sixteenth of August
August the sixteenth
the thirteenth of January
January the thirteenth
the thirty-first of October
October the thirty-first

T 3.16

February third
April sixth
July twelfth
December twenty-fifth
May first
August sixteenth
January thirteenth
October thirty-first

T 3.17

1 A When did man first land on the moon?
B On July the twentieth, 1969.
2 A When's your wedding anniversary?
B November the eighth.
3 A When did the Berlin Wall come down?
B The ninth of November, 1989.
4 A When was your son born?
B July the twenty-first, 2010.
5 A What's the expiry date on your credit card?
B 06 18

UNIT 4

T 4.1 Questions about the diet

1 Q Today we're talking to a couple who are following The Calorie Restriction Diet. So my first question is… Do you eat any meat?
A No, we don't eat any meat at all, but we eat some fish.
2 Q How much fish do you eat?
A We eat a little white fish, but we love shellfish so we eat a lot of prawns.
3 Q Do you eat much fruit?
A Oh yes, we eat a lot of fresh fruit – apples and grapes – everything.
4 Q And do you eat many vegetables?
A Yes, of course, we eat lots of raw vegetables.
5 Q Don't you cook any vegetables at all?
A We cook some. Sometimes we steam a few carrots and a little broccoli.
6 Q And what do you drink?
A Well, we don't drink any tea or coffee, and naturally there's no alcohol in our diet, but we do drink a lot of orange juice.
7 Q How many calories do you have every day?
A About 1,500.
A That's about 1,000 fewer than most people.

T 4.2 Following the diet

Q Tell us some more about the diet.
A Well, I think we have a good diet. We enjoy the food we do eat. For breakfast we have cereal, homemade cereal, we make it ourselves. We have it with fruit. We eat all fruit.
A But we don't eat any dairy products – no milk, no cheese and we don't eat bread so we don't need butter …
A We use olive oil instead. We often have it on salad for lunch with tomatoes and lots of nuts and sometimes green peppers stuffed with rice.
Q So you eat rice. What about pasta and potatoes?
A No, not at all. We don't eat anything made from potatoes.
Q No crisps or chips then. And I'm guessing you eat nothing made with sugar.
A You're right. We make fresh juice to drink, but with no sugar.
Q And nothing alcoholic of course. What about water?
A Well, we don't drink any tap water.
Q Really? Why not?
A It's not good for you. We drink a little mineral water sometimes.
Q You're amazing. Well, I hope you live to be 120, but I'm sure I won't be around to see it.

T 4.3 ***something/someone/somewhere …***

1 A Did you meet anyone nice at the party?
B Yes. I met somebody who knows you!
A Oh, who was that?
B Your ex-boyfriend.
2 A Ouch! There's something in my eye!
B Let me look. No, I can't see anything.
A But I can feel it. Somewhere in the corner of my eye.
3 A Let's go somewhere hot for our holidays.
B But we can't go anywhere that's too expensive.
A I know, but we can afford this package holiday to Turkey.
4 A Where are my glasses? I can't find them anywhere.
B What are they on the top of your head?
A My glasses! Thank you.
5 A It was a great party. Everybody loved it.
B They did. Nobody wanted to go home.
A I know. A few people were still dancing at 3.00 a.m.
6 A Did you get anything nice in the sales?
B No, nothing. I couldn't find anything I liked.
A Why not try shopping online? You can buy everything online these days.

T 4.4 What's the missing word?

Do you know … famous?
The fridge is empty. There's … to eat!
The lights are off. There's … at home.
Pete's a great bloke. … likes him.
We always go … nice to eat.
I can't go to the party. I haven't got … nice to wear!
Has … seen my keys?
I can't find my keys …

T 4.5 My grandfather's shop

My grandfather lived until he was 101 years old. He was a shopkeeper. He had a fish and chip shop in an old village near a big, industrial town in the north of England. He had a son and a daughter. The daughter is my mother. The family lived above the shop.
In those days, fish and chips was the most popular dish in the whole country. My grandfather made the best fish and chips in the area. People came to the village by bus especially to get them. Everybody loved my grandfather because he was such a happy and contented man. He worked hard, but once a week he closed the shop and went to have lunch (not fish and chips!) with friends in the local pub. He didn't retire until he was 78 years old. He said that the secret to a long life was a glass of whisky before going to bed and lots of fish and chips.

T 4.6 **Articles**

My grandfather was a shopkeeper
He lived in the north of England.
He had a fish and chip shop in an old village.
His family lived above the shop.
He made the best fish and chips in the area.
Some people came by bus to the shop.
He closed the shop once a week.
He went to have lunch with friends.
He liked to have a little whisky before bed.

T 4.7 **Unusual restaurants**

1 Alexander

We were on honeymoon and we saw some brochures about this restaurant. It was my wife's birthday so I thought why not – it's expensive, but you don't find many restaurants like this. It was difficult to get a reservation because it only takes twelve people. When we arrived we had drinks on the deck above and someone gave us a talk about how they built the restaurant and then we took off our shoes and descended, – down, down the spiral stairs and into the restaurant. Actually, the restaurant itself isn't very exciting, the decor I mean, but it doesn't need to be because what is totally amazing is the view – it takes your breath away. All around and above your head are hundreds, maybe thousands, of fish, all colours in a blue, blue sea. I was sitting opposite my wife when a turtle appeared just behind her head. In fact we were so busy looking at it all we almost forgot that we were there to eat. The food was delicious, fish of course, but to be honest we felt a bit bad eating white fish, surrounded by white fish. There was just one problem, a guest at the next table. He spoke really loudly and complained about everything. We couldn't find anything to complain about. It was the perfect honeymoon restaurant.

2 Hans

I booked online of course. It's the only way you can book. And I went with my sons – they are five and eight years old – and I thought they would like it a lot. They were very excited. They had the idea that the waiters were robots, so when we arrived and there was nobody there at all they were a bit disappointed. But the whole place was amazing. It was like walking inside a computer, so the boys soon became excited again. We picked up a card and sat down at one of the big round, red tables. The boys loved the touch-screen TVs. They got the idea immediately and started choosing food from the pictures. While we were waiting they were texting their mother to tell her how fantastic it all was. In just a few minutes pots with our meals inside came flying down the spiral tubing in the middle of the table. The boys couldn't believe it, they were shouting with excitement. We all had steak and salad and then the boys had baked bananas with ice cream and chocolate. It was delicious. There was an older lady sitting next to us. She was a bit confused so we helped her. She said, 'I think this is more for young people than people my age'. Maybe she's right.

3 Lucy

I was hungry when I arrived at the restaurant, but when I saw the crane I forgot about being hungry. I was so frightened. The host, David, said 'Don't worry, it's 100% safe'. Huh! I'm sure a few of the other guests felt like me – they looked very pale. Anyway, we sat down at this huge table, fastened our seat belts and up, up, up we went. I couldn't look down. Everyone was saying, 'What a wonderful view', but I just couldn't look. Then one of the waiters put a glass of wine in my hand and I opened my eyes and the view was amazing. People were waving to us from the ground. They probably thought we were mad. The weather was perfect, thank goodness, just a little breeze. I began to enjoy it. The other guests were all great fun. I didn't know anyone at the start, but I soon made some friends and the food was good too, especially the prawns. The chef cooked them in front of us on a tiny cooker. But best of all, was at the end, when everybody learnt my name they started singing 'Lucy in the sky with diamonds'. No diamonds, but I was certainly in the sky. I was quite sorry when we came down to earth again.

T 4.8

a piece of paper
a loaf of bread
a bottle of beer
a can of Coke
a kilo of apples
a litre of petrol
a packet of chewing gum
a pair of jeans
a slice of cake
a bunch of bananas

T 4.9 **Going shopping**

1 **A** Just this copy of *The Times*, please.
B That's £1 exactly.
A Sorry, I only have a £20 note.
B No problem. I've got change.
A Thanks. Oh, and can I have a packet of chewing gum as well?
B OK. That's £1.79 now, please.

2 **A** Excuse me, how much is this pair of socks?
B They're £4.60 a pair.
A OK. Can I have two pairs, please? Have you got any in blue?
B I'm afraid they only come in grey and black.
A Never mind. A black and a grey pair, please.
B That's £9.20 altogether. How would you like to pay?

3 **A** Good morning. Can we have two double espressos, and a latte, please?
B What size latte?
A Just medium, please. Oh, and three slices of chocolate cake. It looks delicious.
B I'm afraid there are only two slices left, but the carrot cake's good too.
A OK. And one slice of carrot cake, then.
B Certainly. That's £11.80.

4 **A** Can you help me? I need something for a very bad cold.
B Yes, of course. Are you allergic to aspirin?
A No, I'm not.
B OK. Take these three times a day.
A Thank you.
B Do you want a bottle or a pack?
A I don't mind. A bottle's fine. And can I have two packets of tissues as well, please?
B Sure. Anything else?
A No, that's all. How much is that?
B That's £5.40 altogether.

5 **A** Five cans of beer and four packets of crisps, please.
B How old are you?
A Er … I'm eighteen.
B Well, you don't look eighteen.
C He is eighteen.
B And you look about twelve! Have you got any ID?
A Not with me, I haven't.
B Then I can't sell you the beer.
A Oh, OK, just the packets of crisps then and two cans of Coke.

6 **A** Good morning. What can I get for you?
B Er- three, no, make that four slices of ham, please. Organic ham.
A OK. That's -er four slices. Anything else?
B Yes, can I have that large piece of cheese?
A The Cheddar?
B That's right. How much is that?
A £8.35. But you don't pay here. You pay at the checkout with your other goods.
B Oh, OK. And can you tell me where the fruit and veg are?
A They're on the first aisle, over there.
B Oh, thanks very much. I'm lost in this place. It's my first time and it's huge.

T 4.10 **Friends for dinner**

1 **A** Would you like some more rice?
B No, thanks. But could I have another piece of bread?
A Of course. Do you want white or brown?

2 **A** Could you pass the salt, please?
B Yes, of course. Do you want the pepper too?
A No, thanks. Just the salt.

3 **A** Can I have some water, please?
B Do you want still or sparkling?
A Just a glass of tap water is fine, thank you.

4 **A** Please, just help yourselves to the dessert.
B We will. It looks fantastic. Did you make it yourself?
A I did. It's my grandmother's recipe.

5 **A** Would anybody like some more ice cream?
B No, but I'd love some more fruit. Is there any left?
A There is a bit. It's all yours.

6 **A** How would you like your coffee?
B Black, no sugar. Have you got any decaf?
A No, sorry. I'm afraid not, but we've got decaf tea. Would that be OK?

7 **A** This is delicious! Would you mind giving me the recipe?
B No, not at all. I got it online. I'll give you the website.
A Thanks. I get lots of my recipes online too.

8 **A** Do you want some help with the washing-up?
B No, of course not. You're our guests!
A Well, I hope you have a dishwasher. There's a lot.

T 4.11 **Polite requests with *can* and *could***

1 **A** Can I have some apple juice, please?
B Sorry, we haven't got any apple juice. Will orange juice do?

2 **A** Could you tell me where Market Street is, please?
B Sorry, I'm afraid I'm a stranger here myself.

3 **A** Can I see the menu, please?
B Here you are. Today's specials are on the board over there.

4 **A** Could I use your iPad for a few minutes, please?
B Eva's using it at the moment. But you can have it after her.

5 **A** Could you lend me £20, please?
B Mmm … I can lend you ten, but not twenty.

6 **A** Can you take me to school, please?
B Goodness, is that the time? We're going to be late!

7 **A** Can you help me with my homework, please?
B OK, but I'm not very good at maths.

8 **A** Could you give me a lift to the station, please?
B Of course. What time's your train?

T 4.12 **Polite requests with *Would you mind ...?***

A Would you mind lending me £20? I'll pay you back tomorrow.
B No, not at all. Is twenty enough?
A Would you mind taking me to school, please? I missed the bus.
B Not again! That's the third time this week!
A Would you mind helping me with my homework? I have no idea how to do it.
B I don't mind helping you, but I'm not doing it for you.
A Would you mind giving me a lift to the station? I've got a lot of heavy bags to carry.
B Not at all. Are you ready to go now?

UNIT 5

T 5.1 **Verb patterns**

Tom
I'm sixteen and I'm fed up with school and exams. I'd like to leave now and get a job, any job. I want to earn some money, but my mum and dad say that I can't leave school. They think I'll regret it later, but I don't think I will.

Abby
I'm a student in my last year at university. I've got debts of nearly £25,000. I'm going to study hard for my exams because I hope to get a well-paid job. I hate owing so much money. I'm going for an interview next Friday. Wish me luck!

Kelly
I'm a paramedic. I love my job, but it's very stressful. I'm looking forward to having a good break. We're going to Spain this summer. I'm planning to do nothing but read on the beach for two whole weeks!

Martin
I work in IT. There's nothing I don't know about computers, but I need a change. I'm thinking of applying for another job with a company in New York. I saw it advertised online and it looks like the job for me. I'd love to work there for a couple of years.

Alison
I've got three kids under seven and my husband works abroad a lot of the time. I enjoy looking after the kids, but I'd love to travel too. Sometimes I get fed up with staying at home all day. I'm looking forward to going back to work in a year or two.

Bill
I'm a retired newsagent and I didn't have a day off for 40 years. Now I like sleeping late and planning holidays on the Internet for me and my wife. I'm pretty good at using a computer. We're going on holiday to Tuscany next year so I'm going to do an evening course in Italian.

T 5.2

1 I want to work in Paris.
I'd like to work in Paris.
2 We like going to Italy for our holidays.
We're thinking of going to Italy for our holidays.
3 She can't leave work early tonight.
4 I hope to see you again soon.
I'd like to see you again soon.
5 He's good at playing sports games on the Wii.
He enjoys playing sports games on the Wii.
6 Are you good at learning foreign languages?
7 We're looking forward to having a few days off soon.
8 I'm fed up with doing housework.
I hate doing housework.

T 5.3

1 I enjoy working in Paris.
2 We're hoping to go to Italy for our holidays.
3 She wants to leave work early tonight.
She'd like to leave work early tonight.
4 I'm looking forward to seeing you again soon.
5 He wants to play sports games on the Wii.
6 Do you want to learn foreign languages?
Do you like learning foreign languages?
7 We're going to have a few days off soon.
We'd love to have a few days off soon.
8 I don't want to do housework.

T 5.4 **Making questions**

1 **A** I hope to go to university.
B What do you want to study?
A I'm going to study philosophy and politics. I'd like to be prime minister.
B I think that's the worst job in the world!

2 **A** One of my favourite hobbies is cooking.
B What do you like making?
A Well, I love baking cakes, all kinds of cakes.
B OK, can I have a huge chocolate cake for my birthday?

3 **A** I'm bored.
B What would you like to do?
A Nothing. I'm happy being bored.
B Well, that's OK then!

4 **A** I'm looking forward to the party.
B Who are you hoping to see there?
A No one special. I just like parties.
B Me too!

5 **A** We're planning our summer holidays.
B Where are you thinking of going?
A We want to go camping this year.
B Ugh! Camping! I hate sleeping in tents.

T 5.5 **Writing for talking**

My dreams for the future
Hello everyone. My name's Susannah – Susie for short. I'm 20 years old. At the moment I'm in my second year at art school and I often dream about my future. I have big plans and I'd like to tell you a bit about them.
My most immediate plans are holiday plans. I'm going to visit my brother who's working in Australia. My mother and I are going to spend Christmas with him in the summer sun. I'm very excited about that.
When I return I need to make a final decision about which course to study next year. I'm still not sure – I'm thinking of doing either fashion design or landscape design. It's difficult because I'm interested in both clothes and gardens. If I choose landscape I'd like to work with my friend Jasper. He's brilliant with gardens and we've already worked on two together. It was great fun and we get on very well.
In five or ten years' time I would like to have my own business and work for myself like my father. He has his own building business. Perhaps I'll do a business course after I finish art school.
Of course, one day I hope to marry and have children. Ideally before I'm 30, but I can't plan when I'll meet the right person and I haven't got a boyfriend at the moment.
In my dreams I see myself at 40 running a successful gardening company with about 20 employees. I'll design beautiful gardens for beautiful people. I'll have a beautiful house, two beautiful children, and of course a husband who's as successful as I am. Who knows, it could even be Jasper!

T 5.6 **Have you got any plans?**

1 Pete and Ben
B Hi Pete! What are you doing this evening?
P Hi Ben. I'm meeting my brother for a drink. Would you like to come?
B Sorry I can't. I'm working late this evening. But ... are you doing anything interesting this weekend?
P Yes, I am. I'm going to stay with an old school friend. It's his birthday and he's having a party.
B Are you going to have a party for your birthday?
P Of course! I'm going to invite all my friends.
B Great! I'll look forward to that! Hey, where are you going on holiday this year?
P I'm going surfing for two weeks in Costa Rica. I'm really excited.
B Wow, that sounds fantastic. I'm not going anywhere this year. I can't afford it.
P Yeah, but that's 'cos you're saving to buy a flat.
B I know. You can't have everything. Give my best to your brother. I'll see you later.

2 Debbie and Ella
E Hey Debbie! It's the weekend. Are you doing anything interesting?
D No, I'm not. I'll give you a ring and maybe we can do something together.
E Sorry, I can't this weekend. I'm going on holiday on Saturday.
D Oh, lucky you! Where to?
E Greece, for a week. Where are you going this year?
D Oh, I can't decide. Perhaps I'll go cycling in France again. Hey, are you back from holiday for my birthday on the 25th?
E Yes, I am. Are you going to have a party?
D I haven't thought about it. Maybe I'll just celebrate at home with a few friends.
E Nice idea! So what about tonight? What are you doing this evening?
D Nothing much. I think I'll just watch a DVD and order a pizza. Hey, why don't you come round and join me?
E OK, I'll do that, but I won't stay late. My plane leaves at eight in the morning.

T 5.7 **Discussing grammar**

1 **A** Have you decided which university to apply for?
B Oh yes, I'm going to apply for Oxford.
A Good luck! That's difficult to get into.

2 **A** I haven't got your mobile number.
B Really? I'll text it to you right now.
A Thanks. Do you have mine?
B Yes, I think so.

3 A We don't have any fruit in the house.
B I'm going shopping this afternoon. I'll get some apples.
A Great. I'll give you the money for them.

4 A My bag is really heavy.
B Give it to me. I'll carry it for you.
A Thanks.
B My goodness. What have you got in here?

5 A Tony's back from holiday.
B Is he? I'll give him a ring.
A I'm seeing him this evening. Do you want to come?

6 A What are we having for supper?
B I'm going to make spaghetti bolognese.
A Not again! We had that twice last week.

T 5.8 What can you say?

1 Why are you looking forward to the weekend?
2 I haven't got your brother's new address.
3 Mary says she hasn't seen you for months.
4 Why are you dressed in old clothes?
5 Congratulations! I hear you've got a new job.
6 Are you doing anything interesting after class?

T 5.9 What can you say?

1 A Why are you looking forward to the weekend?
B Because I'm going to the theatre with friends.

2 A I haven't got your brother's new address.
B Haven't you? I'll give it to you now.

3 A Mary says she hasn't seen you for months.
B I know. I'll call her this evening.

4 A Why are you dressed in old clothes?
B Because I'm going to help my dad in the garden.

5 A Congratulations! I hear you've got a new job.
B Yes, I'm going to work in New York.

6 A Are you doing anything interesting after class?
B No, I'm not. I'm just going home.

T 5.10 *Will you, won't you?*

1 I think you'll pass your driving test. You won't fail again. It's your fourth time.
2 I think my team will win. They won't lose this time. They've got a new manager.
3 I think it'll be warm today. You won't need your jumper. Just take a T-shirt.
4 I think I'll join a gym. I won't go on a diet. I like my food too much.
5 I think they'll get divorced. They won't stay together. They argue all the time.
6 I think I'll go by train. I won't fly. I hate flying.

T 5.11 The 20-somethings!

Leo, aged 28

I had a real shock the other day. My little nephew, he's six, said to me 'Uncle Leo, when you were a little boy did they have telephones?' I couldn't believe it. I said: 'Of course we had telephones. How old do you think I am?' Then he said: 'But did you have mobile phones?' And I thought, 'did we?' I can't remember life without mobile phones, but in fact …-er I think I was about eight when my dad got one. 'Yeah,' I said, 'When I was eight'. 'Aha!' said my nephew 'I knew it. You are old'. I didn't like hearing that! I'm 28 and I don't feel grown up at all. I have a great life – a good job, lots of friends, I go out with them most nights. I go to the gym every morning. I'm going to buy a flat by the river next year. Maybe when I'm in my 30s I'll get married and start a family.

Elsa, aged 26

I finished university and I started training to be a lawyer. I was earning good money and in many ways I had a good life but -er the more I studied law the more I hated it, I was bored and miserable – so I decided to give it all up and go travelling. I was away for a year. I went to Australia, New Zealand, North and South America – it was fantastic, but then I arrived back home. I was now 24 and with no money, no job, and nowhere to live. I moved back with mum and dad – they're wonderful, they don't make me pay rent, but – oh dear – it's like being a little girl again. At the moment I'm working as a waitress just to make a bit of money and my dad keeps asking 'When are you going to find a real job?', and mum says: 'When I was your age I was married with two children'. Married with kids! I don't feel old enough for that! I've got a boyfriend but we're not thinking of getting married. Maybe I'll train to be a teacher, now that's a real job.

Dan, aged 24

When I left home at 18 I thought that was it – 'Goodbye mum and dad'. Now six years later I'm back! My college days were great – I worked hard and played hard but I left with huge debts – over £15,000. I thought, 'No problem, I'll just get a job and pay it back'. I moved into a flat with some friends and I was lucky – I got a job pretty quickly, but … I want to be a journalist and the only way is to begin at the bottom. I'm a very junior reporter for a small local newspaper. I love working there, but I only earn £16,000 a year. I couldn't afford the rent for the flat, so here I am, back with mum and dad. They call us the 'boomerang kids' – you know, kids who grow up, leave home, and then move back again. Lots of my friends are doing the same, my girlfriend is back with her mum too. One day we're hoping to marry and get a place of our own, but that probably won't be for a few years. You can't grow up when you're still at home with your parents. I'm fed up.

T 5.12 An interview with Palina Yanachkina

I = Interviewer, P = Palina

I Today I'm talking to Palina Yanachkina. Palina, it's nice to meet you. Can I ask you some questions?
P Of course.
I I hear that you call yourself the girl with two families. Why is that?
P Well, I have my family back home in the Ukraine and my family here in Ireland.
I Where exactly do you come from?
P I come from the village of Polessye not far from Chernobyl. I was born in 1988 just two years after the nuclear accident there. It was a terrible time for us.
I I can understand that. What happened to your family?
P My parents are farmers and after the accident they couldn't sell any of their produce. No one wanted to buy our meat or vegetables. We were very poor and ill – like many people in the village.
I How awful, how miserable for you all.
P But I was lucky. I had the chance to go to Ireland for a holiday and that was when I met my second family. I loved staying with them, -er they were so kind to me. They looked after me so well.
I Your English is excellent now. Did you speak English then?
P Not a word. But I soon learnt, especially from the children. I got on really well with them.
I So you picked up English bit by bit?
P I had some lessons too and I came back to Ireland many times.
I What are you doing now?
P I'm studying here in Ireland. My wonderful Irish family are paying for my studies. I'm hoping to become a doctor one day and return to my village to help the people there. That's my big hope for the future.
I Well, I'm sure you'll do that one day. Thank you, Palina. I've enjoyed talking to you.

T 5.13 Talking about you

1 Where did you grow up? Do you still live in the same house?
2 How do you get on with your parents?
3 Do you ever fall out with your friends and stop speaking to them?
4 Would you like to be a doctor or nurse and look after people?
5 Are you good at picking up foreign languages?
6 Do you look up lots of words in your dictionary?

T 5.14 Expressing doubt and certainty

1 A Do you think Tom will pass his exams?
B I doubt it. He's fed up with school.
C I know. He has no chance at all. He wants to leave and get a job.

2 A Does Martin earn a lot of money?
B Yes, absolutely. He earns a fortune.
C Mmm … I'm not sure. He wants to change his job.

3 A Are England going to win the World Cup?
B They might do. Anything's possible, but I think it's very unlikely.
A Absolutely! I don't think they have a chance.

T 5.15

1 A Kelly's job is really stressful, isn't it?
B Absolutely. She's a paramedic.
A Is she having a holiday soon?
B I think so. She says she might go to Spain.

2 A Isn't it Rob's birthday next week?
B Yes, definitely. It's on the 21st.
A So he's a Capricorn.
B No, I don't think so. I think he's an Aquarius.

3 A Do you think Anita and Paul are in love?
B Definitely. They're going to get married next June in Hawaii.
A Hawaii! Are you going to the wedding?
B No chance. I can't afford it.

T 5.16 What's your opinion?

1 A Did Leo Tolstoy write *War and Peace*?
B Definitely. He wrote it in 1869.

2 A Is Nicole Kidman American?
B I don't think so. I think she's Australian.

3 A Was Sherlock Holmes a real person?
B Definitely not. He's from a book by a writer called Conan Doyle.

4 A Is the population of China more than 2 billion?
B It might be. I don't know. It's definitely more than 1 billion.

5 A Do some vegetarians eat fish?
B I think so. I have a friend who's vegetarian and she eats fish.

6 A Is the weather going to be nice next weekend?
B I doubt it. It's cold and wet today.

7 A Are you going to be rich and famous one day?
B No chance. I'd like to be a bit richer than now, but I wouldn't like to be famous.

8 A Is your school the best in town?
B Absolutely. It's definitely the best.

UNIT 6

T 6.1 Questions about Mia

1 A Do you like Mia?
B Yes, I do. I like her a lot.

2 A How's Mia?
B She's fine, thanks. Very well.

3 A What's Mia like?
B She's really nice. Very friendly.

4 A What does Mia look like?
B She's tall, and she's got brown eyes and black hair.

T 6.2

1 A What's your teacher like?
B She's great! She helps us a lot.

2 A What sports do you like?
B Cycling and skiing.

3 A What does your brother look like?
B He's got blond hair and blue eyes.

4 A Do you like pizza?
B Mmm, I love it!

5 A What's the weather like today?
B Lovely! Warm and sunny.

6 A How are your parents?
B They're OK. Busy as usual.

T 6.3 What's it like?

T What's Shanghai like?
M It's very big and noisy, but it's very exciting.
T What's the food like?
M It's the best in the world! I just love Chinese food!
T What are the people like?
M They're very friendly, and they really want to do business.
T What was the weather like?
M When I was there, it was hot and humid.
T What are the buildings like?
M There are new buildings everywhere, but if you look hard, you can still find some older ones, too.

T 6.4 Singapore, Shanghai, and Dubai

T What did you think of Singapore? What's it like?
M Well, Singapore is very old. It's older than Shanghai, but it's a lot smaller. Shanghai has a population of 20 million, and it's enormous! Shanghai is much bigger than Singapore, and it's much noisier, too.
T Oh, OK. What about business? What's it like to do business in these places?
M Well, they're both top financial centres, but Singapore is more important. It's better for investment.
T Ah, right. And the buildings? Are they all new?
M Yeah, there are a lot of new buildings in Shanghai, so it's more modern than Singapore, but it isn't as cosmopolitan. Half the population of Singapore are foreigners.
T Wow! Really? What about Dubai? What's that like?
M Dubai is the newest and youngest city, and it's the most modern. I like it because it has a 'can-do' feel to it.
T What about the climate in these places? What was the weather like?
M It's interesting. Singapore is very near the equator, so it's a lot hotter than Shanghai. But it isn't as hot as Dubai. Dubai is the hottest place. When I was there the temperature was over 40 degrees.
T Wow! That's incredible!
M Singapore is very humid, so it's wetter than Shanghai. But Dubai is the driest. It only rains for a few days a year.
T Where did you like most of all? Where was best for you?
M For me Shanghai is the best because it's the busiest and the most exciting. There are so many things to do – the best restaurants, theatres, shops. It's got everything!

T 6.5 Pronunciation

I'm older than Jane.
But I'm not as old as John.
He's the oldest.

T 6.6 Ben and me

A Who's cleverer, you or Ben?
B *Me*, of course! I'm *much* cleverer than Ben. He isn't nearly as clever as me!

T 6.7

A Who's kinder, you or Ben?
B *Me*, of course! I'm *much* kinder than Ben. He isn't nearly as kind as me!
A Who's funnier, you or Ben?
B *Me*, of course! I'm *much* funnier than Ben. He isn't nearly as funny as me!
A Who's better-looking, you or Ben?
B *Me*, of course! I'm *a lot* better looking than *Ben*. He isn't nearly as good looking as me!
A Who's more ambitious, you or Ben?
B *Me*, of course! I'm *much* more ambitious than Ben. He isn't nearly as ambitious as me!

T 6.8 Me and my family

Sally

Well, I'm very like my mum. We're interested in the same kind of things, and we can talk forever. We like the same films and the same books. I look like my mum, too. We have the same hair, the same eyes. And she's the same size as me, so I can wear her clothes! My sister's a bit older than me. Her name's Lena. We're quite different. She's very tidy, and I'm messy. She's much tidier than me. And she's very ambitious. She wants to be a doctor. I'm a lot lazier. I don't know what I want to do.

Jamie

I'm not really like my mum or my dad, but I'm a twin. I've got a twin brother called Rob, and we look a lot like each other. He's just a bit darker than me. I've got blonder hair. His is more kind of fair.
But people are always mixing us up. People come up to me and say hello and start a conversation, and I have no idea who they are. It's quite funny. I just say 'Yeah!' or 'Really?' We're very similar in character. We both love art and theatre and books, but he's a bit moody and quiet. I'm a lot noisier. I guess he's quite shy. Oh, and I'm definitely cleverer than him!

Rachel

People say I'm like my father. Hmm. Not sure about that. We do look the same. We're both quite tall, and I suppose our faces are similar. But my father's a very selfish man, and I hope I'm different from him. I hope I'm a bit kinder. He doesn't talk much. He isn't very cheerful. I'm a lot happier than him. He doesn't sound very nice, does he? He's OK, but there are things about him that I really don't like. I have a sister, Jenny, and we do everything together. I love her to bits. But she's prettier than me and thinner than me, so I hate her!

T 6.9 Synonyms

1 A Jane comes from a very rich family.
B Really? I knew her uncle was very wealthy. They have a house in the south of France, don't they?

2 A Was Sophie angry when you were late?
B Yeah. She was pretty annoyed, it's true. She shouted for a bit, then she calmed down.

3 A Jack's such an intelligent boy!
B Mm. He's very clever for a ten-year old. He has some interesting things to say, as well.

4 A I've had enough of winter now.
B I know. I'm fed up with all these dark nights. I need some sunshine.

5 A Dave and Sarah's flat is small, isn't it?
B Mm. It's tiny. I don't know how they live there. It's only big enough for one person.

6 A Are you happy with your new car?
B Yes, I'm very pleased with it. It goes really well. And it's much more reliable than my old one.

T 6.10 Antonyms

1 A That man was so rude to me!
B Yes, he wasn't very polite, was he?

2 A Some people are so stupid!
B Well, not everyone's as clever as you!

3 A Dave's flat is always so dirty!
B Mm, it isn't very clean, is it?

4 A His wife always looks so miserable!
B Yeah, she never looks very happy, does she?

5 A Their children are so naughty!
B Yes, they aren't very well-behaved, are they?

6 A This lesson is boring!
B True. It isn't very interesting. I can't wait for it to end.

T 6.11 *What's on?*

1 A What shall we do today?
B I'm not sure. How about going to the cinema?
A Mmm … I don't really feel like seeing a film.

2 B OK. Would you like to go to an exhibition?
A That sounds interesting! What's on?
B Well, there's a Van Gogh exhibition.
A Is it any good?
B I think it looks really good!

3 A Where is it on?
B It's on at the Royal Academy.
A What's the nearest underground?
B Piccadilly Circus.
A How much is it?
B It's £12, and £8 for students.
A What time is it open?
B From ten till six.
A Right! Good idea! Let's go!

UNIT 7

T 7.1 **John**

Hi! I'm John. I live in London. I have a flat in Dean Street, Soho. I've lived here for three years. I'm a press photographer. I've worked for *The London Gazette* since 2010. My wife's name is Fay. We've been married for two years. We met at university. Fay's a receptionist at the Ritz Hotel. I get around town on a motorbike. I've had it since I was 25. Fay goes by bus. We don't have any children yet.

T 7.2 **Questions and answers**

1 How long has he lived in the flat? John has lived in the flat for three years.
2 How long did he live in the flat? Karl Marx lived in the flat for five years.
3 Where does he work? John works for *The London Gazette*.
4 How long has he worked there? John has worked there since 2010.
5 What was his job in London? Karl Marx was a foreign correspondent for an American newspaper.
6 Which newspaper did he write for? Karl Marx wrote for *The New York Daily Tribune*.
7 How long has he been married? John has been married for two years.
8 How long was he married? Karl Marx was married for 38 years.

T 7.3 ***for*** **or** ***since*****?**

1 I've known John for three years. We met at university.
2 I last went to the cinema two weeks ago. The film was really boring.
3 I've had this watch since I was a child. My grandpa gave it to me.
4 I lived in New York from 2005 to 2007. I had a great time there.
5 I've lived in this house since 2008. It's got a beautiful garden.
6 We last had a holiday two years ago. We went to Spain.
7 I haven't seen you for ages. What have you been up to?
8 We haven't had a break for over an hour. I really need a coffee.

T 7.4 **Asking questions**

A Where do you live, Susan?
B In a flat near the town centre.
A How long have you lived there?
B For three years.
A Why did you move there?
B Because we wanted to be in a nicer area.

T 7.5

1 **A** What do you do?
B I work for an international company.
A How long have you worked there?
B For two years.
A What did you do before that?
B I worked for a charity.

2 **A** Do you know Dave Brown?
B Yes, I do.
A How long have you known him?
B For five or six years.
A Where did you meet him?
B We were at university together.

T 7.6 **Frieda Hoffman – archaeologist and writer**

I = Interviewer, F = Frieda

Frieda Hoffman was born in Germany, but she has lived most of her life abroad. She has a passion for history and ancient civilizations. Her greatest love is Africa, and she has written several books about ancient Egypt.

I Frieda, you've travelled a lot in your lifetime. Which countries have you been to?
F Well, I've been to a lot of countries in Africa and Asia, but I've never been to South America.
I When did you first go abroad?
F When I was six, my family moved to England.
I Why did you move there?
F Because my father got a job as Professor of History at Cambridge University.
I Have you always been interested in archaeology?
F Yes, I have. When I was ten, there was an exhibition of Tutankhamun, the Egyptian king, in London. My father took me to see it and I was fascinated. After that I knew that I wanted to go to Egypt and be an archaeologist.
I How many times have you been to Egypt?
F Twenty times at least. I go as often as I can.
I Have you ever discovered anything?
F Yes, I've made some very important discoveries. I was the leader of a team that discovered some ancient tombs near Cairo.
I You've written books about Egypt, haven't you? How many books have you written?
F I've written three about the pharaohs. And I've written a book about a journey I made from Cairo to Cape Town.
I How did you travel? By train? By car?
F In a Land Rover, of course!
I In all your travels, have you ever been in any dangerous situations?
F Oh, goodness, yes! I've often been in danger. But in situations like that you learn so much about yourself.

T 7.7

I = Interviewer, F = Frieda

1 **I** You moved to England when you were six. Do you go back to Germany much?
F No, I don't. I've been back a few times to visit relatives, but I've never lived there again. I feel more English than German now.

2 **I** What did you study at university?
F I studied ancient history at Cambridge.
I Did you enjoy it?
F Yes, I did. The course was amazing, and Cambridge was a great place to live.

3 **I** Have you ever had an ordinary job?
F Of course I have! I've done all sorts of things. After university I didn't have any money.
I So what did you do?
F I worked in a restaurant. I hated it!
I Why didn't you like it?
F Because the hours were so long, and the people I was working with were horrible.

4 **I** You said you've often been in danger. What's the most dangerous situation you've ever been in?
F Well, I had a very bad car crash in Cairo. I was seriously injured and broke several bones. I spent three months in hospital. I was very lucky. I nearly died.

T 7.8 **Word endings**

photographer
receptionist
scientist
farmer
artist
politician
musician
accountant
decorator
actor
interpreter
librarian
electrician
lawyer

T 7.9 **Word stress**

Two-syllabled nouns and adjectives

Nouns

danger
kindness
critic
artist
difference

Adjectives

dangerous
healthy
friendly
famous
different

Two-syllabled verbs

invite
explain
discuss
employ
decide
compete

Nouns ending in ***-tion/-sion***

invitation
explanation
competition
ambition
decision

T 7.10 **David Taylor Bews**

I come from Newcastle in England, but now I live in Perth, Australia. I've been here nearly ten years. My wife, Jodie, is Australian and our children, Russell and Alice were born here. Alice is named after my grandmother, her great-grandmother, Alice Bews. She's 89 now and still lives in Newcastle. Lately I've become really interested in my family history back in the UK. I've started speaking to my grandmother about it. I've found out that she was the youngest of nine children and the only one to have been born in England. Her eight brothers and sisters were all born in Scotland. They came from the very north of Scotland, from some islands called the Orkneys. They worked there as farmers over a hundred years ago. My grandmother told me that hundreds of years before that our family's ancestors were actually Norwegian – they came over to Scotland in the 9th century. She says that's why we all have blonde hair in our family. Anyway, it became more and more difficult for my great-grandparents to make a living farming, so they travelled south. They finally arrived in the north of England, in Newcastle with their eight children. Alice was born soon after they arrived.

T 7.11 **Talking to Grandma**

D = David, AB = Alice Bews

D So Grandma, your parents were both born in the Orkney Islands, is that right?
AB Yes, my mother was called Jane. She grew up there and she married when she was just 17.
D And you were her ninth child?
AB Yes, I was the only one born in England. Times were really hard for my mother – you see my father died when I was three. I can't remember him at all.
D So what did your mother do?
AB She worked as a cleaner *and* a dressmaker.
D She had two jobs and a big family, that's …
AB Oh, yes, she was an amazing lady. But my two eldest brothers … -er they got work in the shipyards so that helped too. Ah – all my brothers and sisters have died now – I'm the only one left.
D I know. Did you marry young Grandma?
AB Oh, no. I didn't marry until I was 22.
D That's still young.
AB It wasn't unusual in those days. And I had only three children.
D But now you have lots of grandchildren and great-grandchildren.
AB I do. They live all over the world – not just in Australia.
D I know. I have cousins in New Zealand and America. But cousin Peter still lives near you, doesn't he?
AB Yes, he does. He helps me keep in touch with you all with this 'Skype' thing.
D Yeah, this 'Skype' is amazing, isn't it?
AB Oh, yes. I love it. I talk to all my grandchildren and I've seen all my great-grandchildren. I email sometimes too. Email, Skype, and texting – it's all really wonderful, isn't it?
D It is grandma. It's just great talking to you. I've got lots more questions for next time.

T 7.12 **Question tags**

It's really wonderful, isn't it?
You come from Scotland, don't you?
Life wasn't easy then, was it?
You've lived in England for years, haven't you?

T 7.13 ***It's a lovely day, isn't it?***

1 **A** It's a lovely day, **isn't it?**
B Yes, it is! Beautiful!
A We all love days like this, **don't we?**
B We certainly do!

2 **A** Mummy! Our cat isn't very big, **is she?**
B No, she isn't. She's just a kitten.
A And she loves fish, **doesn't she?**
B She does! It's her favourite food!

3 **A** We had such a good holiday, **didn't we?**
B We did. We had a great time.
A And it wasn't too expensive, **was it?**
B No, it wasn't. It wasn't expensive at all.

4 **A** The baby looks just like her mother, **doesn't she?**
B Uh huh. Same blue eyes, same nose.
A But she's got her father's blonde hair, **hasn't she?**
B Yes, she's very fair.

T 7.14

1 **A** It was a great party last night, wasn't it?
B Yes, it was. I really enjoyed it.

2 **A** Dave knows everything about computers, doesn't he?
B Yes, he does. He can fix them *and* program them.

3 **A** You went to school with my brother, didn't you?
B Yes, I did. We were really good friends.

4 **A** Learning a language isn't easy, is it?
B No, it isn't. It needs a lot of practice and patience.

5 **A** Our English has improved a lot, hasn't it?
B Yes, it has. We're all much better now.

6 **A** We haven't had a break for ages, have we?
B No, we haven't. It's time for one right now.

T 7.15

1 **A** It's horrible weather today, isn't it?
B Awful!
A The rain makes you miserable, doesn't it?
B Yup! And wet!
A Never mind. We need the rain, don't we?
B I suppose so.

2 **A** It's so romantic here, isn't it?
B Yes, it's beautiful!
A And the sea looks so inviting, doesn't it?
B I think I'll go for a swim before breakfast. I've got time, haven't I?
A Of course you've got time! We're on holiday, aren't we?

3 **A** You don't like Ann, do you?
B Er … she's all right.
A But you didn't talk to her all night, did you?
B Well … she was talking to Jim, wasn't she?
A She's very interesting, actually.
B But she never listens, does she? She just talks and talks and talks!

4 **A** I'd love to buy that car!
B But we haven't got any money, have we?
A I thought we had lots.
B But we spent it all on a new kitchen, didn't we?
A Oh, yes! So we did. Never mind.
B We can save up, can't we?
A Er … OK.

5 **S** We had a lovely holiday, didn't we Dave?
D We did. It was very relaxing.
S And the weather was marvellous, wasn't it Dave?
D Yep. We were very lucky.
S And we met some nice people, didn't we Dave?
D We did. Charming people.

6 **A** Kate Burton's a fabulous actor, isn't she?
B Very good.
A And she's got such a good voice, hasn't she?
B Yes, it's amazing!
A She can hit the highest notes, can't she?
B Yeah, I don't know how she does it.

7 **A** We love each other very much, don't we?
B We do.
A And we want to get married one day, don't we?
B One day, yeah.
A And we'll have six children, won't we?
B Er … yeah. Six, that's right.

8 **A** That was a terrible match, wasn't it?
B Awful! Waste of money!
A Albertino played really badly, didn't he?
B He was rubbish! He didn't do a thing right all night, did he?
A We deserved to lose, didn't we?
B I'm afraid so! I don't know why I support them!

UNIT 8

T 8.1 **Interview with Tilly Parkins**

I = Interviewer, TP = Tilly Parkins

I Tilly, I'm sure you have to be very fit and strong to go climbing. How often do you have to train?
TP I don't have to train every day, just two or three times a week, that's enough. I go to the gym. At the weekend I try to get out of the city onto rock, but sometimes I have to work at the hospital.
I What do you do at the hospital?
TP I'm a cardiac technologist. I help doctors treat people with heart diseases.
I Oh, wow! That's interesting. The photograph of Moon Hill Crag is amazing. Was it a difficult climb?
TP Difficult and very beautiful.
I I can see that. It's like a painting. What time of day was it?
TP It was just after dawn. I had to climb very early in the morning. You can't climb later in the day – it's too hot, over 35°C.
I Who took the photograph?
TP A brilliant sports photographer called Adam Pretty.
I He's a brave man.
TP Oh, he didn't have to climb with me. He took the photo from a nearby tourist spot.
I Wise man! Rock climbing is such a dangerous sport and you've climbed in some of the most difficult places in the world. Why do you do it?
TP It's what I love doing. It's my life. It's who I am.

T 8.2 **Questions and answers**

1 'How often does she have to train?'
'Two or three times a week.'
2 'Does she have to work at weekends?'
'Yes, she does sometimes.'
3 'Why did she have to climb Moon Hill Crag just after dawn?'
'Because later it gets too hot and you can't climb in the heat.'
4 'Did Adam have to climb the rock?'
'No, he didn't. He took the photo from a tourist spot.'

T 8.3 **Pronunciation**

1 I have a good job.
I have to work hard.
2 He has a nice camera.
She has to train a lot.
3 We had a good time.
We had to get up early.

T 8.4 **Advice from Annie**

Dear Mark,
Good preparation is the answer. You must prepare well and practise a lot. The first thirty seconds are the most important. You should begin with a personal story. It will relax you and the audience. You should write your speech down, but I don't think you should read it aloud to the group. Just make notes to help you remember it. For more help, you should visit *speechtips.com*.

Dear Paula,
More and more people worldwide have become addicted to this. He must get professional help, but this is difficult because he won't accept that he has

a problem. I think you should show him this letter, and visit the website *olganon.org*. Tell him firmly that he must change his ways or he'll lose his wife and family. Talk to all your friends and family about the problem – you shouldn't suffer alone.

Dear Billy,
These feelings are very common between brothers and sisters. I'm sure your parents love you and your brother just the same, so you shouldn't worry about this. When you're older, you'll get your own phone, and your own clothes! You must talk to your parents about how you feel. And you shouldn't feel jealous of your brother. He's older than you, that's all!

Dear Tracy,
The fact is, that to get to the top in sport you have to train very hard indeed. You should talk to someone else about your doubts. I don't think you should listen to just your friends. You should explain how you feel to your coach and your mother. However, in the end, the decision is yours and yours alone. You must decide your own future.

T 8.5 Giving advice

1 A I can't sleep at night.
B You must do more exercise during the day. Why don't you walk to work? And you shouldn't drink so much coffee just before bedtime.

2 A I don't like my brother's new girlfriend.
B I don't think you should tell your brother. I think you should try to find some good things about her.

3 A I've got an important exam tomorrow, and I'm really nervous.
B I don't think you should study any more today. You must get a good night's sleep tonight. Don't worry. I'm sure you'll pass and if you don't it's not the end of the world.

4 A A boy in my class is bullying me.
B You must tell your teacher or ask your mum to talk to the teacher.

5 A I'm hopeless at all sports.
B You shouldn't worry about that. Lots of people aren't very sporty. Think about all the things you are good at.

6 A I fell over and I think I've twisted my ankle.
B Ooh it looks bad! You must go to the doctor or better still A and E and ask for an X-ray. I'll drive you. I don't think you should walk on it.

7 A My computer's behaving very strangely.
B Mine does that all the time. You should do what I do, turn it off, wait a while, then turn it on again. It's the only thing that ever works for me.

8 A My car's making a funny noise.
B It sounds bad, you shouldn't drive it. You must ring the garage.

T 8.6 Jessica Ennis – Britain's first world heptathlon champion!

I = Interviewer, J = Jessica Ennis

I Nice to meet you, Jessica. Congratulations on your gold medal at the World Athletic Championships in Berlin.
J Thank you very much.
I You won in Berlin, but I know that just a couple of years ago you injured your ankle very badly. Were you worried that your sporting career was over?
J Yes, I was very worried. I missed the Olympics in China and I had to work hard with physios and doctors for nine months – but now I'm fine.
I You're obviously a very determined girl.
J Yeah, my mum always said that from a young age I was very determined. I knew what I wanted.
I Is your mum a big influence in your life?
J Yes, she is. She works for a charity. She helps people with drug problems. You have to have a lot of patience for that. My mum's got that. My dad's a painter and decorator. He was born in Jamaica, er he moved here when he was 13.
I I can see your parents are important to you. I'm sure you have a good coach too.
J Yes, Tony Minichiello. He's a really good coach, but we often fight, I …
I You fight?
J Well, we do spend a lot of time together. He's always saying 'Come on, come on, you must be more aggressive,' and I'm not really like that. He says that I must only think about athletics, he didn't even want me to get a dog.
I Did you get a dog?
J Oh, yeah. I have a beautiful chocolate labrador, called Myla.
I So, do you think that you should have other interests, not just athletics?
J Yeah, but when I'm competing I go into my own little world. I don't see my boyfriend, I …
I You have a boyfriend?
J Yep, Andy. I only spoke to him once on the phone when I was in Berlin. I had to concentrate on competing. I know I won in Berlin, but I can still improve. I have to work on my long jump and javelin, and I know I can run more quickly. It's the small things that make a difference in the end.
I I hope you have time to feel proud of being world champion.
J Oh, yes. I keep my medal by my bed and when I look at it I think 'Oh my goodness, I won. I'm world champion'. Sometimes I can't believe it.
I It's a fantastic achievement. Well done and good luck in the next Olympics.
J Thank you.

T 8.7 Brothers and sisters

1 David

I'm one of three brothers. I'm the middle one. There was just Mark, my elder brother, and me for years. I liked that, I liked being the baby, but then Rob was born when I was seven and I was so jealous. I thought he was our mum's favourite. We had lots of fights as kids, but now it's great. I'd like to have at least three kids – three boys like us would be great.

2 A girl called Peta

My mum and dad called me Peta when I was born because they wanted a boy! Then they had four boys after me. I don't like being the eldest of so many boys and I don't like my name. I'm going to change it to Petra when I'm 18. I quite like the baby, Henry – he's everybody's favourite – but I hate the others. They're annoying and very boring – all they do is play noisy computer games and talk about football. I don't want any children when I grow up – well, maybe one daughter.

3 Stewart (27)

I'm an only child. My mum and dad divorced when I was just three years old so I grew up with just my mum. I love my mum, but I didn't like the situation, I was her whole world. This was difficult for me. Then, when I was thirteen she married again and that was difficult too. It took me a long time to get on with my step-dad. He's really nice, but I was jealous of him for years. I've just got married. My wife's an only child too and we both definitely want to have lots of children.

T 8.8 Symptoms and diagnoses

A I can't stop coughing and blowing my nose.
B You've got a cold.
A I've got a fever and my whole body aches.
B You've got flu.
A It hurts when I walk on it.
B You've got a twisted ankle.
A I keep going to the toilet.
B You've got diarrhoea.
A My glands are swollen, and it hurts when I swallow.
B You've got a sore throat.
A I keep being sick, and I've got terrible diarrhoea.
B You've got food poisoning.
A I start sneezing and itching when I'm near a cat.
B You've got an allergy.

T 8.9 At the doctor's

D = female doctor, E = Edsom

D What seems to be the problem?
E Well, I haven't felt well for a few days. I've had a bad headache and now I've got a sore throat.
D Any sickness or diarrhoea?
E Well, I haven't been sick.
D Do you feel hot?
E Yes, especially at night. I feel hot and I start coughing when I lie down.
D OK, I'll just take your temperature. Ah, yes. You do have a bit of a fever. Now, let me see your throat. Open your mouth wide, please.
E Can you see anything?
D Yes, your throat looks very red. Does this hurt?
E Ow!
D And your glands are swollen. You just have a bit of an infection. You need antibiotics. Are you allergic to penicillin?
E No, I'm not.
D Good. Now, you should take things easy for a couple of days and you must drink plenty of liquids. I'll write you a prescription.
E Thank you. Do I have to pay you?
D No, no. But you'll have to pay for the prescription. It's £7.20.
E Right. Thanks very much. Goodbye.

UNIT 9

T 9.1 The bear and the travellers

1 Where were the travellers walking?
Along a country road.
2 Why were they going to the city?
Because they were looking for work.
3 What did they see in the woods?
They saw a huge bear.
4 What did the men do?
One hid in a tree, the other pretended to be dead.
5 What did the bear do?
It bent down, sniffed, then wandered away.

T 9.2 **The bear and the travellers**

Two travellers were walking slowly along a country road. They were going to the city because they were looking for work. They were tired because they had walked twenty miles and they were hungry because they hadn't eaten all day. Suddenly, in the woods in front of them, they saw a huge bear. The men were terrified. One of them ran away, climbed a tree, and hid.

The other man fell to the ground and pretended to be dead. He had heard that bears don't like eating dead meat. The bear came towards him. It bent down, sniffed him, and whispered something in his ear. Then it wandered away.

After the bear had gone, the other man came down from his tree and went to see how his friend was. He wanted to know what the bear had said to him.

'The bear gave me some advice,' said his companion. 'He said: *Next time you go on a journey, travel with someone who won't leave you at the first sign of danger.*'

The moral of this story is … choose your friends carefully!

T 9.3 **Questions and answers**

1 Why were the travellers tired?
Because they had walked twenty miles.
2 Why were they hungry?
Because they hadn't eaten all day.
3 Why did one of them pretend to be dead?
Because he had heard that bears don't like eating dead meat.
4 When did the other man come down from the tree?
After the bear had gone.
5 What did he want to know?
He wanted to know what the bear had said to his friend.

T 9.4 **Pronunciation**

1 They'd walked twenty miles.
2 One man hid in a tree.
3 The other pretended to be dead.
4 When the bear had gone, the man came down.
5 He felt bad because he'd left his friend.

T 9.5

1 I was nervous on the plane because I'd never flown before.
2 When I'd had breakfast, I went to work.
3 I met a girl at a party. Her face was familiar. I was sure I'd seen her somewhere before.
4 I felt tired all day yesterday because I hadn't slept the night before.
5 My wife was angry with me because I'd forgotten our anniversary.
6 The little girl was crying because she'd fallen over and hurt herself.

T 9.6 **The boy who cried wolf**

Once upon a time there was a shepherd boy who looked after the sheep in the hills near his village. He thought this job was very boring. One day, while he was sitting under a tree, he had an idea. He decided to have some fun, so he went down to the village and shouted 'Wolf! Wolf!' at the top of his voice.

As soon as the villagers heard the boy, they stopped work and raced to the hills to help him. But when they got there, they saw nothing. They returned to their work. After they'd gone, the shepherd boy smiled to himself.

A few days later, the boy did the same thing again. He ran into the village and shouted 'Wolf! Wolf!' The villagers didn't know whether to believe him or not, but they were worried about their sheep so they had to help him. They went back to the hills. Again there was no wolf. They were angry because the shepherd boy had lied again, but he just laughed.

Then, the next day, just as the sun was setting, a wolf really did appear, and it began attacking the sheep. In terror, the boy raced down the hill to the village, shouting 'Wolf! Wolf!' Although the villagers heard his cries, they did nothing to help. This time they really didn't believe him.

The shepherd boy climbed back up the hill to look for the sheep, but the wolf had killed them all. He was so ashamed of himself that he sat down in the moonlight and cried.

The moral of this story is … you should not lie. A liar will not be believed, even when he tells the truth.

T 9.7 **Discussing grammar**

1 When I'd done my homework, I went to bed.
2 After I'd driven 200 miles I stopped for a coffee.
3 As soon as she'd passed her driving test she bought a car.
4 I didn't go to Italy until I'd learned Italian.
5 Although I'd read the book I didn't understand the film.
6 His mother sent him to bed because he'd been naughty.
7 She'd burnt the food, so we went out to eat.
8 She cooked a lovely supper, but unfortunately I'd eaten a large lunch.

T 9.8 **My favourite writer**

I = Interviewer, T = Tom

Part 1

I Tom, you chose Charles Dickens as your favourite writer. Can you tell us a little about him? When was he alive?
T He wrote in the nineteenth century. He was born in England in 1812 and died in 1870.
I What did he write? What sort of books?
T He wrote novels and short stories.
I And tell us … why is he famous?
T At the time he was writing there was a lot of inequality between the rich and the poor. Dickens wanted to change society. He wrote about people who were poor, and hungry, or ill, or who were unfortunate in some way. Dickens created some of the most famous characters in English literature.
I What are his best-known books?
T There are quite a few, but possibly *David Copperfield*, which has a lot of autobiography in it, and *Oliver Twist*, and after that *A Christmas Carol*. In this book we meet a character called Scrooge …
I Ah! The man who hated Christmas!
T That's right. At the beginning of the story Scrooge is a miserable character who refuses to spend any money to help his poor family. But by the end he is a changed man – kind, generous, and full of love for people around him.
I What was Dickens' personal life like?
T Mmm. A mix of good and bad. His parents were poor. Dickens became very rich. He married and had ten children …
I Ten!
T Yes. But he left his wife because he fell in love with an actress. He didn't get divorced – in those days it was impossible, absolutely out of the question. So there was a lot of sadness in his life.
I Oh, dear! Poor Mr Dickens!

T 9.9 **My favourite writer**

I = Interviewer, A = Alice

Part 2

I Now, Alice. You chose Robert Louis Stevenson. Tell us about him. When was he writing?
A Well, he was born in 1850, and he died in 1894, so he was writing just after Dickens, in the second half of the nineteenth century.
I And … what did he write?
A He wrote novels, and poetry, and he was also a travel writer.
I Oh! Quite a lot! Tell us … why is he famous?
A Well, he isn't as famous as Dickens. But he's very popular because he's a *great* story teller. His stories are about adventure, danger, and horror. His heroes are pure, and his villains are dark.
I What are his best-known books?
A There's a children's book called *Treasure Island*, and there's a travel story about going around France, but the most famous is *The Strange Case of Dr Jekyll and Mr Hyde*.
I And they, I suppose, are his most well-known characters?
A Yes. The book was an immediate success. It's about a man who has two sides to his character, one good and one bad. The man, Dr Jekyll, has a battle inside himself between his good side and his evil side.
I This is the psychological idea of someone with a split personality?
A Yes. In everyday speech we say about someone 'Oh, he's a real Jekyll and Hyde', meaning there are two sides to their personality.
I Fascinating! Tell us about his personal life.
A As a child he was often ill. He married an American woman who had children from an earlier marriage, but they didn't have any children together. He travelled a lot, to Europe and the United States. He died very young, when he was just 44.
I Well, thank you, Alice, for telling us about Robert Louis Stevenson.

T 9.10 ***The strange case of Dr Jekyll and Mr Hyde*, by Robert Louis Stevenson**

London, 1886

1 Late one night, a lawyer, Gabriel Utterson, was walking home through dark, silent streets when he saw a man attacking a woman. Utterson ran after him and caught him. The man's name was Mr Hyde, and he looked ugly and evil.
2 Mr Hyde showed no regret for what he had done. To buy the woman's silence, he wrote her a cheque. Utterson noticed that the cheque was signed in the name of Dr Jekyll, a well-known and well-respected man.
3 Utterson was worried. He was Dr Jekyll's lawyer and also his friend. He went to visit him. As soon as he mentioned Mr Hyde, Dr Jekyll turned pale and became angry. Utterson was confused. Who was Mr Hyde?
4 A year passed. One night an old man was murdered as he was walking home. Mr Hyde had struck again! The police went looking for Hyde, but he had disappeared.

5 Again, Utterson went to visit his friend Dr Jekyll. He suspected that Dr Jekyll had helped Mr Hyde to escape. When questioned, the doctor replied in a strange, wild voice that Mr Hyde had gone forever.
6 Over the next few weeks Dr Jekyll's behaviour became more and more unusual. He locked himself in his laboratory and refused to open the door. His servants were worried. When they heard his voice, it sounded different. They asked Utterson for help.
7 Utterson and the servants broke down the door. Mr Hyde was lying dead on the floor. He had taken poison. But why was he wearing Dr Jekyll's clothes? And where was the doctor? Were Dr Jekyll and Mr Hyde one and the same person?
8 On the desk was a letter addressed to Mr Utterson. In it, Dr Jekyll tried to explain himself. He said he believed that inside every human being there was a good side and an evil side.
9 Jekyll had created a potion. When he drank it, his whole body changed. The good, kind doctor became cruel, ugly, and evil. He called this other man Mr Hyde. To change back, he had to drink another potion.
10 But after a time Jekyll found that he liked changing into Mr Hyde. He enjoyed being bad. He became more and more violent and cruel. He took pleasure in hurting innocent people.
11 Finally Dr Jekyll couldn't control Mr Hyde anymore. He began to change into this monster even without taking the potion. Jekyll hoped and prayed that Hyde would disappear. But Hyde always returned.
12 The potion to turn Hyde back into Dr Jekyll no longer worked. It had lost its strength. Dr Jekyll could no longer get rid of the evil Mr Hyde. He had to kill this monster. But to kill Mr Hyde, Dr Jekyll also had to die …

T 9.11

1 I was delighted because I'd won £1,000 in a competition.
2 I was stressed because I had ten bills and no money to pay them.
3 I was proud because I'd worked so hard and passed all my exams.
4 I was amazed because my teachers didn't expect me to pass.
5 I was upset because no one remembered my birthday.

T 9.12

1 **A** Sometimes I feel really lonely.
B Cheer up! You've got me! I'm your best friend!
2 **A** I've got so much to do! And the baby's crying! Help!
B Calm down! You're so stressed! Chill out!
3 **A** Guess what? I've just won £10,000!
B That's fabulous! I'm delighted for you! Can I have some?
4 **A** When I watch the news on TV, I get scared.
B I know what you mean. The world's a scary place.
5 **A** I get upset when people are so horrible.
B Yes, but people can be really nice as well.

T 9.13

A What an amazing film!
B I was scared!
C I was really scared!
D I was SO scared!

T 9.14

I was *so* surprised!
It was *such a* shock!
It was *such an* awful day!
You have *such* crazy ideas!
We had *such* terrible weather!
There were *so many* problems!
I've got *so much* work!

T 9.15

1 That was such a good book! You must read it! I'll lend it to you. You'll really like it.
2 The film was so scary that I couldn't watch it! I hate the sight of blood and people killing each other.
3 Jane and Pete are such nice people! They're always so welcoming and pleased to see you.
4 But their children are so badly-behaved! The parents have no control at all!
5 There were so many people at the party! I didn't manage to talk to everyone.
6 They made such a mess! I'm glad I didn't have to tidy up.
7 I've spent so much money this week! I haven't got a penny left!
8 I've had such an awful day! I need a drink to cheer me up!

UNIT 10

T 10.1 A phone call that changed the world

Fact file

Today, mobile phones are owned by almost six billion people worldwide. In the UK 30 million are sold every year.
The first text message was sent in 1989. Last year 6.1 trillion texts were sent worldwide.
Camera phones have been sold since 2002.
'Smartphones' were introduced in 2007. The mobile phone had become a multimedia gadget.
Over the years a multitude of amazing features have been added, including Internet browsing, email, MP3 players, video, and camera.
In 2008 Apple's iPhone had 500 applications (apps). Now there are over 500,000 apps.
The most expensive mobile is the Goldstriker iPhone 4S EliteGold. It is made of 24ct gold and decorated with over 550 diamonds. It costs £6 million.
100 million mobile phones are thrown away every year.
Some people believe that before long all landline telephones will be replaced by mobile phones.

T 10.2

1 The first mobile phone call was made in 1973 by Martin Cooper.
2 Mobile phones are owned by almost six billion people worldwide.
3 30 million phones are sold in the UK every year.
4 Camera phones have been sold since 2002.
5 A lot of amazing features have been added.
6 The Goldstriker phone is decorated with over 550 diamonds.
7 100 million mobile phones are thrown away every year.
8 Some people believe that eventually all landline telephones will be replaced by mobile phones.

T 10.3

1 Paper was invented in 105 AD by a Chinese government official called T'sai Lun.
2 The printing press was invented in 1440 by a German printer called Johannes Gutenberg.
3 The telephone was invented in 1876 by Alexander Graham Bell. Bell was born in Scotland, but he moved to America and became a scientist and a teacher of the deaf.
4 The radio was invented in 1901 by Guglielmo Marconi, an Italian physicist.
5 Television was invented in 1924 by a Scottish engineer, John Logie Baird.
6 The ball-point pen was invented in 1938 by the Hungarian journalist Laszlo Biro.
7 The Apple PC was invented in 1976 by two American computer engineers, Steve Jobs and Steve Woznak. The name Apple was chosen because it was Job's favourite fruit.

T 10.4 All things online

1 Over 90 trillion emails are sent every year.
2 Nearly 5.5 billion questions are answered by **Google** every day.
3 **eBay** was invented in 1995 by Pierre Omidyar, a French scientist.
4 Nearly 5 billion items have been sold on **eBay** since it began.
5 60,000 new video films are posted on **YouTube** every week.
6 The first **Twitter** message was sent by American businessman, Jack Dorsey, in 2006.
7 **Facebook** has been translated into 76 languages since it began.
8 The online store, **Amazon.com** was founded by Jeff Besoz, in his garage in 1994.

T 10.5 Questions and answers

1 **A** How many emails are sent every year?
B Over 90 trillion. Isn't that amazing?
2 **A** How many questions are answered by Google every day?
B Nearly 5.5 billion. It's incredible.
3 **A** When was eBay invented?
B In 1995.
A Who was it invented by?
B A French scientist called Pierre Omidyar.
4 **A** How many items have been sold on eBay since it began?
B 5 billion. Actually 5 billion and one. I've just bought something!
5 **A** How many films are posted on YouTube every week?
B 60,000 new videos every week.
6 **A** When was the first Twitter message sent?
B In 2006.
A Who was it sent by?
B An American businessman called Jack Dorsey.
7 **A** How many languages has Facebook been translated into?
B 76. And there'll be more.
8 **A** When was Amazon.com founded?
B In 1994.
A Who was it founded by?
B Jeff Besoz.

T 10.6

text message
businessman
newsagent
cellphone

T 10.7

business card
business deal
businessman
business news
computer games
computer program
computer virus
laptop
phone call
phone card
phone number
radio news
radio programme
radio waves
website

T 10.8

1 She has a wonderful job. She's very well-paid.
2 I didn't enjoy that novel. It was really badly-written.
3 You don't need to spend a lot of money on clothes to look well-dressed.
4 Our office is really well-equipped. We have all the latest machines.
5 I hope their children don't come. They're so badly-behaved.
6 Can I have my steak very well-done, please? I don't like it rare.
7 Surely you've heard of Elizabeth Taylor. She was really well-known.

T 10.9

1 **A** Do you ever play computer games?
B No, but my nephew does, all the time.

2 **A** Which websites do you visit most often?
B Google, Wikipedia and BBC recipes. I get all my recipes online now.

3 **A** Do you send a lot of text messages?
B I do. It's a great way to make arrangements. I text all the time.

4 **A** Who does the most housework in your home?
B Not me! My mum always says 'Oh I'll do it, you're so slow.'

5 **A** What size shoes do you take?
B 36. We've got small feet in our family.

6 **A** How do you like your steak?
B I like it rare. I don't like it well-done.

7 **A** Is your school well-equipped?
B Not really. But I think we're getting interactive whiteboards soon.

T 10.10

1 Henry

It's made for me. I'm a frustrated writer. One day maybe I'll write a novel. I write about my thoughts, my work, all my travels and I've even written a kind of work biography. I'm so pleased that I have so many visitors and comments. I feel in touch with the world. I tweet too.

2 Sandy

Yeah, I have an account and I go on it fairly often. I like sharing photos with friends. I love seeing their photos too, and it's a nice way of keeping up to date with them and sometimes making contact with old friends. I don't use it for anything more. Some people communicate a lot about their lives on it – I couldn't do that.

3 Liz

Actually it was a terrible shock. I went back to my machine and the screen was bright purple with large red letters across it saying WARNING. Everything was completely frozen. I rang the helpline and they said they'd had over fifty calls from people with same thing. It had even infected the Stock Exchange. Who are the sad individuals who do this, I want to know!

4 Martin

There aren't many left in my town. Just one, I think, on the High Street. It's because so many people have home computers and laptops these days and there are more and more places where you can access the Internet. I used them a lot when I was travelling.

5 Barry

I do so much online – I think I conduct most of my life online. I book everything – cinema, travel, my sports club; I shop online – clothes, food, presents; I check symptoms if I'm ill (actually, I've stopped doing this because I got too frightened by the answers); I download recipes. I could go on and on. I like the way 'google' has become a verb. I'm always saying 'I'll just google that and find out.'

T 10.11 ***It drives me crazy!***

A = Alan, J = Jack

A Hi Jack! Over here! How was your journey?
J Huh! Not good! Not good at all.
A Why was that?
J Well, there was this girl in the seat behind and she was talking loudly on her mobile phone the *whole* journey. I know *every*thing about her life. I even know what she's going to wear when she goes out on Saturday night *and* I know what she's *not* going to wear.
A That drives *me* mad too! You know, not long ago trains had quiet carriages where you couldn't use your mobile phone.
J Well, they don't anymore. I couldn't read my paper with her yak, yak, yakking behind me. She told the same thing to at least four friends. Then I had this kid opposite me with his mother. He …
A What was *he* doing to annoy you?
J He had one of these mini-computer things …
A A Game Boy!
J Yeah, one of those and he was head down playing this thing all the time – zing, ping, bang – all those noises coming from it. He never looked up once. When his mum asked him to say hello he just grunted, 'Uh!'. So impolite!
A I know. Kids these days, they're so badly-behaved. Did you book your ticket online this time?
J I tried to.
J What happened?
A Well, I followed the instructions, one by one and got right to the end and it asked me for my password. Password? I didn't know I had one for train travel. So I thought 'OK, I'll ring instead.'
A Maybe not the best idea.
J Er- no so I rang the train company and of course I got the usual recorded message – you know the type of thing: 'I'm afraid all our operators are busy at the moment.' Then music and 'Thank you for holding. I'm afraid our operators are still busy.' And more music, so I gave up. I bought a ticket at the station.
A It drives you mad, doesn't it? Life's too short to spend so long on the phone. Still, I usually do enjoy travelling by train.
J Me too, usually. It's better than driving. I hate driving into town these days. There's too much traffic. It's just jam after jam. And it's impossible to find a parking space. Parking's a nightmare! And car parks and parking meters are so expensive.
A I know. I remember when you could park all day for 50p. Come on, let's get out of here. Let's get a coffee.
J OK, but not Starbucks. I can't stand Starbucks.
A Why? I like the coffee.
J It's the size of the cups. They're all huge. Even the small one is too big for me and the biggest is so big, it's enormous, and there's so much choice – latte, skinny latte, soya latte, cappuccino. Frappuccino, single shot, double sh …
A OK! OK! Modern life! There's a small coffee bar round the corner. Let's go there.

T 10.12 **On the phone**

07700 900 333
0049 021 37474
0115 496 0499
0800 142 2466

T 10.13

01632 960200
0207 9460558
029 2018 0763
0061 44 501277

T 10.14

A = Adam, B = Brian, C = Carol, D = Donna, E = Emma, F = Flora

1 Brian and Adam

A Sorry Brian, you're breaking up. I couldn't hear that.
B I know Adam, it's not a good line. But, listen, I'm calling because I can't make it on Thursday. Are you free on Friday?
A Friday? I'm not sure. Can I get back to you?
B Sure. That's fine. Text me. Speak later!

2 Adam and Carol

A Hello, Carol, it's Adam. I'm trying to get hold of Brian.
C I'm afraid he's not in. Have you tried his mobile?
A Yeah. I tried that first but he's not answering.
C It's probably switched off.
A Can you give him a message then?
C Of course.

3 Donna, Emma, and Flora

D I'm afraid Brian's line's busy. Would you like to hold?
E Yes, please.
D It's ringing for you now.
E Thank you.
F Hello. Brian Doyle's office. Flora speaking.
E This is Emma Smith from Digby and Moss Associates.
F Oh, good morning Ms Smith. I'll put you through immediately.

4 Flora and Carol

C Hi, Flora. Can I speak to Brian, please?
F Oh, I'm afraid he has someone with him at the moment. Is it urgent?
C Just tell him Carol rang and I'll see him this evening.
F Will do. I hope there isn't a problem.

UNIT 11

T 11.1 Gareth Malone

1 A When did he start playing the piano?
B When he was three.
2 A How long has he been playing the piano?
B Since he was three.
3 A When did he start teaching singing?
B When he was 23.
4 A How long has he been teaching singing?
B Since he was 23.
5 A When did he make his first TV programme?
B In 2007.
6 A How long has he been making TV programmes?
B Since 2007.
7 A How many programmes has he made?
B Three.
8 A How long has he been living in London?
B For about 30 years.

T 11.2

1 A My sister's working in New York.
B How long has she been working there?
A Only a couple of months.
2 A I'm training to run the marathon.
B How long have you been training?
A Since Christmas. Wish me luck!
3 A My boss is on holiday.
B How long has he been away?
A Two weeks. It's great without him!
4 A I'm learning how to drive.
B How long have you been learning?
A Nearly two years. I've failed my test three times.
5 A I know Maria very well.
B How long have you known her?
A Since we were at school together.
6 A I have the new iPad.
B How long have you had it?
A I only got it yesterday.

T 11.3 ***What have they been doing?***

1 A Why are the students bored?
B Because the teacher's been talking for hours and they haven't understood a word.
2 A Why has he got a sore throat?
B Because he's been singing too much. He's sung every night for the last 3 weeks.
3 A Why are they so tired and dirty?
B Because they've been playing rugby, but they're happy because they've won the match.
4 A Why has he got backache?
B Because he's been digging the garden. He's planted six rows of cabbages.
5 A Why is she covered in paint?
B Because she's been decorating her flat. She's painted two walls already.
6 A Why have they got no money left?
B Because they've been shopping. They've spent over £200.

T 11.4 ***I haven't seen you for ages!***

S = Sophie, M = Mike

S Mike! I'm over here!
M Sophie! You look great! You haven't changed a bit.
S Oh, I don't know. It's been over ten years. I'm definitely older if not wiser.
M Well, you look just the same to me. Come on! We've got over ten years to catch up on and not a lot of time! My plane leaves at 7.00 this evening.
S Tell me about you first. How long have you been working in Madrid? What are you doing there?
M Well, I work for a big international IT company and at the moment I'm based in Madrid. I've been there about eighteen months now.
S Wow, that sounds important. Are you enjoying it?
M Yeah, very much. But there's a chance that I'll have to move to Germany in three months. That's where the headquarters are.
S That sounds interesting too.
M Yeah, but I have a Spanish girlfriend now.
S Ah, I see. What's her name?
M Rosa.You'd like her – she's great fun. We've been going out nearly a year now.
S Whoah! That sounds serious. Does she speak English?
M Oh, yes. Her English is much better than my Spanish. I started going to Spanish lessons six months ago but I still find Spanish pronunciation's really difficult.
S I know.
M Oh, yeah you studied languages, didn't you?
S Yes, I studied French and German at university but I've also been trying learn Swedish for the last few years.
M Swedish! Why? Come on, now it's your turn Sophie. Tell me about you.

T 11.5

S = Sophie, M = Mike

M Tell me about you.
S Well, I got married a year ago to a Swedish guy. Ragnar, Ragnar Hansson.
M Where did you meet him?
S We met while I was working in Stockholm.
M What were you doing there?
S Well, after university I studied fashion design and my first job was in Sweden, as a buyer for H&M Fashion.
M Really! How long did you do that?
S I worked there for over three years. Ragnar was my boss.
M Ah, did you get married in Sweden?
S Yes, we did. My parents came over for the wedding.
M And do you still work in Sweden?
S No, we don't. We've both got new jobs in the UK.
M How long have you been back?
S About ten months. We've been trying to buy a flat since we got back.
M So, where have you been living?
S With my parents. They're lovely, but it's not great and we're expecting a baby next April, so we really need a place of our own.
M Oh, congratulations! I hope you find somewhere soon. Oh, look at the time, I'll have to rush to catch my plane.
S Bye, Mike. It's been great seeing you again. Let's keep in touch from now on.
M Yeah, it's been great. Maybe next time you can meet Rosa and I can meet Ragnar.

T 11.6 Alison's life

I didn't marry until quite late. I met Ben when I was 30 and we didn't marry until I was 33, that was in 2006. We got married in a church near where my mum lives. I had been engaged before that to another boy, Mark, we'd been together over ten years, since school in fact, and I think we just got bored with each other. Ben and I had a great honeymoon, we toured America, we were away for three weeks. And soon after that I found I was pregnant. That was Ellen, our first baby, she was born the year after we got married, and two years after that, in 2009, we had the twins, Tessa and Tom. They've been keeping us busy ever since! I'm exhausted most of the time but they're great fun. I'm really glad I married Ben, he's a great dad. I want it to be forever. My mum and dad divorced when I was just thirteen and I don't want us to do that.

T 11.7 Good news, bad news

1 A My wife had a baby last night.
B Congratulations! Was it a boy or girl?
A A boy. William James.
B How much did he weigh?
A 4.1 kilos.
B Ooh! A big boy! How are mother and baby doing?
A They're fine.
B That's wonderful. Give her my love when you see her.
A I will do. Thanks.
2 A Alfie and I have got engaged.
B That's fantastic news! Congratulations!
A Do you like my ring?
B Wow! Diamonds! It's beautiful. When's the wedding?
A We're thinking of getting married next spring.
B I hope I'm invited.
A Of course you are. I want you to be a bridesmaid.
B Really? I'd love that. I've never been one before.
3 A Have you heard about Bill and Josie?
B No! What's happened?
A Well, they've been having a tough time recently.
B I know, they haven't been getting on well at all.
A Mm. Well, they've finally decided to split up.
B I'm so sorry to hear that. What a shame!
A Yes, I always thought they were so good together.
4 A We lost Grandpa last week.
B I know. Your dad told me. I'm so sorry. He was a lovely man. Everyone was really fond of him.
A He and Grandma were together nearly 60 years.
B That's incredible. How old was he?
A 88.
B And how's your Grandma coping?
A She's OK. She's got her family around her.
B Well, I'm sure you all have wonderful memories of him.

UNIT 12

T 12.1 Real possibilities

A What are you doing this weekend?
B Mmm … if the weather's nice, we'll go for a picnic.
A Ooh! Sounds nice. Where to?
B Not sure. We might go to the park, or we might go to the country.
A Well, I'm sure you'll have fun!

T 12.2

1 A What are you doing this weekend?
B Mmm … if it's sunny, we'll go swimming.
A Ooh! Sounds great! Where to?
B Don't know. We might go to the outdoor pool, or we might go to the river.
A Well, I'm sure you'll have a good time!

2 A What are you doing this weekend?
B Mmm, well … if it rains, we'll go shopping.
A Sounds a good idea! Where to?
B Not sure. We might go to the High Street, or we might go to a shopping centre.
A Well, I'm sure you'll enjoy it!

3 A What are you doing this weekend?
B Mmm … if we have time, we'll see some friends.
A Sounds good! What will you do?
B Don't know. We might go to a restaurant, or we might just go to the pub.
A Well, I'm sure you'll have fun!

T 12.3 *going to* **and** *might*

1 A What are you going to do after school?
B I don't know. I might go home or I might go into town.

2 A Where are you going on your next holiday?
B I'm not sure. I might go to Spain, or I might go to Turkey.

3 A What are you going to study at university?
B I haven't decided. I might study languages, or I might study business.

4 A What are you going to buy Jane for her birthday?
B I'm not sure. I might buy her a T-shirt, or I might buy her some make-up.

5 A When are you going to see your boyfriend again?
B I don't know. I might see him on Friday night, or I might see him on Saturday afternoon.

T 12.4 **Tara and Ben**

1 Tara

When I leave school, first I'm going to have a few weeks' holiday. I'm going to see my brother in Italy. Then I'm going to university. I'm going to study economics. If I do well at university, I'll get a good job and if I get a good job, I'll earn lots of money! I hope so anyway!

2 Ben

I'm not very good at decisions. I don't really know what I want to do. I might go to work for my father. He's got a shop, but that's not very interesting. Or I might go travelling with my friend James. The problem is that I don't have much money. So I might get a job in a bar or a shop and save some. I'm quite good with computers, so I might do a course in computer programming. Who knows?

T 12.5 **Advice, warnings, threats**

1 If you take these pills, you'll feel better.
2 If you eat junk food, you'll get fat.
3 You'll fail your exams if you don't do your homework.
4 Careful! If you touch that, you'll get an electric shock!
5 If you don't do what I say, I'll kill you!

T 12.6 **Lily's dream**

I'd love a baby brother. If I had a baby brother, I would play with him all the time. We'd have a lot of fun. I'd be so happy! I wouldn't ask my mum and dad for anything else!

T 12.7

Sam's Dream

I'd like to be taller. If I were taller, I'd be in the first team at rugby. And if I played really well, I'd be captain. And then if I practised really hard, maybe one day I could play for England! My dad would be so proud of me!

Annie's Dream

I have two young kids. I love them, but I never have any time to myself. If I had a free weekend, I'd stay in bed all day. I'd read magazines and watch TV. Then I'd sleep all night and my children wouldn't wake me. Ah, Heaven!

T 12.8 **Tony's life**

Well, he's not much good at anything. He hasn't had a job since he left school so he hasn't got any money so he can't buy any new clothes. He never looks smart. And he doesn't know what kind of job he wants. He's not ambitious at all so he doesn't apply for many jobs. I think the problem is that he's lazy. He doesn't get up till midday. And he doesn't shave, and he doesn't even shower often. He doesn't look good. Maybe that's why he hasn't got a girlfriend. He's useless!

T 12.9 **If Tony had a job, …**

If Tony had a job he'd have some money.
If he had some money, he could buy some new clothes.
If he had some nice clothes, he'd look smarter.
If he was a bit more ambitious, he would apply for more jobs.
If he weren't so lazy, he'd get up before midday.
If he shaved and showered more, he'd look better.
If he looked better, he might get a girlfriend and that would help him a lot.

T 12.10

1 Jimmy's problem

J = Jimmy, A = Amy

J Amy, can I talk to you for a minute?
A Sure. What about?
J Well, I've got a bit of a problem. You know I'm in my first year at university. I'm really enjoying the course. I love what I'm doing, studying physics, but …
A I was waiting for a but!
J Yes, you're right! But I'm also in a band. There are three of us, and we've been playing together for a couple of years, and we've just got a recording contract, which is something we've been trying to get for ages.
A And you can't do both. Is that it?
J Absolutely! The other guys want me to drop out of university. If the record was a success, we'd go on tour. We might go to Europe for three months, or we might even get to America! That would be amazing!
A But if you dropped out of university and the band wasn't a success, then what would you do?
J Exactly! That's the problem! But if I didn't give the band a chance, I'd regret it for the rest of my life! This is our one big chance!
A But if the band didn't work, you wouldn't have a career.
J And my parents would go crazy! Amy! Help me! What do I do?
A Well, I think you should try with the band. If it doesn't work, it's not the end of the world. You could always go back to university. And you might hit the big time in the music business!

2 Fiona's problem

F= Fiona, J = Jenny

F Jenny! You've got to help me!
J What is it? Are you all right?
F Yes, I'm fine, but I'm having terrible boyfriend trouble.
J What, with Sam? I thought you two were fine?
F We are, sort of. I'm very fond of Sam. We've been going out for over a year, and we do things together, but …
J But, but …
F But … I've met this guy at work, and he's asked me out, and I don't know what to do!
J Wow! This is sudden!
F Well, not really. The thing is, everyone thinks that Sam and I are a couple and we're going to get married. But for me, Sam is more like a brother! I can't marry him! If I married Sam, I'd be so unhappy! But if I broke up with him, he would be heart-broken! I don't know what he'd do.
J But it sounds like you have to say something. If you don't tell him now, it might be worse later. Who's this man at work?
F Well, he's really lovely. His name's Harry. He's my age, and he's very good-looking. We work together, and it's such fun! He really makes me laugh. He isn't pushing me to go out with him, but …
J But you'd really like to. I know.
F And if I don't say anything to him, he might think I don't like him. So what do I do?
J Well, if I were you, I wouldn't say anything to this guy at work yet. Be nice to him, but don't encourage him.
F But he might go out with another girl!
J If he started going out with another girl, then you'd know what sort of man he was. If he likes you, he'll wait. But you have to talk to Sam first.

T 12.11 **A year later**

Jimmy

Well, we made a record, and we went on tour to Japan, and the band's doing really not bad! We haven't hit the big time, but we've had one or two hits, and we're very well-known in some parts of the world. We haven't been to America yet, but we hope to soon.
And my parents have been OK. Well, my mother has. My father keeps saying 'When are you going to get a real job?', but he doesn't approve of anything I do, so that's nothing new. So it was the right decision!

Fiona

Well, I told Sam, and in fact he was fine about it! He also said that he thought we were more like brother and sister! I was quite upset that he wasn't more upset! Anyway, he was all right about it. And of course all our friends said that they had seen this all along …
So I broke up with Sam, and it didn't work out with Harry at all. It turned out that he was engaged to a lovely French girl, and he was just being friendly with me. So I got the situation completely wrong! Never mind. I'm single, but that's fine. I'll just see what happens.

T 12.12 **Note-taking**

Part 1

Generally I am optimistic about the future. If you go back to the beginning of the 19th century most Americans lived for about 50 years. Nowadays life expectancy is nearly 80 years. This is because of great improvements in healthcare and technology. There's no reason why this won't continue far into

the 21st century. The world has changed so much in the last 20 years – we have DNA, microchips and the Internet. We must teach people to use this new technology. I believe that one day everybody will have computers and access to the Internet.
For over two thousand years we have tried to understand our environment, now we are beginning to control it as well. We are learning how to control the weather and one day will learn to control earthquakes and volcanoes. Eventually illness and disease will not exist because we will build new body parts – new livers, kidneys, hearts, lungs – like spare parts for a car.
People say world population is an increasing problem, but if people become more educated and richer, they won't need or want to have so many children and the population of many countries will decrease.
I believe that one day there will be a world government because the resources of the world will have to be managed at a global level. We need to make global decisions. We already have a world language called English and there is now a worldwide communication system called the Internet.

T 12.13

Part 2

I do have some reasons to be pessimistic. I think people will remain fundamentally the same. There will always be stupid people as well as intelligent people. There will always be cruel people who want to fight and wage wars. There will be people who don't understand that we have to look after our world, our forests, our oceans, our atmosphere. There will certainly always be people who think that money is everything. We have the technology, but we need the wisdom to go with it.

T 12.14 Prepositions

1 It wasn't an accident. She broke it on purpose.
2 What's for dinner? I'm starving.
3 He isn't in the office this week. He's away on business.
4 When you go, keep in touch with me via email.
5 Transport workers are on strike for better pay.
6 I don't need other people. I like being by myself.

T 12.15 Thank you and goodbye!

1 **A** Well, it's late. I must be going now. Thank you so much for a lovely evening.
B My pleasure!
A And the food was delicious!
B I'm glad you liked it. I hope you get home all right. Bye!
A Bye! And thanks again!

2 **A** Thank you so much! It was so kind of you.
B That's all right!
A I'm so grateful for all your help.
B Don't mention it!
A Er … Would you mind helping me with just one more thing?
B Of course not! No problem!

3 **A** I hope you have a good flight! Who's meeting you?
B My sister Sarah.
A Remember to give her my love.
B Will do. OK, it's boarding. I have to go now. Bye!
A Right. Look after yourself! Bye!

4 **A** Thanks for having me. I really enjoyed staying with you.
B You're welcome. It was a pleasure. Come back and see us again sometime!
A That's very kind. Maybe next year!
C That would be lovely!

5 **A** Have a safe journey!
B Thanks. I'll text you when I arrive.
A Say hello to your parents from me.
B I will. Oh! The train's leaving!
A OK! Bye! Take care!
B See you soon! Bye!

6 **A** Goodbye! And thanks for everything! It was great fun!
B I really enjoyed being your teacher.
C We learned such a lot with you!
B Thank you! Good luck with your English. Keep practising!
A We will!

Grammar Reference

UNIT 1

1.1 Tenses

This unit has examples of the Present Simple and Present Continuous, the Past Simple, and two future forms: *going to* and the Present Continuous for the future.

All these tenses are covered again in later units.

Present tenses Unit 2
Past tenses Units 3 and 9
Future forms Unit 5

The aim in this unit is to revise what you already know.

Present tenses
She ***lives*** *in London.*
I ***earn*** *$100 a day.*
I'm saving *money for my education.*
*They****'re studying*** *in a language school.*

Past tense
They ***moved*** *to Canada thirty years ago.*
I ***had*** *a bad accident last month.*

Future forms
I'm going to *study for a Master's degree.*
What ***are you doing*** *tonight?*

1.2 Auxiliary verbs

The Present Continuous uses the auxiliary verb *to be* in all forms.

Positive
She ***is*** *reading.*
They ***are*** *watching a film.*

Question
Is *she reading?*
What ***are*** *they watching?*

Negative
He ***isn't*** *learning French.*
I'm not *sleeping.*

Verb forms with no auxiliary verb
In the Present Simple and the Past Simple there is no auxiliary verb in the positive. We use the auxiliary verb *do* in the questions and negatives.

Positive
They live in Australia.
He arrived yesterday.

Question
Do *they live in London?*
Where ***did*** *Bill go?*

Negative
I ***don't*** *work in New York.*
We ***didn't*** *watch TV.*

1.3 Questions

1 *Yes/No* questions have no question word.
Are you hot? *Yes, I am./No, I'm not.*
Does he speak English? *Yes, he does./No, he doesn't.*

2 Questions can begin with a question word.

what	where	which	how	who	when	why	whose

Where*'s the station?*
Why *are you laughing?*
Whose *is this coat?*
How *does she go to work?*

3 *What, which,* and *whose* can be followed by a noun.
What *size do you take?*
Which *coat is yours?*
Whose *book is this?*

4 *Which* is generally used when there is a limited choice.
Which *is your pen? The black one or the blue one?*

This rule is not always true.
What / ***Which*** | *newspaper do you read?*

5 *How* can be followed by an adjective or an adverb.
How big *is his new car?*
How fast *does it go?*

How can also be followed by *much* or *many.*
How much *is this sandwich?*
How many *brothers and sisters have you got?*

UNIT 2

2.1 Present Simple

Form

Positive and negative

I You We They	live don't live	near here.
He She It	lives doesn't live	

Question

Where	do	I you we they	live?
	does	he she it	

	Short answer
Do you like Peter?	***Yes, I do.***
Does he speak French?	***No, he doesn't.***

Use

The Present Simple is used to express:

1 a habit.
I ***get up*** *at 7.30.*
Jo ***smokes*** *too much.*

2 a fact which is always true.
Vegetarians ***don't eat*** *meat.*
We ***come*** *from Spain.*

3 a fact which is true for a long time.
I ***live*** *in Oxford.*
She ***works*** *in a bank.*

2.2 Present Continuous

Form

am/is/are + *-ing* (present participle)

Positive and negative

I	'm (am) 'm not	working.
He She It	's (is) isn't	
You We They	're (are) aren't	

Question

What	am	I	wearing?
	is	he she it	
	are	you we they	

	Short answer	
Are you going?	***Yes**, I **am**./**No**, I'**m not**.*	NOT ~~*Yes, I'm.*~~
Is Anna working?	***Yes**, she **is**./**No**, she **isn't**.*	NOT ~~*Yes, she's.*~~

Use

The Present Continuous is used to express:

1 an activity happening now.

*They'**re playing** football in the garden.*
*She can't talk now because she'**s washing** her hair.*

2 an activity happening around now, but perhaps not at the moment of speaking.

*He'**s studying** maths at university.*
*I'**m reading** a good book at the moment.*

3 a planned future arrangement.

*I'**m seeing** the doctor at 10.00 tomorrow.*
*What **are** you **doing** this evening?*

2.3 Present Simple and Present Continuous

1 Read the right and wrong sentences.

*Fraser **comes** from Scotland.*
NOT ~~*Fraser is coming from Scotland.*~~
*I'**m reading** a good book at the moment.*
NOT ~~*I read a good book at the moment.*~~

2 Some verbs express a state, not an activity, and are usually used in the Present Simple only.

*She **likes** the Rolling Stones.*
NOT ~~*She's liking the Rolling Stones.*~~
*I **know** what you mean.*
NOT ~~*I'm knowing what you mean.*~~

Similar verbs are *think, agree, understand, love*.

2.4 *have got/have*

Form

Positive

I/You/We/They	have 've got	two sisters.
He/She	has 's got	

Negative

I/You/We/They	don't have haven't got	any money.
He/She	doesn't have hasn't got	

Question

Do	I/you/ we/they	have	a new car?
Does	he/she		
Have	I/you/ we/they	got	a new car?
Has	he/she		

Short answer

Do you have an iPhone?	***Yes, I do./No, I don't.***
Have you got an iPhone?	***Yes, I have./No, I haven't.***

Note

We can use contractions (*'ve* and *'s*) with *have got*, but not with *have*.
*I'**ve got** a sister.*
*I **have** a sister.* NOT ~~*I've a sister.*~~

Use

1 *Have* and *have got* mean the same. *Have got* is more informal. We use it a lot when we speak, but not so much when we write.

***Have** you **got** the time?*
*The UK **has** a population of 60 million.*

In American English, *have* + *do/does* is much more common.

2 *Have* and *have got* express possession.

I have I've got	a new car.
She has She's got	three children.
He has He's got	blond hair.

3 When *have* + noun expresses an activity or a habit, *have* (not *have got*) is used. Look at these sentences.

*I **have** a shower every day.*
NOT ~~*I've got a shower every day.*~~

What time do you have lunch?
NOT ~~*What time have you got lunch?*~~

4 In the past tense, we use *had* with *did* and *didn't*.

*I **had** a bicycle when I was young.*
***Did** you **have** a nice weekend?*
*I **didn't have** any money when I was a student.*

3.1 Past Simple

Form

The form of the Past Simple is the same for all persons.

Positive

I He/She/It You We They	finished arrived went	yesterday.

Negative

The negative of the Past Simple is formed with *didn't*.

I He/She/It You We They	didn't (did not) arrive	yesterday.

Question

The question in the Past Simple is formed with *did*.

When	did	she/you/they/etc.	arrive?

	Short answer
Did you go to work yesterday?	***Yes, I did.***
Did it rain last night?	***No, it didn't.***

Spelling of regular verbs

1 The normal rule is to add *-ed* or *-d*.
work/work**ed** start/start**ed** live/liv**ed** love/lov**ed**

2 Some short verbs with only one syllable double the consonant.
stop/sto**pped** plan/pla**nned**

3 Verbs ending in a consonant + *-y* , change the *-y* to *-ied*.
stud**y**/stud**ied** carr**y**/carr**ied**

But …
play/play**ed** enjoy/enjoy**ed**

There are many common irregular verbs. See the list on p158.

Use

The Past Simple expresses a completed past action. Notice some of the time expressions.

*We **played** tennis last Sunday.*
*I **worked** in London in 2007.*
*John **left** two minutes ago.*

3.2 Past Continuous

Form

was/were + verb *-ing* (present participle)

Positive and negative

I/He/She/It	was wasn't (was not)	working.
You/We/They	were weren't (were not)	

Question

What	was	I he she it	doing?
	were	you we they	

	Short answer
Were you working yesterday?	***Yes, I was./No, I wasn't.***

Use

1 The Past Continuous expresses a past activity that has duration.
*I had a good time while I **was living** in Paris.*
*You **were making** a lot of noise last night. **Were** you **having** a party?*

2 The activity was in progress *before*, and probably *after*, a time in the past.
*'What **were** you **doing** at 8.00 last night?' 'I **was watching** TV.'*
*When I woke up this morning, the sun **was shining**.*

3.3 Past Simple and Past Continuous

1 The Past Simple expresses completed past actions. The Past Continuous expresses activities in progress. Compare these sentences.
*I **washed** my hair last night.*
*I **was washing** my hair when you **phoned**.*
*'What **did** you **do** at the weekend?' 'I **played** tennis.'*
*We **were playing** tennis when it **started** to rain.*

2 A Past Simple action can interrupt a Past Continuous activity in progress.
*When I **phoned** Simon he **was having** a shower.*
*I **was doing** my homework when Jane **arrived**.*

3 In stories, the Past Continuous can describe the scene. The Past Simple tells the action.
*It **was** a beautiful day. The sun **was shining** and the birds **were singing**, so we **decided** to go for a picnic. We **put** everything in the car …*

3.4 Prepositions in time expressions

at	**in**	**on**
at six o'clock at midnight at Christmas at the weekend	in 2007 in the morning/ afternoon/evening in summer in two weeks' time	on Saturday on Monday morning on Christmas Day on January 18th

no preposition	
two weeks ago yesterday evening this afternoon	next month tomorrow morning tonight

UNIT 4

4.1 Expressions of quantity

Count and uncount nouns

1 It is important to understand the difference between count and uncount nouns.

Count nouns	Uncount nouns
a cup	water
a girl	sugar
an apple	milk
an egg	music
a pound	money

We can say *three cups*, *two girls*, *ten pounds*. We can count them. We cannot say ~~*two waters*~~, ~~*three musics*~~, ~~*one money*~~. We cannot count them.

2 Count nouns can be singular or plural.

*This **cup** is full.*
*These **cups are** empty.*

Uncount nouns can only be singular.

*The **water** is cold.*
*The **weather was** terrible.*

much **and** ***many***

1 We use *much* with uncount nouns in questions and negatives.

*How **much money** have you got?*
*There isn't **much milk** left.*

2 We use *many* with count nouns in questions and negatives.

*How **many people** were at the party?*
*I didn't take **many photos** on holiday.*

some **and** ***any***

1 *Some* is used in positive sentences.

*I'd like **some** sugar.*

2 *Any* is used in questions and negatives.

*Is there **any** sugar in this tea?*
*Have you got **any** brothers and sisters?*
*We don't have **any** washing-up liquid.*
*I didn't buy **any** apples.*

3 We use *some* in questions that are requests or offers.

*Can I have **some** cake?*
*Would you like **some** tea?*

4 The rules are the same for *someone*, *anything*, *anybody*, *somewhere*, etc.

*I've got **something** for you.*
*Hello? Is **anybody** here?*
*There isn't **anywhere** to go in my town.*

a few **and** ***a little***

1 We use *a few* with count nouns.

*There are **a few biscuits** left, but not many.*

2 We use *a little* with uncount nouns.

*I only have **a little time**.*

a lot/lots of

1 We use *a lot/lots of* with both count and uncount nouns.

*There's **a lot of butter**.*
*I've got **lots of friends**.*

2 *A lot/lots of* can be used in questions and negatives.

*Are there **lots of tourists** in your country?*
*There isn't **a lot of butter**, but there's enough.*

4.2 Articles – *a*, *an*, and *the*

1 The indefinite article *a* or *an* is used with singular, count nouns to refer to a thing or an idea for the first time.

*We have **a cat** and **a dog**.*
*There's **a supermarket** in Adam Street.*

2 The definite article *the* is used with singular and plural, count and uncount nouns when both the speaker and the listener know the thing or idea already.

*We have a cat and a dog. **The cat** is old, but **the dog** is just a puppy.*
*I'm going to **the supermarket**. Do you want anything?* (We both know which supermarket.)

Indefinite article

The indefinite article is used:

1 with professions.

*I'm **a teacher**.*
*She's **an architect**.*

2 with some expressions of quantity.

a pair of ***a little*** ***a couple of*** ***a few***

3 with some expressions of frequency.

once a week ***three times a day***

4 in exclamations with *what* + a count noun.

***What a** lovely **day**!*
***What a pity**!*

Definite article

The definite article is used:

1 before seas, rivers, hotels, pubs, theatres, museums, and newspapers.

the Atlantic ***the British Museum***
The Times ***the Ritz***

2 if there is only one of something.

the sun ***the Queen*** ***the Government***

3 with superlative adjectives.

*He's **the richest man** in the world.*
*Jane's **the oldest** in the class.*

No article

There is no article:

1 before plural and uncount nouns when talking about things in general.

I like potatoes.
Milk is good for you.

2 before countries, towns, streets, languages, magazines, meals, airports, stations, and mountains.

I had lunch with John.
I bought Cosmopolitan *at Victoria Station.*

3 before some places and with some forms of transport.

at home	in/to bed	at/to work
at/to school/university	by bus	by plane
by car	by train	on foot

*She goes to work **by bus**.*
*I was **at home** yesterday evening.*

4 in exclamations with *What* + an uncount noun.

***What** beautiful **weather**!* ***What** loud **music**!*

Note

In the phrase *go home*, there is no article and no preposition.

*I went **home** early.* NOT ~~*I went to home.*~~

5.1 Verb patterns

Here are four verb patterns. There is a list of verb patterns on p158.

1 Verb + *to* + infinitive
*They **want to buy** a new car.* *I'd **like to go** abroad.*

2 Verb + *-ing*
*We **love going** to parties.* *I **enjoy travelling** abroad.*

3 Verb + *-ing* or + *to* + infinitive with no change in meaning
*It **started to rain/raining**.*
*I **continued to work/working** in the library.*

4 Verb + preposition + *-ing*
*We're **thinking of moving** house.*
*I'm **looking forward to having** more free time.*

like doing and *would like to do*

1 *Like doing* and *love doing* express a general enjoyment.
*I **like working** as a teacher.* = I am a teacher and I enjoy it.
*I **love dancing**.* = This is one of my hobbies.

2 *Would like to do* and *would love to do* express a preference now or at a specific time.
*I'd **like to be** a teacher.* = When I grow up, I want to be a teacher.
*Thanks. **I'd love to dance**.* = At a party. I'm pleased you asked me.

Question	Short answer
Would you like to dance?	*Yes, I would./Yes, I'd love to.*
Would you like to come for a walk?	*Yes, I would./No, thank you.*

Note
No, I wouldn't is not common because it is impolite.

5.2 Future forms

will

Form

will + infinitive without *to*
Will is a modal auxiliary verb. There is an introduction to modal auxiliary verbs on p143. The forms of *will* are the same for all persons.

Positive and negative

I/He/She/It/You/We/They	'll (will) won't	come. help you. invite Tom.

Question
*What time **will** he/you/they **be back**?*

	Short answer
Will you help me?	***Yes, I will.***

Note
No, I won't is impolite. It means 'I don't want to help you.'
A polite way of saying '*no*' here is '*I'm afraid I can't.*'
'*Will you give me a lift?*' '*Sorry, **I'm afraid I can't.***'

Use

Will is used:

1 to express a future intention made *at* the moment of speaking.
*'It's Jane's birthday.' 'Is it? **I'll buy** her some flowers.'*
***I'll give** you my phone number.*
*'Do you want the blue or the red pen?' '**I'll take** the red one.'*

2 to express an offer.
***I'll carry** your suitcase.* *We**'ll do** the washing-up.*

3 to express a future fact. The speaker thinks it is sure to happen in the future.
***I'll be** 30 next week.* ***It will be** a nice day tomorrow.*

This use is called the pure future. The speaker is talking about the future without expressing an intention, plan, or personal opinion.

going to

Form

am/is/are + *going* + *to* + infinitive

Positive and negative

I	'm (am) 'm not	going to leave.
He/She It	's (is) isn't	
You We They	're (are) aren't	

Question

When	am	I	going to arrive?
	is	he/she/it	
	are	you/we/they	

	Short answer
Are they going to get married?	*Yes, they **are**./No, they **aren't**.*

Use

Going to is used:

1 to express a future decision, intention, or plan made *before* the moment of speaking.
*How long **are** they **going to stay** in Rome?*
*She **isn't going to have** a birthday party.*

2 when we can see or feel now that something is certain to happen in the future.
*Look at these clouds! It's **going to rain**.*
*Watch out! You**'re going to drop that vase**.*

will or *going to*?

Look at the use of *will* and *going to* in these sentences.

*I'm **going to make** a chicken casserole for dinner.*
(I decided this morning and bought everything for it.)
*What can I cook for dinner? Er ... I know! **I'll make** a chicken casserole!* (I decided at the moment of speaking.)

Present Continuous

The Present Continuous for the future is used:

1 to express a planned future arrangement.
***I'm meeting** my cousin for lunch.*
*'What **are you doing** this weekend?'*
*'**We're having** a party. Can you come?'*

2 with the verbs *go* and *come*.
***She's coming** on Friday.*
***I'm going** home early tonight.*

Sometimes there is little or no difference between *going to* and the Present Continuous to express a future arrangement.
*We**'re seeing** a film this evening.*
*We're **going to** see a film this evening.*

UNIT 6

6.1 *What ... like?*

Form

what + *to be* + subject + *like*?

A ***What's*** *your teacher* ***like?*** **B** *She's very patient.*
A ***What are*** *his parents* ***like?*** **B** *They're very kind.*
A ***What*** *was your holiday* ***like?*** **B** *Wonderful. We swam a lot.*
A ***What*** *were the beaches* ***like?*** **B** *OK, but some were dirty.*

Note

1 We don't use *like* in the answer.
She's patient. NOT ~~*She's like patient.*~~

2 *Like* in this question is a preposition, not a verb:
'What's Jim ***like?****' 'He's intelligent and kind, and very good-looking.'*

3 In these sentences *like* is a verb:
'What does Jim ***like?****' 'He* ***likes*** *motorbikes and playing tennis.'*

Use

1 *What ... like?* means 'Describe somebody or something. Tell me about it. I don't know anything about it.'

2 *How's your mother?* asks about health. It doesn't ask for a description.
'How's your mother?' 'She's very well, thank you.'

6.2 Comparative and superlative adjectives

Form

1 Look at the chart.

		Comparative	Superlative
Short adjectives	cheap small *big	cheaper smaller bigger	cheapest smallest biggest
Adjectives that end in -*y*	funny early heavy	funnier earlier heavier	funniest earliest heaviest
Adjectives with two syllables or more	careful boring expensive interesting	more careful more boring more expensive more interesting	most careful most boring most expensive most interesting
Irregular adjectives	far good bad	further better worse	furthest best worst

*For short adjectives with one vowel + one consonant, double the consonant: *hot/hotter/hottest; fat/fatter/fattest.*

2 *Than* is often used after a comparative adjective.
I'm ***younger than*** *Barbara.*
Barbara's ***more intelligent than*** *Sarah.*

Much can come before the comparative to give emphasis.
She's ***much nicer than*** *her sister.*
Is Tokyo ***much more modern than*** *London?*

3 *The* is used before superlative adjectives.
He's ***the funniest*** *boy in the class.*
Which is ***the tallest*** *building in the world?*

Use

1 Comparatives compare one thing, person, or action with another.
She's ***taller*** *than me.*
London's ***more expensive*** *than Rome.*

2 We use superlatives to compare somebody or something with the whole group.
She's the ***tallest*** *in the class.*
It's the ***most expensive*** *hotel in the world.*

3 *As ... as* shows that something is the same or equal.
Jim's ***as tall as*** *Peter.*
I'm ***as worried as*** *you are.*

4 *Not as ... as* shows that something isn't the same or equal.
*She is****n't as tall as*** *her mother.*
*He is****n't*** *nearly* ***as clever as*** *me!*

UNIT 7

7.1 Present Perfect

Form

have/has + *-ed* (past participle)
The past participle of regular verbs ends in *-ed*. There are many common irregular verbs. See the list on p158.

Positive and negative

I You/We/They	've (have) haven't	won a competition.
He/She/It	's (has) hasn't	

Question

Have	I you/we/they	been to the United States?
Has	he/she/it	

	Short answer
Have you been to Las Vegas?	***Yes,*** *I* ***have./No,*** *I* ***haven't.***
Has she ever written a novel?	***Yes,*** *she* ***has./No,*** *she* ***hasn't.***

Note

We cannot use *I've, they've, he's*, etc. in short answers.
Yes, I have. NOT ~~*Yes, I've.*~~
Yes, we have. NOT ~~*Yes, we've.*~~

Use

1 The Present Perfect expresses an action or state which began in the past and continues to the present.
I've known *John for six years.*
How long ***have*** *you* ***worked*** *for* The London Gazette*?*

The time expressions *for* and *since* are common with this use. We use *for* with a period of time, and *since* with a point in time.
We've lived here ***for*** *three years.* (a period of time)
They've lived here ***since*** *2010.* (a point in time)

Note
In many languages, this use is expressed by a present tense. But in English, we say:
Peter ***has been*** *a teacher for ten years.*
NOT ~~*Peter is a teacher for ten years.*~~

2 The Present Perfect connects the present and the past. It expresses experiences in life before now.
*I****'ve met*** *a lot of famous people.* (before now)
She ***has won*** *a lot of awards.* (in her life)
*I****'ve travelled*** *a lot in Africa.* (in my life)
*She****'s written*** *three books.* (up to now)

The action can continue to the present, and probably into the future.
*He****'s made*** *six TV programmes.* (So far. He'll probably make more.)

Ever and *never* are common with this use.
Have you ***ever*** *been to Africa?*
I've ***never*** *played poker.*

3 The Present Perfect expresses a past action with results in the present. It is often a recent past action.
*I****'ve lost*** *my wallet.* (I haven't got it now.)
*The taxi****'s arrived****.* (It's outside the door now.)
Has *the postman* ***been****?* (Is there a parcel for me?)

The adverbs *just*, *already*, and *yet* are common with this use.

Yet is used in questions and negatives.
She's ***just*** *had some good news.*
I've ***already*** *had breakfast.*
Has the postman been ***yet****?*
It's 11.00 and she hasn't got up ***yet****.*

7.2 Present Perfect and Past Simple

1 Read and compare the use of the Past Simple and the Present Perfect in these sentences.
I ***lived*** *in Paris for two years, from 2007–2009.* (The action is finished.)
*I****'ve lived*** *in London since 2009.* (I still do. The action is not finished.)
*I****'ve been*** *to Scotland.* (This is an experience in my life.)
I ***went*** *with my husband two years ago.* (At a definite past time.)
*'****Have you ever flown*** *in a helicopter?' 'Yes, I* ***have****.'*
'Where ***did*** *you* ***fly****?' 'I* ***flew*** *over New York.'*
*'Oh dear, I****'ve broken*** *my glasses.'*
'What happened?'
'I ***dropped*** *them.'*

2 These are common time expressions used with the Past Simple and the Present Perfect.

Past Simple	Present Perfect
last week yesterday the day before yesterday in 1999 on July 21st three months ago for two weeks (but now ended)	since Monday ever never just already yet for two weeks (and continues)

UNIT 8

8.1 *have to*

Form
has/have + *to* + infinitive

Positive and negative

I You/We/They	have don't have	to	work hard.
He/She It	has doesn't have		

Question

Do	I/you/we/they	have to	work hard?
Does	he/she/it		

	Short answer
Do *you* ***have to*** *wear a uniform?*	*Yes, I* ***do****.*
Does *he* ***have to*** *go now?*	*No, he* ***doesn't****.*

Past of *have to*
The past tense of *have to* is *had to*, with *did* and *didn't* in the question and the negative.
I ***had to*** *get up early this morning.*
Why ***did*** *you* ***have to*** *work last weekend?*
I ***didn't have to*** *do any housework when I was a child.*

Use
1 *Have to* expresses strong obligation. The obligation comes from 'outside' – perhaps a law, a rule at school or work, or someone in authority.
You ***have to*** *pass a driving test if you want to drive a car.* (That's the law.)
I ***have to*** *start work at 8.00.* (My company says I must.)
The doctor says I ***have to*** *do more exercise.*

2 *Don't/doesn't have to* expresses absence of obligation (it isn't necessary).
You ***don't have to*** *do the washing-up. I've got a dishwasher.*
She ***doesn't have to*** *work on Monday. It's her day off.*
I ***didn't have to*** *get up early this morning, but I did get up because it was such a lovely day.*

Note
Have got to is more informal. It usually expresses an obligation on one particular occasion.
*Look at the time! I****'ve got to go****.*
*I'm going to bed. I****'ve got to get up*** *early tomorrow.*
*She****'s got to work*** *hard. Her exams start next week.*
The forms of *have got to* + infinitive are the same as *have got* + noun. See p137.

8.2 Introduction to modal auxiliary verbs

Form

These are modal auxiliary verbs.

can	could	must	shall	should	will	would

They have certain things in common:

1 They go with another verb and add meaning.
*He **can** play the guitar.*
*I **must** wash my hair.*

2 There is no *'s* in the third person singular. The form is the same for all persons.
*She **can dance** very well.*
*He **should try** harder.*
*It **will rain** soon.*
*We **must hurry**.*

3 There is no *do/does* in the question.
Can she sing?
***Shall we go** now?*

4 There is no *don't/doesn't* in the negative.
*I would**n't** like to be a teacher.*
*They ca**n't** speak French.*

Note
will not = won't
*It **won't** rain tomorrow.*

5 Most modal verbs refer to the present and future. Only *can* has a past tense form, *could*.
*I **could** swim when I was three.*

8.3 *should*

Form

should + infinitive without *to*
The forms of *should* are the same for all persons.

Positive and negative

I You/We/They He/She	should shouldn't	do more exercise. tell lies.

Question
***Should** I/she/they see a doctor?*
*Do you think I/he/we **should** see a doctor?*

	Short answer
Should I phone home?	***Yes,** you **should.***
Should I buy a motorbike?	***No,** you **shouldn't.***

Use

1 *Should* is used to express what the speaker thinks is the best thing to do. It expresses mild obligation, or advice.
*I **should** do more work.* (This is my opinion.)
*You **should** do more work.* (This is my advice.)
*Do you think we **should** stop?* (I'm asking for your opinion.)

2 *Shouldn't* expresses negative advice.
*You **shouldn't** sit so close to the TV. It's bad for your eyes.*

3 *Should* expresses the opinion of the speaker, and it is often introduced by *I think* or *I don't think*.
***I think** politicians **should** listen more.*
***I don't think** people **should** get married until they're 21.*

8.4 *must*

Form

must + infinitive without *to*
The forms of *must* are the same for all persons.

Positive and negative

I You/We/They He/She	must mustn't	try harder. steal.

Note
Questions with *must* are possible, but *have to* is more common.
*What time **do we have to** leave?*

Use

1 *Must* expresses strong obligation. Generally, this obligation comes from 'inside' the speaker.
*I **must** have a shower.* (I think this is necessary.)
*We **must** get a new car.*

2 *You must …* can express a strong suggestion.
***You must** see the Monet exhibition. It's wonderful.*
***You must** give me a call when you're next in town.*

UNIT 9

9.1 Past Perfect

Form

had + *-ed* past participle.
The past participle of regular verbs ends in *-ed*. There are many common irregular verbs. See the list on p158.

Positive and negative

I He/She/It You/We/They	'd (had) hadn't	arrived.

Question

Had	I he/she/it we/you/they	left already?

Short answer
Yes, I ***had****.*
No, they ***hadn't****.*

Use

1 We use the Past Perfect to express an action in the past which happened before another action in the past.
When I arrived at the theatre, the play ***had*** *already* ***started****.*

2 We use the Past Simple to express actions in the order they happened. Look at these actions in the Past Simple.

Action 1	Action 2
The bear ***went****.*	*The man* ***came*** *down from the tree.*
John ***left*** *the party.*	*I* ***arrived****.*
They ***walked*** *a long way.*	*They* ***were*** *tired.*

Notice how they are expressed using the Past Perfect.

Action 2	Action 1
The man came down from the tree …	*after the bear* ***had gone****.*
When I arrived at the party …	*John* ***had left****.*
They were tired …	*because they****'d walked*** *a long way.*

3 If it is clear that one action was completed before, it isn't necessary to use the Past Perfect.
I tidied up after everyone ***went*** *home.*
I tidied up after everyone ***had gone*** *home.*

9.2 Conjunctions

We use conjunctions to join sentences.

1 *when, while, as soon as, after, before, as,* and *until*, are conjunctions of time. They can go in two places in the sentence.
When *I arrived home, Tom was cooking the meal.*
Tom was talking to me ***while*** *he was cooking the meal.*
As soon as *I arrived home, Tom started cooking the meal.*
Tom cooked the meal ***after*** *I arrived/I'd arrived home.*
He had cooked the meal ***before*** *I arrived home.*
As *he was talking, I was thinking about the last time we'd met.*
He didn't start cooking the meal ***until*** *I arrived home.*

2 *so* is a conjunction of result.
He was bored ***so*** *he went for a walk.*
because is a conjunction of reason.
He went for a walk ***because*** *he was bored.*

3 *but* and *although* are conjunctions which join contrasting ideas.
It was raining, ***but*** *we played tennis.*
Although *it was raining, we played tennis.*

9.3 *so, such (a), so many, so much*

Form

so **+ adjective/adverb**
I was ***so*** *scared.*
He always drives ***so*** *fast.*

such a **+ adjective + singular noun**
She's ***such a*** *nice person.*

such **+ adjective + plural/uncountable noun**
The Smiths are ***such*** *friendly neighbours.*

so many **+ plural nouns**
Some children have ***so many*** *toys.*

so much **+ uncountable nouns**
Footballers earn ***so much*** *money these days.*

Use

So and *such* are used for emphasizing an adjective or noun. They are used more in spoken than written English. They are often exclamations, with an exclamation mark (!).
He works so hard! is stronger than *He works very hard.*

UNIT 10

10.1 The passive

Form

am/is/are was/were has/have been will	+ *-ed* (past participle)

The past participle of regular verbs ends in *-ed*. There are many common **irregular past participles**. See the list on p158.

Present
English ***is spoken*** *all over the world.*
100 million mobile phones ***are thrown away*** *every year.*
Fiat cars ***aren't made*** *in France.*
Where is coffee ***grown****?*

Past
The first text message ***was sent*** *in 1989.*
They ***weren't injured*** *in the accident.*
When ***was*** *television* ***invented****?*

Present Perfect
A lot of new features ***have been added****.*
*The bank****'s been robbed****!*
We ***haven't been invited*** *to the wedding.*

will
10,000 cars ***will be produced*** *next year.*
The cars ***won't be sold*** *in the UK.*

	Short answers
Are cars made in your country?	***Yes****, they* ***are./No****, they* ***aren't****.*
Has my car been repaired?	***Yes****, it* ***has./No****, it* ***hasn't****.*
Will landline phones be replaced by mobiles?	***Yes****, they* ***will./No****, they* ***won't****.*

Note
The passive infinitive (*to be* + *-ed*) is used after modal auxiliary verbs and other verbs which are followed by an infinitive.
Driving should ***be banned*** *in city centres.*
The house is going ***to be knocked down****.*

Use

1 The rules for tense usage in the passive are the same as in the active.
Present Simple to express habit:
My car ***is serviced*** *regularly.*
Past Simple to express a finished action in the past:
America ***was discovered*** *by Christopher Columbus.*
Present Perfect to express an action which began in the past and continues to the present:
'Smartphones' ***have been sold*** *since 2007.*

2 The object of an active verb becomes the subject of a passive verb. Notice the use of *by* in the passive sentence.

Object
Active *Shakespeare wrote* *Hamlet*.
Passive *Hamlet* *was written* ***by*** *Shakespeare.*
Subject

3 The passive is not just another way of expressing the same sentence in the active. We choose the active or the passive depending on what we are more interested in.
Hamlet ***was written*** *in 1600.* (We are more interested in *Hamlet*.)
Shakespeare ***wrote*** Hamlet *in 1600.* (We are more interested in who wrote it.)

Note
The subject of an active sentence is not mentioned in the passive sentence if it is not really important.

Active *People speak German in parts of Italy.*
Passive *German is spoken in parts of Italy.*
NOT ~~*German is spoken in parts of Italy by people.*~~

UNIT 11

11.1 Present Perfect Continuous

Form
has/have + been + -ing (present participle)

Positive and negative

I You We They	've (have) haven't	been working.
He She It	's (has) hasn't	

Question

How long	have	I you we they	been working?
	has	he she it	

	Short answer
Have you been running?	***Yes, I have./No, I haven't.***

Use
The Present Perfect Continuous is used:

1 to express an activity which began in the past and continues to the present.
*He****'s been teaching*** *music for years.*
*It****'s been raining*** *for days.*

2 to refer to an activity with a result in the present.
I'm hot because ***I've been running****.*
I haven't got any money because ***I've been shopping****.*

Note

1 Sometimes there is little or no difference in meaning between the Present Perfect Simple and Continuous.
How long ***have you worked*** *here?*
How long ***have you been working*** *here?*

2 Some verbs have the idea of a long time – *wait, work, learn, travel, play*.
These verbs can often be found in the Present Perfect Continuous.
I've been waiting *for hours.*
Some verbs don't have the idea of a long time – *find, start, buy, die, lose, break, stop*. It is unusual to find these in the Present Perfect Continuous.
I've bought *a new dress.*
My cat ***has died****.*
*My radio****'s broken****.*

3 Verbs that express a state – *like, love, know, have* (for possession), are not found in the Present Perfect Continuous.
*We****'ve known*** *each other for a few weeks.*
NOT ~~*We've been knowing each other for a few weeks.*~~

4 If the sentence gives a number or a quantity, the Present Perfect Simple is used. The Continuous is not possible.
I've been writing *emails all morning.* ***I've written*** *twenty.*
NOT ~~*I've been writing twenty.*~~

12.1 First conditional

Form

If + Present Simple, *will* + infinitive without *to*

Positive and negative

*If I work hard, **I'll pass** my exams.*
***If** we **don't hurry** up, we'**ll be** late.*
***If** you're late, I **won't wait** for you.*

Question

*What **will** you do **if** you don't go to university?*

	Short answer
***Will** you go to university **if** you pass your exams?*	***Yes,** I **will.***
	No,** I **won't.

Notes

1. English uses a present tense in the condition clause, not a future form.
   ***If** it rains, **I'll stay** home.* NOT ~~*If it will rain …*~~
   ***If** I work hard, **I'll pass**.* NOT ~~*If I'll work hard …*~~
2. The condition clause (*if*) can come at the beginning of the sentence or at the end. Notice the use of the comma.
   ***If** I work hard, I'll pass my exams.*
   *I'll pass my exams **if** I work hard.*

Use

The first conditional is used to express a possible condition and a probable result in the future.

***If** it's sunny, we'**ll go** for a picnic.*
*You'**ll get** wet if you **don't take** an umbrella.*

If* and *when

If expresses a possibility that something will happen.
When expresses what the speaker sees as certain to happen.
***When** I get home, I'll have a shower.* NOT ~~*If I get home*~~

12.2 *might*

Form

might + infinitive without *to*
Might is a modal auxiliary verb. For an introduction to modal auxiliary verbs, see p143.
The forms of *might* are the same for all persons.

Positive and negative

I He It We	might might not	go to the party. be late. rain tomorrow. go out for a meal tonight.

Note

The negative is often expressed with *I don't think* + *will*.
*I **don't think it'll** rain tomorrow.*

Question

The inverted question *Might you …?* is unusual. It is very common to ask a question with *Do you think … + will …?*

Do you think	it'll rain? they'll come to our party?

	Short answer
Do you think it'll rain?	***It might.***

Use

Might is used to express a future possibility. It means *will perhaps*.
It contrasts with *will*, which expresses a future certainty.

*England **will** win the match.*
(I am sure they will.)
*England **might** win the match.*
(It's possible, but I'm not sure.)

12.3 Second conditional

Form

If + Past Simple, *would* + infinitive without *to*
Would is a modal auxiliary verb. There is an introduction to modal auxiliary verbs on p143.
The forms of *would* are the same for all persons.

Positive and negative

***If** I had more money, **I'd** (would) buy a new computer.*
***If** she knew the answer, she'**d** tell us.*
***If** I didn't like you, I **wouldn't** talk to you.*

Question

*What **would** you do **if** you had a year off?*

	Short answer
Would you travel round the world?	***Yes,** I **would.***
	No,** I **wouldn't.
If they had the money, would they buy a new car?	***Yes,** they **would.***
	No,** they **wouldn't.

Notes

1. As with the first conditional, the condition clause can come at the beginning or the end of the sentence.
   ***If I had** more time, I'd help.*
   *I'd help **if I had** more time.*
2. *Were* is often used instead of *was* in the condition clause.
   *If I **were** you, I'd go to bed.*
   *If he **were** taller, he'd be a policeman.*
3. The use of the past tense (*If I had*) and *would* does not refer to past time. It expresses distance from the present and unreality because it is different from the facts we know.
   If I had … (but I don't have …)
   I would … (but I won't …)

Use

1. The second conditional is used to express an unreal or improbable condition and its result. The use of the past forms show that is not reality.
   ***If I were** the President, **I'd stop** all war.* (But I'm not the President. = reality)
   ***If I lived** in a big house, **I'd have** a party.* (But I live in a small flat.)
2. The phrase, *If I were you, I'd …*, is often used to give advice.
   ***If I were** you, **I'd** call the doctor.*

First and second conditional

The first conditional is possible and probable.
The second conditional is improbable and sometimes impossible.
***If** I **win** the tennis match, **I'll be** so happy.* (I think it's possible.)
***If** I **won** the tennis match, **I'd be** so happy.* (But I don't think I will.)

Word list

Here is a list of most of the new words in the units of *New Headway Pre-Intermediate, Fourth edition* Student's Book.

adj = adjective
adv = adverb
conj = conjunction
coll = colloquial
n = noun
opp = opposite
pl = plural
prep = preposition
pron = pronoun
pp = past participle
v = verb
US = American English

UNIT 1

aboriginal *adj* /ˌæbəˈrɪdʒənl/
accident *n* /ˈæksɪdənt/
amazing *adj* /əˈmeɪzɪŋ/
another time /əˈnʌðə(r) taɪm/
art gallery *n* /ɑːt ˈgæləri/
as many as /əz ˈmeni əz/
attractive *adj* /əˈtræktɪv/
blind date *n* /ˌblaɪnd ˈdeɪt/
borrow *v* /ˈbɒrəʊ/
Bulgaria *n* /bʌlˈgeəriə/
charity *n* /ˈtʃærəti/
check-up *n* /ˈtʃek ʌp/
cheek *n* /tʃiːk/
Cheers! /tʃɪəz/
chopsticks *pl n* /ˈtʃɒpstɪks/
coach *n* /kəʊtʃ/
cosmopolitan *adj* /ˌkɒzməˈpɒlɪtən/
couple *n* /ˈkʌpl/
dates *pl n* /deɪts/
embarrass *v* /ɪmˈbærəs/
excited *adj* /ɪkˈsaɪtɪd/
first impressions *n* /fɜːst ɪmˈpreʃnz/
flat *adj* /flæt/
gang *n* /gæŋ/
Goodness! /ˈgʊdnɪs/
greet *v* /griːt/
Have a good weekend! /hæv ə gʊd ˌwiːkˈend/
hurry *n* /ˈhʌri/
impress *v* /ɪmˈpres/
interview *n* /ˈɪntəvjuː/
it doesn't matter /ɪtˈ dʌz(r)nt ˈmætə(r)/
journey *n* /ˈdʒɜːni/
mainly *adv* /ˈmeɪnli/
marathon *n* /ˈmærəθən/
Master's degree *n* /ˈmɑːstərz dɪˈgriː/
messenger *n* /ˈmesɪndʒə(r)/
mistakes *pl n* /mɪˈsteɪks/
more and more /mɔː(r) ənd mɔː(r)/
my pleasure /maɪ ˈpleʒə(r)/
nervous *adj* /ˈnɜːvəs/
never mind /ˈnevə(r) maɪnd/
noise *n* /nɔɪz/
Not a great look! /ˈnɒt ə greɪt lʊk/
nothing much /ˈnʌθɪŋ mʌtʃ/
notice *n* /ˈnəʊtɪs/
oldest *adj* /ˈəʊldɪst/
opening *n* /ˈəʊpənɪŋ/
percentage *n* /pəˈsentɪdʒ/
Pleased to meet you. /pliːzd tə miːt ju/
progress *v* /ˈprəʊgres/
raisins *pl n* /ˈreɪznz/
readers *pl n* /ˈriːdəz/
reporter *n* /rɪˈpɔːtə(r)/
seat *n* /siːt/
shake *v* /ʃeɪk/
shapes *pl n* /ʃeɪps/
show round *v* /ʃəʊ ˈraʊnd/
Shut up! /ʃʌt ˈʌp/
signs *pl n* /saɪnz/
so many things /səʊ ˈmeni θɪŋz/
successful *adj* /səkˈsesfl/
sunshine *n* /ˈsʌnʃaɪn/
suppose *v* /səˈpəʊz/
survey *n* /ˈsɜːveɪ/
swap *v* /swɒp/
table manners *pl n* /ˈteɪbl mænəz/
terrible *adj* /ˈterəbl/
theatre *n* /ˈθɪətə(r)/
to have in common *v* /tə hæv ɪn ˈkɒmən/
train *v* /treɪn/
Turkish *adj* /ˈtɜːkɪʃ/
wear *v* /weə(r)/
wise *adj* /waɪz/
worry *v* /ˈwʌri/

UNIT 2

actually *adv* /ˈæktʃuəli/
afraid *adj* /əˈfreɪd/
architect *n* /ˈɑːkɪtekt/
article *n* /ˈɑːtɪkl/
average *n* /ˈævərɪdʒ/
behave *v* /bɪˈheɪv/
bright-red *adj* /braɪt red/
Cheer up! /tʃɪə(r) ʌp/
chill out *v* /tʃɪlˈaʊt/
clubs *pl n* /klʌbz/
currently *adv* /ˈkʌrəntli/
dance music *n* /dɑːns ˈmjuːzɪk/
deaf *adj* /def/
depend on *v* /dɪˈpend ɒn/
depressed *adj* /dɪˈprest/
download *v* /daʊnˈləʊd/
electro music *n* /ɪˈlektrəʊ ˈmjuːzɪk/
energetic *adj* /enəˈdʒetɪk/
enthusiastic *adj* /ɪnθjuːziˈæstɪk/
envious *adj* /ˈenviəs/
extraordinary *adj* /ɪkˈstrɔːdnri/
failures *pl n* /ˈfeɪljəz/
feel at home /fiːl ət həʊm/
festivals *pl n* /ˈfestɪvlz/
flavour *n* /ˈfleɪvə(r)/
fortune *n* /ˈfɔːtʃuːn/
gig *n* /gɪg/
grateful *adj* /ˈgreɪtfl/
grow *v* /grəʊ/
happiness *n* /ˈhæpinəs/
health *n* /helθ/
huge *adj* /hjuːdʒ/
image *n* /ˈɪmɪdʒ/
jars *pl n* /dʒɑːz/
jealous *adj* /ˈdʒeləs/
jogging *n* /ˈdʒɒgɪŋ/
joy *n* /dʒɔɪ/
lie-in *n* /ˈlaɪ ɪn/
lipstick *n* /ˈlɪpstɪk/
major *adj* /ˈmeɪdʒə(r)/
marketing *n* /ˈmɑːkɪtɪŋ/
Mind your own business! /ˈmaɪnd jə əʊn ˌbɪznəs/
neighbours *pl n* /ˈneɪbəz/
obviously *adv* /ˈɒbviəsli/
on the way /ɒn ðə weɪ/
on their own /ɒn ðeə(r) ˈəʊn /
opportunity *n* /ˌɒpəˈtjuːnəti/
ordinary *adj* /ˈɔːdnri/
planning *n* /ˈplænɪŋ/
pleasure *n* /ˈpleʒə(r)/
products *pl n* /ˈprɒdʌkts/
relationship *n* /rɪˈleɪʃnʃɪp/
remarkable *adj* /rɪˈmɑːkəbl/
satisfaction *n* /sætɪsˈfakʃən/
saxophone *n* /ˈsæksəfəʊn/
score *n* /skɔː(r)/
secret *n* /ˈsiːkrət/
selling *n* /selɪŋ/
silver *n* /ˈsɪlvə(r)/
single *n* /ˈsɪŋgl/
smart *adj* /smɑːt/
stressed *adj* /strest/
suspicious *adj* /səˈspɪʃəs/
tea parties *pl n* /ˈtiː pɑːtiz/
tour *v* /tɔː(r)/
unemployed *adj* /ˌʌnɪmˈplɔɪd/
unusual *adj* /ʌnˈjuːʒəl/
young people *n* /jʌŋ ˈpiːpl/

UNIT 3

activate *v* /ˈæktɪveɪt/
admire *v* /ədˈmaɪə(r)/
adventure *n* /ədˈventʃə(r)/
adventurer *n* /ədˈventʃərə(r)/
appreciate *v* /əˈpriːʃieɪt/
argument *n* /ˈɑːgjəmənt/
beat *v* /biːt/
bite *n* /baɪt/
bleed *v* /bliːd/
cabin crew *n* /ˈkæbɪn kruː/
chute *n* /ʃuːt/
coast *n* /kəʊst/
companion *n* /kəmˈpæniən/
crime *n* /kraɪm/
damage *v* /ˈdæmɪdʒ/
dangerous *adj* /ˈdeɪndʒərəs/
dearly *adv* /ˈdɪəli/
endanger *v* /ɪnˈdeɪndʒə(r)/
enormous *adj* /ɪˈnɔːməs/
explode *v* /ɪkˈspləʊd/
explosion *n* /ɪkˈspləʊʒn/
fame *n* /feɪm/
fangs *pl n* /fæŋz/
flight attendant *n* /flaɪt əˈtendənt/
folk hero *n* /fəʊk ˈhɪərəʊ/
forest *n* /ˈfɒrɪst/
forestry *adj* /ˈfɒrɪstri/
fountain *n* /ˈfaʊntɪn/
furiously *adv* /ˈfjʊəriəsli/
guide *n* /gaɪd/
guns *pl n* /gʌnz/
half-time *n* /ˌhɑːf ˈtaɪm/
hammock *n* /ˈhæmək/
headline *n* /ˈhedlaɪn/
hostile *adj* /ˈhɒstaɪl/
injured *adj* /ˈɪndʒəd/
jungle *n* /ˈdʒʌŋgl/
knives *pl n* /naɪvz/
land *v* /lænd/
length *n* /leŋθ/
locker *n* /ˈlɒkə(r)/
lost his cool /lɒst hɪz kuːl /
mend *v* /mend/
monkeys *pl n* /ˈmʌŋkiz/
overhead *adj* /ˈəʊvəhed/
PA system *n* /piː ˈeɪ sɪstəm/
permission *n* /pəˈmɪʃn/
quit *v* /kwɪt/
react *v* /riˈækt/
record *v* /rɪˈkɔːd/
refuse *v* /rɪˈfjuːz/
robbery *n* /ˈrɒbəri/
runway *n* /ˈrʌnweɪ/
sleeping pill *n* /ˈsliːpɪŋ pɪl/
snake *n* /sneɪk/

source n /sɔːs/
star v /stɑː(r)/
strike n /straɪk/
sympathy n /'sɪmpəθi/
taxiing v /'tæksiɪŋ/
temper n /'tempə(r)/
terrified adj /'terɪfaɪd/
theft n /θeft/
thieves pl n /θiːvz/
tribe n /traɪb/
trip n /trɪp/
vase n /vɑːz/
web page n /'web peɪdʒ/
worldwide adj /'wɜːldwaɪd/

UNIT 4

allergic adj /ə'lɜːdʒɪk/
ambition n /æm'bɪʃn/
aspirin n /'æsprɪn/
automated adj /'ɔːtəmeɪtɪd/
beauty n /'bjuːti/
branches pl n /brɑːntʃɪz/
breeze n /briːz/
broccoli n /'brɒkəli/
brochure n /'brəʊʃə(r)/
calorie n /'kæləri/
cans pl n /kænz/
chemist's n /'kemɪsts/
chewing gum n /'tʃuːɪŋ gʌm/
complain v /kəm'pleɪn/
connect v /kə'nekt/
coral n /'kɒrəl/
courage n /'kʌrɪdʒ/
crane n /kreɪn/
crystal-blue n /'krɪstl bluː/
dairy n /'deəri/
decaffeinated adj /ˌdiː'kæfɪneɪtɪd/
décor n /'deɪkɔː/
delicious adj /dɪ'lɪʃəs/
descend v /dɪ'send/
dessert n /dɪ'zɜːt/
diners pl n /'daɪnəz/
direct debit n /dəˌrekt 'debɪt/
disappointed adj /ˌdɪsə'pɔɪntɪd/
excitement n /ɪk'saɪtmənt/
expressions pl n /ɪk'spreʃnz/
fasten v /'fɑːsn/
fry v /fraɪ/
give (someone) a lift v /gɪv ə lɪft/
grill v /grɪl/
hang v /hæŋ/
heights n /haɪts/
help yourself /help jə'self/
homemade adj /ˌhəʊm 'meɪd/
honeymoon n /'hʌnimuːn/
industrial adj /ɪn'dʌstriəl/
lend v /lend/
limit n /'lɪmɪt/
loaf n /ləʊf/
loudly adv /laʊdli/
magical adj /'mædʒɪkl/
Maldives n /'mɔːldaɪvz/
mangoes pl n /'mæŋgəʊz/
meaning n /'miːnɪŋ/
nuts pl n /nʌts/
off-licence n /'ɒf laɪsns/
patent n /'peɪtnt/
pick up v /pɪk 'ʌp/
platform n /'plætfɔːm/
portion n /'pɔːʃn/
postman n /'pəʊstmən/
pots pl n /pɒts/
prawns pl n /prɔːnz/
programmer n /'prəʊgræmə(r)/
raw adj /rɔː/
restriction n /rɪ'strɪkʃn/
retire v /rɪ'taɪə(r)/
roast v /rəʊst/
robots pl n /'rəʊbɒts/
romantic adj /rəʊ'mæntɪk/
round adj /raʊnd/
seat belts pl n /'siːt belts/
sharks pl n /ʃɑːks/
shellfish n /'ʃelfɪʃ/
shopkeeper n /'ʃɒpkiːpə(r)/
sitting n /'sɪtɪŋ/
slices pl n /slaɪsɪz/
snack bar n /'snæk bɑː(r)/
software n /'sɒftweə(r)/
sparkling adj /'spɑːklɪŋ/
spectacular adj /spek'tækjələ(r)/
speechless adj /'spiːtʃləs/
spiral stairs pl n /'spaɪrəl steəz /
steam v /stiːm/
still adj /stɪl/
sting rays pl n /'stɪŋreɪz/
sunken adj /'sʌŋkən/
tap water n /'tæp wɔːtə(r)/
tip n /tɪp/
tonnes pl n /tʌnz/
touch-screen n /'tʌtʃ skriːn/
tropical fish pl n /'trɒpɪkl fɪʃ/
turtles pl n /'tɜːtlz/
underwater adj /ˌʌndə'wɔːtə(r)/
washing-up n /ˌwɒʃɪŋ 'ʌp/
weigh v /weɪ/
whisky n /'wɪski/

UNIT 5

advertise v /'ædvətaɪz/
afterwards adv /'ɑːftəwədz/
amazed adj /ə'meɪzd/
apply v /ə'plaɪ/
arrange v /ə'reɪndʒ/
Belarus n /ˌbelə'ruːs/
billion /'bɪljən/
biochemistry n /ˌbaɪəʊ'kemɪstri/
boomerang n /'buːməræŋ/
boss n /bɒs/
camping n /'kæmpɪŋ/
Capricorn n /'kæprɪkɔːn/
celebrate v /'seləbreɪt/
communicate v /kə'mjuːnɪkeɪt/
contaminate v /kən'tæmɪneɪt/
cycling n /'saɪklɪŋ/
debts pl n /dets/
delighted adj /dɪ'laɪtɪd/
disaster n /dɪ'zɑːstə(r)/
divorced adj /dɪ'vɔːst/
driving test n /'draɪvɪŋ test/
exams pl n /ɪg'zæmz/
experts pl n /'ekspɜːts/
fall out v /fɔːl 'aʊt/
farmers pl n /'fɑːməz/
fed up adj /ˌfed 'ʌp/
fluent adj /'fluːənt/
full-time adj /ˌfʊl 'taɪm/
get on v /get 'ɒn/
grown-up adj /ˌgrəʊn 'ʌp/
heavy adj /'hevi/
hope n /həʊp/
immediately adv /ɪ'miːdiətli/
jumper n /'dʒʌmpə(r)/
lawyer n /'lɔːjə(r)/
look after v /lʊk 'ɑːftə(r)/
look up v /lʊk 'ʌp/
lucky adj /'lʌki/
medicine n /'medsn/
miserable adj /'mɪzrəbl/
miss v /mɪs/
mushrooms n /'mʌʃruːmz/
nephew n /'nefjuː/
newsagent n /'njuːzeɪdʒənt/
nuclear adj /'njuːkliə(r)/
owe v /əʊ/
paramedic n /ˌpærə'medɪk/
petrol n /'petrəl/
philosophy n /fɪ'lɒsəfi/
phrase book n /'freɪz bʊk/
pick v /pɪk/
pretty good /'prɪti gʊd/
prime minister n /ˌpraɪm 'mɪnɪstə(r)/
produce n /'prɒdjuːs/
run out of v /rʌn 'aʊt ɒv/
regret v /rɪ'gret/
stressful adj /'stresfl/
supper n /'sʌpə(r)/
surfing n /'sɜːfɪŋ/
test n /test/
traffic jams pl n /'træfɪk dʒæmz/
warm welcome /wɔːm 'welkəm/

UNIT 6

annoyed adj /ə'nɔɪd/
blond adj /blɒnd/
bring up v /brɪŋ 'ʌp/
busier adj /'bɪziə(r)/
busiest adj /'bɪziɪst/
calm down v /kɑːm daʊn/
career n /kə'rɪə(r)/
cheerful adj /'tʃɪəfl/
citizen n /'sɪtɪzn/
climate n /'klaɪmət/
creative adj /kri'eɪtɪv/
culture shock /'kʌltʃə ʃɒk/
customers pl n /'kʌstəməz/
darker adj /'dɑːkə(r)/
democratic adj /ˌdemə'krætɪk/
development n /dɪ'veləpmənt/
driest adj /'draɪɪst/
equator n /ɪ'kweɪtə(r)/
experience n /ɪk'spɪəriəns/
fair adj /feə(r)/
financial adj /faɪ'nænʃl/
florist's shop n /'flɒrɪsts ʃɒp/
foreign adj /'fɒrən/
friendly adj /'frendli/
generation n /ˌdʒenə'reɪʃn/
heartbreaking adj /'hɑːtbreɪkɪŋ/
hectic adj /'hektɪk/
herbal adj /'hɜːbl/
honest adj /'ɒnɪst/
humid adj /'hjuːmɪd/
incredible adj /ɪn'kredəbl/
intelligent adj /ɪn'telɪdʒənt/
investment n /ɪn'vestmənt/
Kenya n /'kenjə/
largest adj /'lɑːdʒɪst/
messy adj /'mesi/
mix up v /mɪks 'ʌp/
moody adj /'muːdi/
multicultural adj /ˌmʌlti'kʌltʃərəl/
nationality n /ˌnæʃə'næləti/
pharaohs pl n /'feərəʊz/
Philippines n /'fɪlɪpiːnz/
qualities pl n /'kwɒlətiz/
reliable adj /rɪ'laɪəbl/
religion n /rɪ'lɪdʒən/
reveal v /rɪ'viːl/
safe adj /seɪf/
salary n /'sæləri/
selfish adj /'selfɪʃ/
serve v /sɜːv/
shy adj /ʃaɪ/
skies pl n /skaɪz/
society n /sə'saɪəti/
South American adj /saʊθ ə'merɪkən/
surrounded adj /sə'raʊndɪd/
system n /'sɪstəm/
temperature n /'temprətʃə(r)/
thankful adj /'θæŋkfl/
tidy adj /'taɪdi/
twin n /twɪn/
wealthy adj /'welθi/
well-behaved adj /ˌwel bɪ'heɪvd/
wetter adj /'wetə(r)/

UNIT 7

accountant *n* /ə'kaʊntənt/
acres *pl n* /'eɪkəz/
ancestors *pl n* /'ænsestəz/
Ancient Civilisations *n pl* /'eɪnʃənt ˌsɪvəlaɪ'zeɪʃnz/
archaeology *n* /ˌɑːki'ɒlədʒi/
aristocracy *n* /ˌærɪ'stɒkrəsi/
charming *adj* /'tʃɑːmɪŋ/
compete *v* /kəm'piːt/
correspondent *n* /kɒrɪ'spɒndənt/
crash *n* /kræʃ/
decorator *n* /'dekəreɪtə(r)/
discover *v* /dɪ'skʌvə(r)/
Duchess *n* /'dʌtʃəs/
Duke *n* /djuːk/
economist *n* /ɪ'kɒnəmɪst/
electrician *n* /ɪˌlek'trɪʃn/
employ *v* /ɪm'plɔɪ/
estate *n* /ɪ'steɪt/
exhibition *n* /ˌeksɪ'bɪʃn/
fascinated *adj* /'fæsɪneɪtɪd/
film industry *n* /'fɪlm ɪndəstri/
flower shows *pl n* /'flaʊə(r) ʃəʊz/
great-grandmother *n* /greɪt 'grænmʌðə(r)/
historian *n* /hɪ'stɔːriən/
inherit *v* /ɪn'herɪt/
interpreter *n* /ɪn'tɜːprɪtə(r)/
kindness *n* /'kaɪn(d)nəs/
librarian *n* /laɪ'breəriən/
magnificent *adj* /mæg'nɪfɪsnt/
musician *n* /mju'zɪʃn/
ninth /naɪnθ/
parkland *n* /'pɑːklænd/
passion *n* /'pæʃn/
persuade *v* /pə'sweɪd/
philosopher *n* /fɪ'lɒsəfə(r)/
politician *n* /ˌpɒlə'tɪʃn/
press photographer *n* /pres fə'tɒgrəfə(r)/
receptionist *n* /rɪ'sepʃənɪst/
royalty *n* /'rɔɪəlti/
running *v* /'rʌnɪŋ/
scientist *n* /'saɪəntɪst/
several *pron* /'sevrəl/
shipyards *pl n* /'ʃɪpjɑːdz/
similarities *pl n* /ˌsɪmə'lærətiz/
situated *adj* /'sɪtʃueɪtɪd/
situation *n* /ˌsɪtʃu'eɪʃn/
suite *n* /swiːt/
trials *pl n* /'traɪəlz/
vast *adj* /vɑːst/

UNIT 8

achievement *n* /ə'tʃiːvmənt/
aftershave *n* /'ɑːftəʃeɪv/
aggressive *adj* /ə'gresɪv/
allergy *n* /'ælədʒi/
antibiotic *n* /ˌæntibaɪ'ɒtɪk/
audience *n* /'ɔːdiəns/
baseball *n* /'beɪsbɔːl/
blouse *n* /blaʊz/
boisterous *adj* /'bɔɪstərəs/
casual wear *n* /'kæʒuəl weə(r)/
chatty *adj* /'tʃæti/
climbers *pl n* /'klaɪməz/
cling on *v* /klɪŋ 'ɒn/
competitive *adj* /kəm'petətɪv/
contest *n* /'kɒntest/
determined *adj* /dɪ'tɜːmɪnd/
diagnosis *n* /ˌdaɪəg'nəʊsɪs/
diarrhoea *n* /ˌdaɪə'rɪə/
dive *v* /daɪv/
endlessly *adv* /'endləsli/
equipment *n* /ɪ'kwɪpmənt/
exhausting *adj* /ɪg'zɔːstɪŋ/
fever *n* /'fiːvə(r)/
figure *n* /'fɪgə(r)/
fit *adj* /fɪt/
flu *n* /fluː/
food poisoning *n* /'fuːd pɔɪzənɪŋ/
gentle *adj* /'dʒentl/
glands *pl n* /glændz/
go-karting *n* /'gəʊ kɑːtɪŋ/
gold medal *n* /ˌgəʊld 'medl/
gymnastics *n* /dʒɪm'næstɪks/
haulage *n* /'hɔːlɪdʒ/
heat *n* /hiːt/
heptathlon *n* /hep'tæθlən/
high jump *n* /'haɪ dʒʌmp/
hopeless *adj* /'həʊpləs/
horse-riding *n* /'hɔːs raɪdɪŋ/
infection *n* /ɪn'fekʃn/
javelin throw *n* /'dʒævlɪn θrəʊ/
Labrador *n* /'læbrədɔː(r)/
liquids *pl n* /'lɪkwɪdz/
long jump *n* /'lɒŋ dʒʌmp/
nerves *pl n* /nɜːvz/
patient *n* /'peɪʃnt/
penicillin *n* /ˌpenɪ'sɪlɪn/
physiotherapist *n* /ˌfɪziəʊ'θerəpɪst/
polite *adj* /pə'laɪt/
pouring *n* /pɔːrɪŋ /
prescription *n* /prɪ'skrɪpʃn/
racing *n* /'reɪsɪŋ/
recover *v* /ˌrɪ'kʌvə(r)/
rock climbing *n* /'rɒk klaɪmɪŋ/
sailing *n* /'seɪlɪŋ/
sensitive *adj* /'sensətɪv/
shot put *n* /'ʃɒt pʊt/
sickness *n* /'sɪknəs/
skydiving *n* /'skaɪdaɪvɪŋ/
sneeze *v* /sniːz/
sore *adj* /sɔː(r)/
sporty *adj* /'spɔːti/
squash *n* /skwɒʃ/
suit *n* /sjuːt/
swallow *v* /'swɒləʊ/
swollen *adj* /'swəʊlən/
symptoms *pl n* /'sɪmptəmz/
thermometer *n* /θə'mɒmɪtə(r)/
tourist spot *n* /'tɔːrɪst spɒt/
twisted *adj* /'twɪstɪd/
untidy *adj* /ʌn'taɪdi/

UNIT 9

absolutely *adv* /'æbsəluːtli/
address *v* /ə'dres/
advice *n* /əd'vaɪs/
anniversary *n* /ˌænɪ'vɜːsəri/
ashamed *adj* /ə'ʃeɪmd/
attack *v* /ə'tæk/
autobiography *n* /ˌɔːtəbaɪ'ɒgrəfi/
badly-behaved *adj* /'bædli bɪ'heɪvd/
battle *n* /'bætl/
behaviour *n* /bɪ'heɪvjə(r)/
bend down *v* /bend 'daʊn/
best-known *adj* /best 'nəʊn/
best-seller *adj* /ˌbest'selə(r)/
break down *v* /breɪk 'daʊn/
burn *v* /bɜːn/
case *n* /keɪs/
cheque *n* /tʃek/
childhood *n* /'tʃaɪldhʊd/
compliment *n* /'kɒmplɪmənt/
cruel *adj* /'kruːəl/
disgusting *adj* /dɪs'gʌstɪŋ/
escape *v* /ɪ'skeɪp/
evil *adj* /'iːvəl/
fables *pl n* /'feɪblz/
fact *n* /fækt/
familiar *adj* /fə'mɪliə(r)/
fascinating *adj* /'fæsɪneɪtɪŋ/
fiction *n* /'fɪkʃn/
get rid of *v* /get 'rɪd əv/
homesick *adj* /'həʊmsɪk/
immediate *adj* /ɪ'miːdiət/
innocent *adj* /'ɪnəsnt/
lend *v* /lend/
lie *v* /laɪ/
literature *n* /'lɪtrətʃə(r)/
master *n* /'mɑːstə(r)/
monster *n* /'mɒnstə(r)/
moonlight *n* /'muːnlaɪt/
murder *n* /'mɜːdə(r)/
narrative *n* /'nærətɪv/
novels *pl n* /'nɒvlz/
pale *adj* /peɪl/
personality *n* /ˌpɜːsə'næləti/
poetry *n* /'pəʊətri/
potion *n* /'pəʊʃn/
pray *v* /preɪ/
pretend *v* /prɪ'tend/
psychological *adj* /ˌsaɪkə'lɒdʒɪkl/
publish *v* /'pʌblɪʃ/
race *v* /reɪs/
romance *n* /'rəʊmæns/
run away *v* /rʌn 'əweɪ/
servants *pl n* /'sɜːvənts/
shepherd *n* /'ʃepəd/
sight *n* /saɪt/
sniff *v* /snɪf/
split personality *n* /ˌsplɪt pɜːsə'næləti/
strength *n* /streŋθ/
success *n* /sək'ses/
suspect *v* /sə'spekt/
take pleasure *v* /teɪk 'pleʒə(r)/
terror *n* /'terə(r)/
tiring *adj* /'taɪərɪŋ/
traveller *n* /'trav(ə)lə/
true *adj* /truː/
ugly *adj* /'ʌgli/
upset *adj* /ʌp'set/
villagers *pl n* /'vɪlɪdʒəz/
villains *pl n* /'vɪlənz/
wander away *v* /'wɒndə(r) ə'weɪ/
well-respected *adj* /wel rɪ'spektɪd/
whether *conj* /'weðə(r)/
whisper *v* /'wɪspə(r)/
wild *adj* /waɪld/
wolf *n* /wʊlf/

UNIT 10

access *v* /'ækses/
arrangements *pl n* /ə'reɪndʒmənts/
badly-written *adj* /'bædli 'rɪtn/
ballpoint pen *n* /'bɔːlpɔɪnt pen/
basement *n* /'beɪsmənt/
battery *n* /'bætəri/
blogger *n* /'blɒgə(r)/
browsing *v* /braʊzɪŋ/
chronologically *adv* /ˌkrɒnə'lɒdʒɪkli/
commercial *adj* /kə'mɜːʃl/
complaint *n* /kəm'pleɪnt/
copy *v* /'kɒpi/
database *n* /'deɪtəbeɪs/
decorate *v* /'dekəreɪt/
directory enquiries *n* /də'rektəri ɪŋ'kwaɪriːz/
easily *adv* /'iːzəli/
employee *n* /ɪm'plɔɪiː/
engineer *n* /ˌendʒɪ'nɪə(r)/
estimate *v* /'estɪmeɪt/
evolution *n* /ˌevə'luːʃn/
fairly *adv* /'feəli/
fashionable *adj* /'fæʃnəbl/
fears *pl n* /fɪəz/
feature *n* /'fiːtʃə(r)/
flatmate *n* /'flætmeɪt/
found *v* /faʊnd/
gadget *n* /'gædʒɪt/
introduce *v* /ˌɪntrə'djuːs/
keeping up to date /'kiːpɪŋ ʌp tə deɪt/
landline *n* /'lændlaɪn/
last *v* /lɑːst/
latest *adj* /'leɪtɪst/
launch *v* /lɔːntʃ/
luxury *n* /'lʌkʃəri/
middle-aged *adj* /ˌmɪdl 'eɪdʒd/
mini-computer *n* /mɪni 'kəmpjuːtə(r)/
multimedia *adj* /ˌmʌlti'miːdiə/

multitude *n* /ˈmʌltɪtjuːd/
nightmare *n* /ˈnaɪtmeə(r)/
operators *pl n* /ˈɒpəreɪtəz/
overcrowded *adj* /ˌəʊvəˈkraʊdɪd/
oversized *adj* /ˈəʊvəsaɪzd/
own *v* /əʊn/
password *n* /ˈpɑːswɜːd/
pocket-sized *adj* /ˈpɒkɪt saɪzd /
predict *v* /prɪˈdɪkt/
printing press *n* /ˈprɪntɪŋ pres/
rare *adj* /reə(r)/
recorded message *n* /rɪˈkɔːdɪd ˈmesɪdʒ/
reignite *v* /ˌriːɪgˈnaɪt/
replace *v* /rɪˈpleɪs/
replicate *v* /ˈreplɪkeɪt/
routine *adj* /ruːˈtiːn/
search engines *pl n* /ˈsɜːtʃ endʒɪnz/
searchable *adj* /ˈsɜːtʃəbl/
skinny latte *n* /skɪni ˈlæteɪ/
smartphone *n* /ˈsmɑːtfəʊn/
social networking *n* /səʊʃl ˈnetwɜːkɪŋ/
store *n* /stɔː(r)/
switch off *v* /swɪtʃ ˈɒf/
throw away *v* /θrəʊ ˈəweɪ/
trillion /ˈtrɪljən/
user-friendly *adj* /ˌjuːzə ˈfrendli/
variety *n* /vəˈraɪəti/

UNIT 11

academy *n* /əˈkædəmi/
antiques *pl n* /ænˈtiːks/
awards *pl n* /əˈwɔːdz/
backache *n* /ˈbækeɪk/
based in /beɪst ɪn/
blind *adj* /blaɪnd/
boarding school *n* /ˈbɔːdɪŋ skuːl/
bridesmaid *n* /ˈbraɪdzmeɪd/
bury *v* /ˈberi/
buyer *n* /ˈbaɪə(r)/
catch up *v* /kætʃ ˈʌp/
cave *n* /keɪv/
chance *n* /tʃɑːns/
choir *n* /ˈkwaɪə(r)/
choirmaster *n* /ˈkwaɪəmɑːstə(r)/
classical *adj* /ˈklæsɪkl/
colleague *n* /ˈkɒliːg/
coma *n* /ˈkəʊmə/
coping *v* /ˈkəʊpɪŋ/
covered *adj* /ˈkʌvəd/
demand *v* /dɪˈmɑːnd/
diamond *n* /ˈdaɪəmənd/
digging *v* /ˈdɪgɪŋ/
drama *n* /ˈdrɑːmə/
elite *adj* /ɪˈliːt/
engaged *adj* /ɪnˈgeɪdʒd/
entertain *v* /ˌentəˈteɪn/
exact *adj* /ɪgˈzækt/
expecting a baby /ɪkˈspektɪŋ ə ˈbeɪbi/
expel *v* /ɪkˈspel/
fantastic news /fænˈtæstɪk njuːz/
fond of /ˈfɒnd əv/
generosity *n* /ˌdʒenəˈrɒsəti/
Great to hear from you! /greɪt tə hɪə(r) frɒm ju/
great-grandson *n* /greɪt ˈgrænsʌn/
guy *coll* /gaɪ/
headquarters *n* /ˌhedˈkwɔːtəz/
hit series *n* /hɪt ˈsɪəriːz/
install *v* /ɪnˈstɔːl/
it's been ages /ɪts bɪn eɪdʒɪz/
keep in touch *v* /kiːp ɪn tʌtʃ/
kidnap *v* /ˈkɪdnæp/
leading role *n* /ˈliːdɪŋ rəʊl/
lifestyle *n* /ˈlaɪfstaɪl/
meanness *n* /ˈmiːnnəs/
millionaires *pl n* /ˌmɪljəˈneəz/
model *n* /ˈmɒdl/
modest *adj* /ˈmɒdɪst/
nan *n* /næn/
overdose *n* /ˈəʊvədəʊs/
paralysed *adj* /ˈpærəlaɪzd/
party-loving *adj* /ˈpɑːti ˈlʌvɪŋ/
passionate *adj* /ˈpæʃənət/
photograph *v* /ˈfəʊtəgrɑːf/
plague *v* /pleɪg/
plant *v* /plɑːnt/
popular *adj* /ˈpɒpjələ(r)/
postgraduate *n* /ˌpəʊstˈgrædʒuət/
pregnant *adj* /ˈpregnənt/
presenter *n* /prɪˈzentə(r)/
promises *pl n* /ˈprɒmɪsɪz/
pronunciation *n* /prəˌnʌnsiˈeɪʃn/
proof *n* /pruːf/
prove *v* /pruːv/
ransom *n* /ˈrænsəm/
release *v* /rɪˈliːs/
remarry *v* /ˌriːˈmæri/
rush *v* /rʌʃ/
serious *adj* /ˈsɪəriəs/
show tunes *pl n* /ʃəʊ tjuːnz/
split up *v* /splɪt ˈʌp/
stroke *n* /strəʊk/
Swedish *adj* /ˈswiːdɪʃ/
sweetheart *n* /ˈswiːthɑːt/
terribly *adv* /ˈterəbli/
the arts *pl n* /ðiː ˈɑːts/
tough *adj* /tʌf/
tragedy *n* /ˈtrædʒədi/
tragic *adj* /ˈtrædʒɪk/
Tudor *adj* /ˈtjuːdə(r)/
upbringing *n* /ˈʌpbrɪŋɪŋ/
wealth *n* /welθ/
What a shame! /wɒt ə ˈʃeɪm/
widowed *adj* /ˈwɪdəʊd/

UNIT 12

a click of the fingers /ə ˈklɪk əv ðə ˈfɪŋgəz/
alien *n* /ˈeɪliən/
angle *n* /ˈæŋgl/
atmosphere *n* /ˈætməsfɪə(r)/
axis *n* /ˈæksɪs/
block *v* /blɒk/
body parts *pl n* /ˈbɒdi pɑːts/
burn out *v* /bɜːn ˈaʊt/
collapse *v* /kəˈlæps/
cool *v* /kuːl/
crossroads *n* /ˈkrɒsrəʊdz/
decrease *v* /dɪˈkriːs/
dilemmas *pl n* /dɪˈleməz/
Earth *n* /ɜːθ/
earthquake *n* /ˈɜːθkweɪk/
economics *n* /ˌekəˈnɒmɪks/
electric shock *n* /ɪˌlektrɪk ˈʃɒk/
encourage *v* /ɪnˈkʌrɪdʒ/
evaporate *v* /ɪˈvæpəreɪt/
expand *v* /ɪkˈspænd/
express *v* /ɪkˈspres/
extreme *adj* /ɪkˈstriːm/
first team *n* /ˈfɜːst tiːm/
flash *n* /flæʃ/
fundamentally *adv* /ˌfʌndəˈmentəli/
galaxy *n* /ˈgæləksi/
gas *n* /gæs/
global *adj* /ˈgləʊbl/
good-looking *adj* /ˌgʊd ˈlʊkɪŋ/
government *n* /ˈgʌvənmənt/
gravity *n* /ˈgrævəti/
harmful *adj* /ˈhɑːmfl/
healthcare *n* /ˈhelθkeə(r)/
helium *n* /ˈhiːliəm/
hemisphere *n* /ˈhemɪsfɪə(r)/
hold *v* /həʊld/
hydrogen *n* /ˈhaɪdrədʒən/
improbable *adj* /ɪmˈprɒbəbl/
improvement *n* /ɪmˈpruːvmənt/
in touch /ɪn ˈtʌtʃ/
increasing *adj* /ɪnˈkriːsɪŋ/
infinite *adj* /ˈɪnfɪnət/
junk food *n* /ˈdʒʌŋk fuːd/
life expectancy *n* /ˈlaɪf ɪkˌspektənsi/
Mars *n* /mɑːz/
Mercury *n* /ˈmɜːkjəri/
metal *n* /ˈmetl/
microchips *pl n* /ˈmaɪkrəʊtʃɪps/
Milky Way *n* /ˌmɪlki ˈweɪ/
miraculous *adj* /mɪˈrækjələs/
moons *pl n* /muːnz/
observable *adj* /əbˈzɜːvəbl/
oceans *pl n* /ˈəʊʃnz/
on purpose /ɒn ˈpɜːpəs/
permanently *adv* /ˈpɜːmənəntli/
pessimistic *adj* /ˌpesɪˈmɪstɪk/
picnic *n* /ˈpɪknɪk/
pills *pl n* /pɪlz/
planet *n* /ˈplænɪt/
precious *adj* /ˈpreʃəs/
radiation *n* /ˌreɪdiˈeɪʃn/
require *v* /rɪˈkwaɪə(r)/
rotate *v* /rəʊˈteɪt/
rotation *n* /rəʊˈteɪʃn/
row *n* /raʊ/
skyscrapers *pl n* /ˈskaɪskreɪpəz/
solar system *n* /ˈsəʊlə sɪstəm/
starving *adj* /stɑːvɪŋ/
suitable *adj* /ˈsjuːtəbl/
support *v* /səˈpɔːt/
threats *pl n* /θrets/
time scale *n* /ˈtaɪmskeɪl/
universe *n* /ˈjuːnɪvɜːs/
Venus *n* /ˈviːnəs/
volcano *n* /vɒlˈkeɪnəʊ/
wage *v* /weɪdʒ/
warm *v* /wɔːm/
warning *n* /ˈwɔːnɪŋ/
wisdom *n* /ˈwɪzdəm/
wonders *pl n* /ˈwʌndəz/

Pairwork Student A

UNIT 2 *p16*

PRACTICE

Speaking – exchanging information

3 Work with a partner. Answer questions about Ilona.

Where/from?	Hungary
Where/live?	in a flat in Budapest
... a big family?	yes – three brothers and two sisters
What/do?	student – studying politics
What/like doing/ free time?	going to art galleries, having driving lessons, playing poker
What/doing now?	having a meal in a restaurant with friends

Ask questions about Bill and Christina. Complete the chart.

Where/from?	
Where/live?	
... a big family?	
What/do?	
What/like doing/ free time?	
What/doing now?	

UNIT 5 *p41*

PRACTICE

When can we meet?

3 Work with a partner. Arrange to meet in the next week. Look at your diary.

What are you doing on Monday evening?

I'm meeting Katie in town. Are you doing anything on Monday afternoon?

	morning	afternoon	evening
Monday	study		meet Katie in town
Tuesday	study	visit Uncle Chris	
Wednesday	study		go to the cinema with Jenny
Thursday	study		cook meal for Mum and Dad
Friday	study	have piano lesson	

UNIT 10 *p85*

EVERYDAY ENGLISH

Roleplay

7 Work in pairs. You are going to have three telephone conversations.

PHONE CALL 1	PHONE CALL 2	PHONE CALL 3
Call a friend's mobile.	You are a receptionist at a Marketing company. A client calls to speak to Duncan Jones (your manager).	You work at an IT company. You are on a business trip and need information from a colleague (Marco). Call the office and ask to speak to Marco.
You can't meet on Tuesday – suggest Thursday instead.	Try to connect them.	You have tried Marco's mobile, but he didn't answer.
Agree what to do.	Duncan is busy.	Decide what to do.
	Make a suggestion.	

UNIT 11 *p88*

SPEAKING

Tense review

When was Charlotte Church born?

She was born in 1986.

7 Work with a partner. You have different information about Charlotte Church's life and career. Ask and answer questions to complete the text.

Charlotte Church's life and career

Charlotte Church is an ordinary girl with an extraordinary singing voice. She was born in _______ (*Where?*) in 1986. She's been singing in public since she was _______ (*How long?*), when she sang at a seaside holiday camp. She had to be dragged off stage. When she was 11, she rang a TV talent show and sang _______ (*What?*) down the phone. She's been singing on TV shows ever since and has also given concerts at The London Palladium, and The Royal Albert Hall. She performed in front of the US president when she was just _______ (*How old … when?*).

She has sold over 10 million albums worldwide and has earned _______ (*How much?*). Charlotte is a classical singer, but she likes all kinds of music. She'd love to sing her favourite opera *Madame Butterfly*, but she has also been trying to become a pop singer. She has released _______ pop albums (*How many?*) so far, *Tissues and Issues* in 2005 and *Back to Scratch* in 2010.

Charlotte is not just a singer. She's recently been hosting her own TV chat show *The Charlotte Church Show* for which she won an award. Overall she's won eight awards for her singing and TV appearances.

At 19 Charlotte began a relationship with the _______, Gavin Henson (*Who?*). They had two children, Ruby in 2007 and Dexter in 2009, but split up in 2010.

Pairwork Student B

UNIT 2 *p16*

PRACTICE

Speaking – exchanging information

3 Work with a partner. Ask questions about Ilona. Complete the chart.

Where/from?	
Where/live?	
... a big family?	
What/do?	
What/like doing/ free time?	
What/doing now?	

Answer questions about Bill and Christina.

Where/from?	the United States
Where/live?	in a house on the beach in LA
... a big family?	no – just one daughter
What/do?	Bill – IT consultant Christina – writes travel guides
What/like doing/ free time?	walking on the beach, going swimming, doing yoga
What/doing now?	shopping in a supermarket

UNIT 5 *p41*

PRACTICE

When can we meet?

3 Work with a partner. Arrange to meet in the next week. Look at your diary.

What are you doing on Monday afternoon?

I'm playing tennis with Joe. Are you doing anything on Tuesday afternoon?

	morning	afternoon	evening
Monday	study	play tennis with Joe	
Tuesday	study		watch football at Dan's house
Wednesday	study	visit Tom in hospital	
Thursday	study		
Friday	study		

UNIT 10 *p85*

EVERYDAY ENGLISH

Roleplay

7 Work in pairs. You are going to have three telephone conversations.

PHONE CALL 1

A friend will call your mobile.

↓

The line is bad – ask your friend to repeat what they said.

↓

Agree what to do.

PHONE CALL 2

You are an important customer for a Marketing company. Call the company and ask to speak to Duncan Jones.

↓

You need to speak to him as soon as possible.

↓

Decide what to do.

PHONE CALL 3

You work at an IT company. A colleague calls to speak to another colleague (Marco).

↓

Marco is not there. He is visiting a customer. He has his mobile with him.

↓

Make a suggestion.

UNIT 11 *p88*

SPEAKING

Tense review

7 Work with a partner. You have different information about Charlotte Church's life and career. Ask and answer questions to complete the text.

Where was Charlotte Church born?

She was born in Cardiff, Wales.

Charlotte Church's life and career

Charlotte Church is an ordinary girl with an extraordinary singing voice. She was born in Cardiff, Wales in _______ (*When?*). She's been singing in public since she was three years old, when she sang at a _______ (*Where?*). She had to be dragged off stage. When she was 11, she rang a TV talent show and sang 'Pie Jesu' down the phone. She's been singing on TV shows ever since and has also given concerts _______ (*Where?*). She performed in front of the US president when she was just 14.

She has sold _______ (*How many?*) albums worldwide and has earned over £11 million. Charlotte is a classical singer, but she likes all kinds of music. She'd love to sing her favourite opera _______ (*What?*), but she has also been trying to become a pop singer. She has released two pop albums so far, *Tissues and Issues* in 2005 and *Back to Scratch* in 2010.

Charlotte is not just a singer. She's recently been hosting her own TV chat show *The Charlotte Church Show* for which she won an award. Overall she's won _______ awards (*How many?*) for her singing and TV appearances.

At 19 Charlotte began a relationship with the Welsh rugby star, Gavin Henson. They had two children, Ruby in 2007 and Dexter in 2009, but split up in _______ (*When?*).

Extra materials

UNIT 3 *p24*

PRACTICE

Talking about the news

7 Choose one of the stories and read it. Make sure you understand all the words.

Work in small groups. Tell your story to the others. DON'T read it! The other students can ask questions.

Texting woman falls into fountain

A woman who fell into a fountain while she was shopping is becoming an international hit on YouTube.

A video of her falling into the water went online last Friday, and since then 1.8 million people have watched it.

The woman was in a shopping mall in Nottingham in the UK. She was walking along the mall and texting at the same time, so she wasn't looking where she was going. Security cameras filmed her as she fell into a fountain. Fortunately the water wasn't very deep. When she climbed out of the fountain, she finished sending her text, then carried on walking down the mall.

Chinese vase sells for £53 million

A woman who lives in a suburb of north-west London was clearing out the house of her brother who recently died. She found a vase that her brother kept on a shelf in his dining room.

She said that her brother was very fond of the vase, although she didn't really like it herself.

A local antique shop thought it was worth about £800. So she asked an auction house to look at it, and they discovered it was from the Qianlong period, and dated it from the mid 18th century.

Yesterday it sold for £53 million to a Chinese buyer. The woman's son said that his mother was at first surprised, then amazed, then totally breathless.

Granny stops robbery

Janet Powell, a 71-year-old grandmother, yesterday stopped a robbery at a mobile phone shop in Birmingham.

At 9.30am Mrs Powell was doing her shopping. She heard a noise on the other side of the street. 'At first I thought it was a mugger,' she said, 'so I crossed the street. I wanted to do something to help.'

Then she realized that six men had hammers, and they were trying to smash the windows of a mobile phone shop. 'That made me more angry!' said Janet.

She attacked the men with her shopping bag, and shouted for help.

Police arrived and all six men were arrested.

The app that saved an iPad

A thief who stole an iPad led police straight to his door, as the owner had an app called 'Find my iPad'.

Ronald Bowe, 59, from Gateshead, stole the hand-held computer from a bag in St Nicholas's Cathedral, Newcastle, while its owner, Xin Shi, was praying.

Mr Xin reported the theft to the police, then realised he could use the app to find out where his iPad was. The GPS app gives the location of the computer.

Police followed the app to Bowe's house, where they found a bag containing the iPad, a mobile phone, a wallet, and a bank card.

Bowe was found guilty and will be sentenced at a later date.

UNIT 3 *p26*

READING AND SPEAKING

What do you think?

20 October

STEVEN SLATER ADMITS GUILT

The American flight attendant, who received world-wide attention in the summer and became a media and Internet sensation, appeared in court yesterday.

He admitted that he lost his temper, put the lives of passengers in danger, and caused damage to the plane when he activated the emergency chute.

Slater will have one year of counselling for anger management and treatment for alcohol abuse. If he doesn't complete the treatment, he could go to prison for one to three years.

He also has to pay a fine of $10,000 to JetBlue for damage to the plane.

Slater is currently unemployed.

EVERYDAY ENGLISH

Agree with me

5 Choose two of the conversations and decide where question tags can be added. Act them to the class.

1 A It's horrible weather today.
B Awful!
A The rain makes you miserable.
B Yup! And wet!
A Never mind. We need the rain.
B I suppose so.

2 A It's so romantic here!
B Yes, it's beautiful!
A And the sea looks so inviting!
B I think I'll go for a swim before breakfast. I've got time.
A Of course you've got time! We're on holiday!

3 A You don't like Ann.
B Er … she's all right.
A But you didn't talk to her all night.
B Well … she was talking to Jim.
A She's very interesting, actually.
B But she never listens! She just talks and talks and talks!

4 A I'd love to buy that car!
B But we haven't got any money!
A I thought we had lots.
B But we spent it all on a new kitchen.
A Oh, yes! So we did. Never mind.
B We can save up.
A Er … OK.

5 Sally We had a lovely holiday, Dave.
Dave We did. It was very relaxing.
Sally And the weather was marvellous, Dave.
Dave Yup. We were very lucky.
Sally And we met some nice people, Dave.
Dave We did. Charming people.

6 A Kate Burton's a fabulous actor.
B Very good.
A And she's got such a good voice!
B Yes, it's amazing!
A She can hit the highest notes!
B Yeah, I don't know how she does it.

7 A We love each other very much.
B We do.
A And we want to get married one day.
B One day, yeah.
A And we'll have six children.
B Er … yeah. Six, that's right.

8 A That was a terrible match!
B Awful! Waste of money!
A Albertino played really badly!
B He was rubbish! He didn't do a thing right all night.
A We deserved to lose!
B I'm afraid so! I don't know why I support them!

UNIT 12 *p97*

LISTENING AND SPEAKING

Discussion

5 Look at the situations. Talk together. What would you do?

Dilemma 1 You've been offered a job on the other side of the world. You would earn a lot of money, but you'd have to leave all your family and friends.

Dilemma 2 Your friend James is always in trouble. He says to you one day, 'If anyone asks you, tell them I was with you last night. OK?'

Dilemma 3 You go to a party where you meet someone and fall totally and hopelessly in love. At the end of the evening, he/she says to you, 'Let's get married tonight!'

Dilemma 4 At work your boss gives you lots of praise and a pay rise for an idea you had. In fact it was a colleague's idea that you stole.

Dilemma 5 You have neighbours who you really don't get on with. They are on holiday when you see that their house is on fire.

Dilemma 6 A well-known politician is telling the press stories about his/her childhood. In fact, you went to school with this politician and you know that what he/she is saying is all lies.

Dilemma 7 You are shopping in a supermarket. When you come out, you realise that you accidentally put something in your bag and didn't pay for it.

UNIT 3 *p107*

WRITING – Building a story

A fishy tale

Ten days ago businessman, Andrew Cheatle, was walking on the beach near his home in Worthing, Sussex, when he lost his mobile phone. It fell into the water and unfortunately a wave took it out to sea. One week later fisherman, Glen Kerley, was on his boat catching fish to sell in the market. The same day, back on land, he was preparing the fish for sale when he noticed something metal inside a cod fish. It was a mobile phone. Glen couldn't believe it. The phone was smelly and dirty, but amazingly it still worked so Glen called some of the contact numbers. Soon he had a reply.

Andrew was out shopping for a new mobile phone with his girlfriend, Rita Smith, when her phone rang. Incredibly she said 'It's for you! It's a call from your phone.' Glen told Andrew the fishy tale of how he found the phone. They met the next day and he returned it to an amazed Andrew, who still uses it.

Irregular verbs

Base form	Past Simple	Past participle
be	was/were	been
become	became	become
begin	began	begun
break	broke	broken
bring	brought	brought
build	built	built
buy	bought	bought
can	could	been able
catch	caught	caught
choose	chose	chosen
come	came	come
cost	cost	cost
cut	cut	cut
do	did	done
drink	drank	drunk
drive	drove	driven
eat	ate	eaten
fall	fell	fallen
feel	felt	felt
fight	fought	fought
find	found	found
fly	flew	flown
forget	forgot	forgotten
get	got	got
give	gave	given
go	went	gone/been
grow	grew	grown
have	had	had
hear	heard	heard
hit	hit	hit
keep	kept	kept
know	knew	known
learn	learnt/learned	learnt/learned
leave	left	left
lose	lost	lost
make	made	made
meet	met	met
pay	paid	paid
put	put	put
read /riːd/	read /red/	read /red/
ride	rode	ridden
run	ran	run
say	said	said
see	saw	seen
sell	sold	sold
send	sent	sent
shut	shut	shut
sing	sang	sung
sit	sat	sat
sleep	slept	slept
speak	spoke	spoken
spend	spent	spent
stand	stood	stood
steal	stole	stolen
swim	swam	swum
take	took	taken
tell	told	told
think	thought	thought
understand	understood	understood
wake	woke	woken
wear	wore	worn
win	won	won
write	wrote	written

Verb patterns

Verb + *-ing*	
like love enjoy hate finish stop	swimming cooking

Note

We often use the verb *go* + *-ing* for sports and activities.

I **go swimming** every day.
I **go shopping** at the weekend.

Verb + *to* + infinitive	
choose decide forget promise manage need help hope try want would like would love	to go to work

Verb + *-ing* or *to* + infinitive	
begin start	raining/to rain

Verb + preposition + *-ing*	
think of look forward to	going

Modal auxiliary verbs	
can could must had to shall should will would	go arrive

Phonetic symbols

Consonants

1	/p/	as in	**pen** /pen/
2	/b/	as in	**big** /bɪg/
3	/t/	as in	**tea** /tiː/
4	/d/	as in	**do** /duː/
5	/k/	as in	**cat** /kæt/
6	/g/	as in	**go** /gəʊ/
7	/f/	as in	**four** /fɔː/
8	/v/	as in	**very** /'veri/
9	/s/	as in	**son** /sʌn/
10	/z/	as in	**zoo** /zuː/
11	/l/	as in	**live** /lɪv/
12	/m/	as in	**my** /maɪ/
13	/n/	as in	**now** /naʊ/
14	/h/	as in	**happy** /'hæpi/
15	/r/	as in	**red** /red/
16	/j/	as in	**yes** /jes/
17	/w/	as in	**want** /wɒnt/
18	/θ/	as in	**thanks** /θæŋks/
19	/ð/	as in	**the** /ðə/
20	/ʃ/	as in	**she** /ʃiː/
21	/ʒ/	as in	**television** /'telɪvɪʒn/
22	/tʃ/	as in	**child** /tʃaɪld/
23	/dʒ/	as in	**German** /'dʒɜːmən/
24	/ŋ/	as in	**English** /'ɪŋglɪʃ/

Vowels

25	/iː/	as in	**see** /siː/
26	/ɪ/	as in	**his** /hɪz/
27	/i/	as in	**twenty** /'twenti/
28	/e/	as in	**ten** /ten/
29	/æ/	as in	**bag** /bæg/
30	/ɑː/	as in	**father** /'fɑːðə/
31	/ɒ/	as in	**hot** /hɒt/
32	/ɔː/	as in	**morning** /'mɔːnɪŋ/
33	/ʊ/	as in	**football** /'fʊtbɔːl/
34	/uː/	as in	**you** /juː/
35	/ʌ/	as in	**sun** /sʌn/
36	/ɜː/	as in	**learn** /lɜːn/
37	/ə/	as in	**letter** /'letə/

Diphthongs (two vowels together)

38	/eɪ/	as in	**name** /neɪm/
39	/əʊ/	as in	**no** /nəʊ/
40	/aɪ/	as in	**my** /maɪ/
41	/aʊ/	as in	**how** /haʊ/
42	/ɔɪ/	as in	**boy** /bɔɪ/
43	/ɪə/	as in	**hear** /hɪə/
44	/eə/	as in	**where** /weə/
45	/ʊə/	as in	**tour** /tʊə/

OXFORD
UNIVERSITY PRESS

Great Clarendon Street, Oxford, OX2 6DP, United Kingdom

Oxford University Press is a department of the University of Oxford. It furthers the University's objective of excellence in research, scholarship, and education by publishing worldwide. Oxford is a registered trade mark of Oxford University Press in the UK and in certain other countries

First published in 2013
2017 2016 2015 2014 2013
10 9 8 7 6 5 4 3 2 1

ISBN: 978 0 19 477276 1 Student's Book
ISBN: 978 0 19 476969 3 iTutor DVD-ROM
ISBN: 978 0 19 472039 7 Oxford Online Skills
ISBN: 978 0 19 477275 4 Student's Book Pack

Printed in Spain by Orymu, S.A.

This book is printed on paper from certified and well-managed sources.

ACKNOWLEDGEMENTS

The authors and publisher are grateful to those who have given permission to reproduce the following extracts and adaptations of copyright material: p.14 Fictitious interview with Mamy Rock (Ruth Flowers) and article based on factual information, www.mamyrock.com. Reproduced by permission; p.15 Fictitious interview with Fraser Doherty and article based on factual information, www.superjam.co.uk. Reproduced by permission; pp.66 & 67 From 'So what happened when two families swapped children?' by Tessa Cunningham, *Daily Mail* 11 August 2010. Reproduced by permission; pp.42 & 43 Interview with Palina Yanachkina is fictitious and is reproduced by permission of Palina Yanachkina. Article adapted from 'First person: Palina Yanachkina 'I have two families'' by Danielle Wrate, 5 May 2008, *The Guardian*. Copyright Guardian News & Media Ltd 2008. Reproduced by permission; pp.50 & 51 From 'The British Dream' by Tim Pozzi, 19 July 2008, timesonline.co.uk. Reproduced by permission of NI Syndication; pp.58 & 59 Article about Chatsworth reproduced by permission of the Chatsworth House Trust; pp.65 Interview with Jessica Ennis is fictitious and is based on factual information from *The Observer*, 15 November 2009. Reproduced by permission of JCCM Ltd; pp.82 & 83 Extracts adapted from 'A first time for everything' by Tom Meltzer, 23 October 2009, *The Guardian*. Copyright Guardian News & Media Ltd 2009. Reproduced by permission; pp.87 Information about Gareth Malone reproduced by permission of Curtis Brown; p.18 'Money' Words and Music by Berry Gordy JR and William Robinson JR © 1958. Reproduced by permission of EMI Music Publishing (WP) Ltd, London W8 5SW.

Sources: p.11 'Blind date' Source: www.guardian.co.uk; pp.26 & 27 'Emergency exit for flight attendant who lost his cool' Source: *The Evening Standard;* p.41 'I still can't believe I'm a grown-up!' Source: *The Times;* pp.26 & 27 'Steven Slater thanks public' Source: www.telegraph.co.uk/news

Additional information: p.63 Interview with Tilly Parkins is fictitious and is based on factual information; Tapescript 5.12 Fictitious interview with Palina Yanachkina reproduced by permission; Tapescript 8.1 Fictitious interview with Tilly Parkins is based on factual information. Tapescript 8.6 Fictitious interview with Jessica Ennis is fictitious and is based on factual information from *The Observer*, 15 November 2009. Reproduced by permission of JCCM Ltd.

Commissioned photography by: Gareth Boden pp.8 (man in street), 10 (Sally, Dominic, piano), 12 (dictionaries), 20, 31, 37, 46, 53 (leaflets/flyers), 54, 89.

Illustrations by: Ian Baker p.69; Fausto Bianchi/Beehive Illustration p.72; Gill Button pp.24, 29, 52, 68, 76, 81, 92; Katriona Chapman/The Bright Agency pp.70, 71; Simon Cooper/The Organisation pp.41, 44 (throw something away etc), 88; Tom Croft pp.13, 21 (John and Maria), 84, 101; Lucy Davey/The Artworks p.17; Maxwell Dorsey/Meiklejohn Illustration Ltd pp.16, 44 (look after a baby, etc.), 95; Penko Gelev pp.74, 75; Andy Hammond/Illustration p.106; Martin Sanders pp.22, 42, 60; Tony Sigley pp.26, 65, 107

We would also like to thank the following for permission to reproduce the following photographs: Alamy pp.8 (mobile phone/Mark Bassett), 18 (bubbles/Laurel), 28 (Photo Cornwall), 32 (fish & chips/numb), 33 (Fish and Chips sign/Mick Sinclair), 33 (shopkeeper/Trinity Mirror/Mirrorpix), 49 (Marilou/Jon Feingersh/Blend Images), 53 (Inca gold/Peter Horree), 56 (canoeing/TMI), 59 (long gallery/Ros Drinkwater), 60 (Alice Bews/Ian Shaw), 70 (Alice/Lebrecht Music and Arts Photo Library), 73 (Dr Jekyll and Mr Hyde/AF archive), 80 (ball-point pen/bobo), 80 (radio/Marc Arundale), 83 (Facebook/David J. Green – Lifestyle 2), 92 (couple/Andrey Kekyalyaynen), 93 (gravestone/Jeff Morgan 05), 115 (CJG – Lifestyle); By kind permission of Linda Barnicott, *My Hometown, Pittsburgh Remembered Series*, 1993/www.lindabarnicott.com p.110; Oliver Beatson, released on Public Domain licence on Wikipedia, 2009 p.99 (Life Cycle of the Sun); Camera Press, London pp.88 (young Charlotte Church/Paul Massey), 91 (young Jean Paul Getty III/Photography by Brian Aris), 152 & 154 (Charlotte Church/Sean Cook); Courtesy of Chatsworth House Trust pp.58 (D.Vintiner), 59 (dining room/D.Vintiner); Corbis pp.7 (Aboriginal art – blue painting/Ralph A. Clevenger), 9 (Zac/Simon Marcus/Comet), 9 (Katie and Beth older/Tim Hale Photography/Comet), 9 (Katie and Beth younger/moodboard), 16 (Bill and Christina/Philip Lee Harvey/cultura), 18 (parent and toddler/Ben Hupfer), 18 (meditating/Hans Huber/Westend61), 18 (child blowing/hsimages/Westend61), 25 (flood/Rehan Khan/epa), 25 (African children football/Christian Liewig/TempSport), 25 (crowd raising hands/Imaginechina), 25 (tents/Gideon Mendel For Action Aid/In Pictures), 25 (women queuing/Peter Turnley), 25 (earthquake rescue worker/WEDA/epa), 25 (footballers/Neil Marchand/Liewig Media Sports), 25 (helicopter/Rehan Khan/epa), 34 (Alexander/Bill Varie/Somos Images), 34 (Dinner in the Sky/Karoly Arvai/Reuters), 35 (man reaching at 's Baggers Restaurant/Daniel Karmann/epa/Corbis Wire), 38 (Tom/Rick Barrentine/Comet), 38 (Alison/Ocean), 39 (Bill/Beau Lark), 47 (Shanghai/Xiaoyang Liu/Flirt), 47 (Dubai/Jose Fuste Raga/Terra), 49 (Sally/Maskot), 58 (house and grounds/Peter Scholey/Robert Harding World Imagery), 60 (father and children/Ocean), 61 (Mika/Comet), 67 (football boots/Image Source), 70 (Hamlet/Bettmann), 70 (Oliver Twist/John Springer Collection), 70 (Sherlock Holmes/Bettmann), 73 (Charles Dickens/Bettmann), 73 (Robert Louis Stevenson/Bettmann), 80 (television/Lawrence Manning/Spirit), 80 (paper/Klaus Tiedge/Fancy), 82 (Henry/Blue Jean Images/Collage), 82 (background/ImageZoo), 91 (Jean Paul Getty II/Bettmann), 94 (Christine Schneider), 95 (Sigrid Olsson/PhotoAlto), 96 (Sam/Peter Muller/cultura), 97 (Tony and his dad/E. Audras/Onoky), 97 (Jimmy/Ocean), 108 (Norbert Schaefer), 110 (historical Pittsburgh/SuperStock), 111 (John F Kennedy/Ted Spiegel), 151 (Bill and Christina/Philip Lee Harvey/cultura), 153 (Bill and Christina/Philip Lee Harvey/cultura); Keith Ducatel – www.KeithDucatel.com pp.22, (Ed Stafford & jungle), 23 (Cho), 23 (Ed Stafford paddling); Jude Edginton – www.judeedginton.com pp.66 (the Cafearo & Tibbett families); Getty Images pp.6 (Anton/Zia Soleil/Iconica), 6 (New York/Fredrik Skold/The Image Bank), 7 (Rowenna/NWDA), 9 (Pete/Johner Royalty-Free), 9 (Judy and Kenny/Severin Schweiger/Cultura), 9 (Damian and Toby/Marcy Maloy/Photodisc), 12 (Jill Fromer/Photodisc), 14 (Ruth Flowers/Mark Ralston/AFP), 14 (jam pot/Peter Dazeley/Photographer's Choice), 16 (Ilona/Chev Wilkinson/Cultura), 18 (teenagers on beach/Image Source), 18 (canoeing/Erik Isakson), 18 (men chatting/Martin Barraud), 18 (couple working/Zero Creatives), 21 (businessman and woman/John Giustina/Iconica), 23 (snake/Mark Moffett/Minden Pictures), 23 (night/James p. Blair/National Geographic), 25 (world/Fry Design Ltd), 25 (press photographers/Christopher Pillitz/Reportage), 25 (leaders/AFP), 25 (reporter/Yellow Dog Productions), 25 (fashion/AFP), 25 (tennis/AFP), 27 (on beach/New York Daily News), 34 (Hans/Jupiterimages/Comstock Images), 34 (Lucy/Westend61), 35 (Ithaa Undersea Restaurant/Jon Nicholson), 35 (cutlery/Steve Wisbauer/Stockbyte), 36 (trolley foreground/Fuse), 38 (Abby/Stockbyte), 38 (Kelly/Mike Powell/Stone+), 39 (Martin/DreamPictures/Riser), 40 (Pete/Hill Street Studios/Harmik Nazarian/Blend Images), 40 (Debbie/WIN-Initiative), 41 (Leo/B2M Productions/Photodisc), 41 (Elsa/Hola Images), 41 (Dan/Dougal Waters/Photodisc), 42 (field background/Ingmar Wesemann), 43 (clover/Burazin), 45 (undecided woman/Hill Creek Pictures/UpperCut Images), 45 (hand and placards/Image Source), 47 (Singapore/Keith Mcgregor/Digital Vision), 48 (Agnes/Andreas Kindler), 48 (Kevin/Simon Wilkinson), 49 (Marcel/Jupiterimages/FoodPix), 49 (Jamie/Mark Scoggins), 50 (pavement/Richard Newstead), 55 (Karl Marx/Hulton Archive), 56 (Frieda Hoffmann/Vicky Kasal/Photodisc), 56 (jeep/Michael Poliza), 56 (Great Wall/Martin Puddy/Asia Images), 56 (desert/Patrice Hauser), 56 (archaeology in Egypt/Khaled Desouki/AFP), 60 (Victorian family/Nigel Dobinson/SSPL), 62 (Adam Pretty/Stone), 63 (Tilly Parkins/Adam Pretty), 63 (football/Ryan McVay/Photodisc), 63 (golf clubs/Stockbyte), 64 (Jupiterimages/Comstock Images), 65 (Jeff J Mitchell), 69 (doctor/Chris Whitehead/Digital Vision), 69 (stethoscope/Stockbyte), 77 (cinema/altrendo images), 77 (man clinging/Antonio R. Ramos/Flickr Select), 78 (discarded phones/SSPL), 79 (icons/Jim Snyder), 80 (Mac computer/SSPL), 82 (Sandy/PhotoAlto/Michele Constantini), 82 (Liz/Adrian Weinbrecht/Cultura), 82 (Barry/LWA/Riser), 85 (Clerkenwell/the Agency Collection), 88 (mature Charlotte Church/Gareth Cattermole), 90 (background/Gyro Photography/amanaimagesRF), 90 (Jean Paul Getty I/Hulton Archive), 91 (mature Jean Paul Getty III/Bruno Vincent), 91 (Balthazar Getty/Kevin Winter), 93 (baby/Rosemarie Gearhart/the Agency Collection), 93 (engagement/John Slater/StockImage), 93 (divorce/Peter Dazeley/Photographer's Choice RF), 96 (Lily/Lynn Koenig/Flickr), 96 (Annie/Marcy Maloy/Photodisc), 97 (Fiona/Cosmonaut Creative Media, LLC/Vetta), 99 (our Solar System/Stocktrek Images), 104 (Dougal Waters), 105 (Oliver Lopez Asis), 109 (Student/amana productions inc), 109 (paper background/Jill Fromer/Photodisc), 110 (Pittsburgh now/VisionsofAmerica/Joe Sohm), 116 (student/Andrew Rich), 116 (globe/Doug Armand/Photographer's Choice RF), 117 (Erik Dreyer), 151 (Ilona/Chev Wilkinson/Cultura), 152 (telephoning/Clerkenwell/the Agency Collection), 153 (Ilona/Chev Wilkinson/Cultura), 154 (telephoning/Clerkenwell/the Agency Collection), 156 (Nico Hermann); iStockphoto pp.7 (Aboriginal art Kangaroo/Paul Pegler), 11 (balloons/robstyle1), 11 (rice bowl/Floortje), 26 (panel pins/Chromatika Multimedia), 26 (cork board/sorendls), 27 (torn paper/Trevor Hunt), 27 (torn paper/Trevor Hunt), 27 (Jon Helgason), 35 (sky background/Peter Firus), 36 (shelves background/Vladimir Maravic), 43 (Belarus flag/popjop), 48 (crowd/jan kranendonk), 49 (paper family/maerorls), 49 (Rachel/Juanmonino), 50 (street sign/Alan eisen), 65 (Jamie Farrant), 67 (ballet shoes/millionhope), 70 (book/DNY59), 73 (pile of books/Alan Crawford), 73 (feather/ryan burke), 78 (globe/Edward Grajeda), 80 (ipad/TommL), 82 (Martin/ImageSource), 83 (virus/Philip Barker), 86 (page of music/Joanne Green), 86 (ribbon of notes/redfrog), 96 (genie/Ruslan Kokarev), 96 (lamp/Sergey Kulikov), 96 (smoke/Chanyut Sribua-rawd), 97 (signpost/scibak), 100 (notebook/Floortje), 110 (frame/Victor Martello); Mary Evans Picture Library p.55 (Dean Street – 19th century); Oxford University Press, Charles Dickens, *David Copperfield*, Oxford Bookworms Library, 2008 p.73; Courtesy of Ping Pong Ltd www.pingpongdimsum.co.uk p.10 (restaurant); Press Association Images pp.27 (planes/Rick Maiman/AP), 27 (press conference/Seth Wenig/AP), 78 (Martin Cooper/Eric Risberg/AP), 155 (Seth Wenig/AP); Rex Features pp.14 (Fraser Doherty/Nick Cunard), 35 (family at 's Baggers Restaurant/Action Press), 55 (blue plaque/Stuart Clarke), 79 (Goldstriker iphone/Stuart Hughes), 82 (Cyberia/Patrick Barth), 111 (Caroline Kennedy/Startraks Photo), 114 (Courtesy Everett Collection), 158 (David McHugh); Royalty-free pp.43, 98 (earth/Corbis), 112 (Goodshoot); Science Photo Library pp.80 (telephone/Sheila Terry), 80 (printing press/CCI Archives), 99 (Milky Way/Mark Garlick), 99 (background/Royal Observatory, Edinburgh/AAO), 99 (the universe/NOAO/AURA/NSF); Splash News p.26 (inside plane); Solo Syndication p.30; Adapted from listings published in *Time Out* Magazine. Logo reprinted by permission of *Time Out* p.53; Photographs of Gareth Malone © Twenty Twenty Television 2009 pp.86–87; Muir Vidler/The Times/NI Syndication pp.50 (Burkham Mehmet, Stroud Green Road shops), 51 (Ming Liang Chen, Mehul Shah, Luz-Elena Lamprea); By kind permission of Palina Yanachkina and the Quaid family/Press22/Sean Curtin pp.42–43.

Photos and illustrations sourced by: Suzanne Williams/Pictureresearch.co.uk

Although every effort has been made to trace and contact copyright holders before publication, this has not been possible in some cases. We apologise for any apparent infringement of copyright and, if notified, the publisher will be pleased to rectify any errors or omissions at the earliest possible opportunity.